HEART OF THE CARIBOO-CHILCOTIN

VICTORIA • VANCOUVER • CALGARY

HEART
OF THE
CARIBOO-
CHILCOTIN

STORIES WORTH KEEPING

EDITED BY DIANA WILSON

Heritage House Publishing Company Ltd.
#108 – 17665 66A Avenue
Surrey, BC V3S 2A7
www.heritagehouse.ca

Library and Archives Canada Cataloguing in Publication
Heart of the Cariboo–Chilcotin: stories worth keeping/
edited by Diana Wilson.

ISBN 13: 978-1-894-974-08-0
ISBN 10: 1-894974-08-5
  I. Cariboo Region (B.C.)—Literary collections. 2. Chilcotin River
Region (B.C.) Literary collections. I. Wilson, Diana, 1958– II. Title.

FC3845.C3H42 2006   971.1'75   C2005-907758-1

Cover design by Frances Hunter and Erin Woodward.
Interior design by Frances Hunter.
Cover photo by Chris Harris.

Printed in Canada

Heritage House acknowledges the financial support for its publishing
program from the Government of Canada through the Book Publishing
Industry Development Program (BPIDP), Canada Council for the Arts,
and the British Columbia Arts Council.

The Canada Council | Le Conseil des Arts
for the Arts | du Canada

BRITISH COLUMBIA
ARTS COUNCIL
We acknowledge the support of the Province of British Columbia
through the British Columbia Arts Council

This book has been printed on 100% post-consumer recycled paper,
processed chlorine free and printed with vegetable-based dyes.

Contents

Foreword 7   *Introduction* 10

JEAN E. SPEARE   The Captive Girl   13

F.W. LINDSAY   Dusty Nuggets from a
Miner's Diary   19

VISCOUNT MILTON &
W.B. CHEADLE   Original Tourist   27

AGNES C. LAUT   The Cariboo Road   39

VEERA BONNER   Portrait of a Pioneer Family   45

SAGE BIRCHWATER   Chiwid   53

HARRY MARRIOTT   Riding up the Road   69

OLIVE SPENCER LOGGINS   Danger Comes Calling   81

BILL RILEY & LAURA LEAKE   Rookie Cop at Soda Creek   93

ERIC COLLIER   To Heal the Land   101

RICHMOND P. HOBSON JR.   Unexplored Territory   111

HILARY PLACE   Davey Anderson   129

ALAN FRY   Wet Summer   137

ELDON LEE   We Were Brothers   151

TODD LEE   High Noon in a
Cow-town Court   165

DIANA FRENCH   The Mechanics   173

IRENE STANGOE   Looking Back with Irene   179

D.A. HOLLEY   Pioneer Doctor   185

CHILCO CHOATE   Gang Ranch Cowboy   193

HILARY PLACE   Almost Made the Big Time   205

PAUL ST. PIERRE   Everything You Need
to Make a Ranch   215

PAUL ST. PIERRE   How Red Lost the Ranch   219

TERRY GLAVIN   We Never Gave In   223

Photo credits 239   *Acknowledgements* 239

Dedicated to the Memory
of Art Downs

Foreword

People who care about the Cariboo–Chilcotin are sufficiently maverick-minded to make up their own minds about things. They are not the sort to be swayed by fancy words, cheerleading or politicians—or literary types.

So I'll refrain from superlatives about the worldwide success of Eric Collier's *Three Against the Wilderness*, or the importance of Alan Fry's 1970 novel *How A People Die* (published one year after Harold Cardinal's *The Unjust Society: The Tragedy of Canada's Indians*), or the cleverness of Paul St. Pierre's stories that generated the first worthwhile CBC drama series from British Columbia, *Cariboo Country*.

I'll leave it instead to Hilary Place of Dog Creek to define what the heck this book is about.

> The Cariboo–Chilcotin is not just a geographic
> designation: it's also a state of mind. It seems that it
> requires a certain type of person to feel at home and
> be suited to the Cariboo–Chilcotin. This doesn't mean
> that all the Cariboo–Chilcotin's residents are the
> same, by any means, but rather the opposite. They are
> strong-willed and have different outlooks than their
> neighbour, certainly, but should that neighbour need
> help, it is always forthcoming. The early years of the
> Cariboo–Chilcotin produced some of the most unique
> pioneers this country has ever seen.

That's the literary terrain you're about to enter. Much of the writing is uplifting, bemused and anecdotal, but that doesn't mean it's not also sophisticated. Whether it's a monologue by Augusta Tappage or reportage by Terry Glavin, everyone is trying to speak the truth, and that's as sophisticated as one can get.

I once owned land for a spell near the Marguerite cable ferry, just south of the Indian reserve, on the west side of the Fraser, but I've never roped a calf, I've never fought a forest fire or even fired a gun. What I have done over the past few decades is look at the literature of British Columbia. And the more I read, the more I can say without equivocation that it's high time we had a Cariboo–Chilcotin equivalent to *Raincoast Chronicles*, the down-to-earth series that has documented everyday coastal life since the early '70s.

That's why I welcome the appearance of *Heart of the Cariboo– Chilcotin*. If it serves as the initial volume for a series that will reflect the lives and times of a unique place, that sounds like progress to me.

It's always easy to complain about omissions from any anthology. I started to do so when I first flipped through this collection. But when someone has the nerve to go ahead and get a job done, to get the ball rolling—whether it's Eric Collier re-introducing beavers at Meldrum Creek or folks banding together to make an extraordinary road all the way to Bella Coola without government support—you gotta stand back and respect the gumption it takes to make progress.

When I was living between Williams Lake and Quesnel, on our impractical 25 acres, we were poor enough, and dumb enough, and crazy enough to dig a 40-foot well by hand. Our Cariboo neighbours must have thought we were nuts. But we got water.

This anthology gets the job done, too. If *Heart of the Cariboo* was a deluxe, 1,000-page doorstopper, maybe it could be all things to all people, but you have to figure not many people would fork out to buy it. So I'm not going to bellyache about omissions, not when I think so much of the writing is excellent.

You will find your own favourites; I won't try to prejudice you by naming mine.

Few British Columbians, or Canadians at large, recognize that the Cariboo–Chilcotin has a rich literary history. Precious few people know the province's first published poet, James Anderson ("the Robert Service of the Cariboo gold rush"), lived, wrote and acted in theatricals in Barkerville.

Even more original, Father Jean-Marie Le Jeune of Kamloops, as a member of the Oblates of Mary Immaculate, published a mimeographed Chinook newsletter, the *Kamloops Wawa*, that described itself as "the queerest newspaper in the world." First published on May 2, 1891, the *Wawa* was "Indian news" printed in both the English alphabet and a bizarre form of shorthand developed in 1867 by two French clerics, the Duploye brothers. Thanks to the *Wawa*'s wide circulation, many Natives and non-Natives in the B.C. Interior became literate as Duployan readers.

Skipping ahead, a fellow named Art Downs published his first story called "The Saga of the Upper Fraser Sternwheelers" in 1950 in *Cariboo Digest*, a regional magazine published in Quesnel since 1945. With Wes Logan, Art Downs bought the *Cariboo Digest* from Alex Sahonovich in 1955 and became its editor. It evolved into *BC Outdoors*, a successful blend of history, wildlife and conservation that served a broad readership.

Art Downs didn't believe in fishing derbies or trophies, but he recognized the importance of tourism. He deplored clear-cut logging and was a tireless conservationist and grassroots organizer. Downs eschewed the city and affected a down-to-earth bluntness that disguised his intelligence, if you weren't paying much attention. Along the way he served as president of the B.C. Wildlife Federation, director of the Canadian Wildlife Federation and a member of the Pacific Salmon Commission.

Selling *BC Outdoors* in 1979, he and his wife, Doris, turned to publishing books "by B.C. writers for B.C. readers" under their Heritage House imprint in Surrey. Art Downs died at his home in Surrey on August 13, 1996, but not before he passed along his Heritage House operation to Rodger Touchie—publisher of this book.

So *Heart of the Cariboo–Chilcotin* is emanating from a publishing operation that dates back to Quesnel in the '40s and '50s.

My guess is, that's all that needs to be said.

Alan Twigg
Publisher of BC BookWorld *and*
author of 11 books

INTRODUCTION

Although the town of my childhood, Vanderhoof, is a half-day's journey up the road beyond the Cariboo–Chilcotin, I'm no stranger to cold winters and short growing seasons.

I've been to a cattle auction. I've spent days on horseback. I am acquainted with the profound loneliness that can be experienced in a remote landscape. Growing up in the Interior of the province, I was always keenly aware of how isolated we were—how our vital and palpable lives were largely unknown to outsiders, and unsung. This is one of the reasons I became a writer: I wanted to tell the world that we were here, and who we were, and how we lived.

As soon as I began diving into more than 75 non-fiction volumes about the Cariboo–Chilcotin to find selections for this anthology, I felt an instant spark of connection with these voices. Here was everything I was familiar with, writ large. At the same time, I was able to find aspects of the Cariboo–Chilcotin that are unique to that region. I was able to stand outside, to some extent, and view the region through its stories, marvelling at what I saw.

I hope this volume expresses a fresh vision of what is distinct and remarkable about the Cariboo–Chilcotin and its people.

When I was asked to make selections for this anthology, my first task was to establish criteria for inclusion: memorable characters, an authentic sense of place, situations that both entertain and give insight into the human condition, and that indefinable, haunting quality that makes a story last in a reader's mind. I also wanted to present a broad spectrum from different periods, places, occupations and perspectives.

The diverse voices I chose capture the multi-faceted spirit of a geographically varied region. They tell the story of a harshly beautiful and remote area, of First Nations on the cusp of change and how that change is met; of gold miners seeking adventure and finding heart-ache more often than riches; of travellers on the famous Cariboo Road, and the first tourists to the area.

As men laid down their picks to take up the plow, ranching began to thrive, as did the cowboy mystique—more the stuff of romance than reality. And with the growth of permanent communities came an uneasy compromise with modernization—always with a rural spin that some call resistance to change and others call country charm.

Here are stories about intricate tensions: Aboriginals and Whites, lawbreakers and law, conquerors and conservationists. Here are stories about difference and the common ground where the voices harmonize—with grit, humility, humour, sharing and self-sacrifice—in a timeless striving to build a place to call home.

In order to preserve the authenticity and the history of the period in which the stories were written, I have chosen not to alter the text to reflect modern-day attitudes. Spellings may vary according to historical conventions.

Although it was tempting to put some of the most humourous material at the outset, I've opted for a chronological arrangement to show the region developing over time, with history carrying forward to enrich each story with a sense of building complexities.

With a 40-year history of publishing Cariboo–Chilcotin books, Heritage House has maintained an ongoing affinity for the stories from British Columbia's central Interior. We hope to bring you more, and we welcome your comments and suggestions.

Diana Wilson
Victoria, 2006

THE CAPTIVE GIRL

from *The Days of Augusta*
by Jean E. Speare

*Mary Augusta Tappage was born in 1888 in Soda Creek
and died in 1978. Over 30 years ago, Jean E. Speare, herself of
Cariboo pioneering stock, spent many hours with this diminutive
Shuswap woman, listening to her stories and the oral history
of her people. Jean transcribed these "memories of a lifetime"
for* The Days of Augusta, *a book that Bennet Schiff of the
Smithsonian Institute describes as "a contemporary classic of
oral literature." The following story from that book is a rare
glimpse back through the veil of time to when Natives lived close
to the land, competing for power and resources. Here is one
frightening event in a young girl's life.*

In her Native oral tradition, Mary Augusta Tappage passed on the stories she inherited about life in the early days of her people.

It is a long time ago, but they used to steal women then. Yes, I'll tell you about it. I'll tell you about one woman who was taken. My grandmother told me this and it's true.

There were three women. Well, two women and one of them had a daughter with her. Well, the daughter, I guess, she was about thirteen. In those days, they got married early. She was married or about to get married, so I guess she was a woman, really.

They went out to pick saskatoons. There were no more berries down Soda Creek, so they went "way out."

Going up this hill, they saw some trees tied up together like this, you know, and this woman who didn't have a daughter with her, she got afraid.

She said, "Let's go back. This don't look right."

But this other woman said, "Oh, I guess some kids came along and tied the trees like that."

Anyhow, the first woman I guess decided to stay on, even though she didn't feel just so. But they had lunch with them and they had reached good saskatoon country just this side of Big Lake. That's quite a ways, you know. But this woman I guess she kept thinking those trees tied up was a warning.

Anyhow, they picked berries and they had lunch and sometime later, they went to bed under a tree.

They didn't know this man was watching them. They didn't know there were other men nearby. I guess they were coming to steal some women, coming from a long distant country. Some said Cree and some said *sicom*—that's my language—it means far-off people. And Cree is supposed to be in Alberta. But which of those I don't know.

But anyhow, there was one man there. He didn't want to hurt these women, so that night, I guess when the other men had gone to sleep, he got up and went to where these women were sleeping. He poked one of them on her forehead ... with a stick. She woke up and she looked up and there was a man making signs to her, telling her not to talk and to go home. That was no place here for them.

Well, she understood it, this woman without a daughter. And the next morning, she wanted to come home to Soda Creek. Well, this other woman was determined to pick berries and of course her daughter would stay with her.

Well, that's when these men took her daughter. The other woman, the smart one, she ran off. She didn't show herself. She could hear this girl screaming and the old lady, too. The old lady hung on to her daughter, and they told her to let go. But she wouldn't. So they killed her and took the girl. They didn't care for nobody, you know.

Anyhow, they took the girl. She wasn't really a girl, but they thought she was single. They didn't know she was married or about to be. So they took her a long way back to their country and they put her with a woman of their own tribe. This woman had her own hut or tent—it was too early for tents—it must have been a hut of some sort and she had to guard and look after this girl.

Well anyhow, soon they found out she was to be a mother. Well this let them out, see? They hadn't counted on this. But they put her there and this woman was good to her. Yes, nice to her. I guess their language was different, is all.

In the meantime, the woman who was smart enough to run away told the people at Soda Creek what had happened. They went looking for the girl. But they never found her. They just found where she had been made to dance and had lost the feathers out of her headband. And I guess they found the mother, killed.

So the girl stayed with this woman in the hut, and she stayed there and stayed there till her child was born. And when they found out it was a boy, they took it away and threw it in the river.

"If this boy grows up, he might kill us all," they said. "Might as well kill it and throw it away. If it was a girl, we would have kept it. It would have done us no harm." That is what they were saying to this woman. So they took it.

It broke the girl's heart, you know, to see her baby taken away and thrown in the water.

Anyway, I guess the woman in the hut pitied the girl. She made up her mind to help her escape. She started making moccasins for her to wear and dried food to carry with her and then she told the girl to go.

So she took off.

She came to a river that she had to cross and there about the centre was a log jam—logs all piled up from when the river starts to get higher. Well, she made it to the log jam, how I don't know. Maybe by swimming. And then she heard dogs barking and men shouting. They were looking for her. They found out she had escaped. But she hid in the log pile.

The dogs came down and smelled her tracks where they had gone into the water. And the men came running behind carrying long sticks with sharp points on and they were trying to find her. But they couldn't see her. But she was looking at them; looking at them.

Well finally they gave up and went home. She waited and waited until there was no more noise and then she came out. She was wet and her moccasins and her lunch were all gone. She had sunk down you know on that log pile and was all wet.

She rested awhile, I guess, and then she took off, went on her way. She knew what she had to do. She knew where she had to go.

So she kept a-coming, kept a-coming. She was hungry, you know. She saw some wild chickens. She stoned them. Killed them. She skinned them off, peeled them off and hung them over her shoulders to dry while she was walking. Only way she could eat them, you know, was dried. She didn't have no matches. She had nothing.

When they were kind of dry, she would eat them. It was her lunch, you know.

She kept a-coming and a-coming until she got 'way up into this big valley and she knew she was close to home. She kept a-coming until she landed at Soda Creek, right down here.

Her people were all across the river. They used to live across the river then. And I guess she was pretty weak by this time, but she tried, and she raised her arms and waved to them. And they saw her, yes, they saw her wave.

She laid down then, all sore, all hungry and so weak that she laid down. She laid down to wait.

They came across in canoes and they had blankets—buckskin blankets—there were no blankets as we know them. They loaded her into the canoe and took her home. They looked after her until she got better. They give her lots of fish soup, I guess. It would make her strong again.

And she lived. How long she lived after that, it doesn't say, but she lived in spite of everything.

My grandmother told me this. It's true.

DUSTY NUGGETS FROM A MINER'S DIARY

from *The Cariboo Story*
by F.W. Lindsay

Cariboo historian F.W. Lindsay dedicated The Cariboo Story
*"to no particular race, but rather to a particular brand of man.
The fighter, the individualist and the eccentric who would rather
struggle with the wilderness and suffer the discomforts of an
uncivilised frontier than stagnate in the more refined and gentle
atmosphere of the farms and counting houses of the old world
and the eastern states and provinces of the new world."*

*Born in 1903, Lindsay himself thrived on the rough
conditions of frontier Cariboo, working as a jack-of-all-trades
and running a newspaper in Quesnel. He collected old
manuscripts and pioneer diaries, self-publishing them in
small volumes to preserve their history. The following diary
from* The Cariboo Story *illuminates a darker side of the
gold rush. Lindsay writes: "This one battered diary, though
incomplete, gives us the true story of a miner—and likewise of
a thousand miners. Not one of the few who struck it rich, but
one of the many who found hardship and disappointment ...
The diary is not quoted in full, but excerpts have been chosen
which sketch the action and shade in the details. Like many a
modern story, the ending is left to the reader's imagination."*

June, 1862.

Thurs. 12. (163—202) Still at the Forks
Got a Job to Pack 80 lbs
Weight to onters Creek 50
miles distance for iour y
Reseve 30 cents per lb
for Mr Kemble a Boston
Man

Fri. 13. (164—201) Lett the Forks 7 am
with 100 lb Weight

This is a fragment of the original 1862 diary excerpted here.

February 1862

TUES. 17   Left Southampton per the Shannon, a fine steamer.

WED. 18   Taken with bad sea sickness.

THURS. 19   Got over sea sickness through taking sundry bottles of Barclay's stout.

April 1862

TUES. 8   Panama a fine old city but very dirty. English stout & ale 1 dollar per bottle. This place noted for broken bottles, fat pigs and open water closets.

SAT. 26   Arrived at San Francisco. Put up at the Waverly Hotel.

MON. 28   Sunday went to concert. Monday got drunk.

May 1862

THURS.1   Left Friscoe by the Serrio Nevada. Very much crowded. Man put in irons for stealing a pair boots. Crying and swearing all night.

WED. 7   Arrived at Asquamalt 4 am. Walk to Victoria. Camped on rock valley. Swarms of Indians.

THURS.8   Victoria is a very fine town of 4 years standing. Some fine land.

MON. 12   Left Victoria by the Enterprise. Arrived at New Westminster on the Fraser River. Camped on the hill facing the landing. This is a fine country.

TUES. 13   Still at Westminster. Plenty of fish, salmon and sturgeon. Saw one caught weighing 180 lbs. It is sold cheap enough. For 2 meals for 4 men price 1s. 6d.

THURS. 15   Bad news from the diggings. No provisions on the road.

FRI. 16.   Left Westminster by the Flying Dutchman a small steamer up the Fraser.

Sat. 17   Arrived Harrison River 8 am. Left by the Union another small steamer, 3 months since leaving England. Got to Douglas 7 pm.

Mon. 19   Left Douglas 7 am with about 70 lbs. weight on back. Up ·some steep hills. Very hot. Walk 8 miles and stopped for dinner. 2 lbs. beef—4 men. Camped at the 14 mile stone. Bread, tea and Indian meal for supper.

Tues. 20   Struck tent at 6 am. Wrote name on the 21 mile post. Dinner at a stream near the 23 mile post. Mush and tea. One of our party shot a squirrel and cooked it.

[No Date] Steamer Lady of the Lake—crossed Anderson's Lake. Crossed Seaton Lake in Champion. Camped.

Fri. 23   Struck tent 6 am. Walked 11 mi. by fine running stream.

Sat. 24   Struck tent 5 am. At Lillooet 1/2 past 6 am. Queen's birthday. Drank her health. Walked 13 miles. Cam'd on Fraser. Fine spring. Very heavy country.

Sun. 25   Camped near farm. Got some milk. Quite a treat. 1s. 6d. a qt.

Mon. 26   Struck tent 5 am. Milk for breakfast. Walked about 20 mi. Steep mountains. Passed about 10 mules. Pitched tent near Bonapart river.

Tues. 27   Shot 1 rook and 1 hawk for dinner. Quite a treat, being on short fare. 1 lb. rice between 5 men for breakfast. Walked 15 mi. Tented on farm land. Bought 12 lbs. flour and 6 lbs. beans of a packer.

Thurs. 29 Walk 19 mi. Camped by Bonapart River and found we had taken wrong road. Lost about 20 mi. Bought flour and beans from one of the Hudson's Bay Company trains.

June 1862

Mon. 2   Walked 13 miles. One of our men lame.

Tues. 3   Struck tent 3 am. Breakfast on the road. Walked 10 mi and tented on Williams Lake. Bought fish and duck of Indians. Cash short and bad news—things very high in price.

WED. 4   Struck tent 7 am. Quite out of food, with exception of a little Indian meal. Down in spirits. Thinking of home and those left behind. Bought 2 lb. meat on road. Bad news from the miners. Men returning for want of funds.

FRI. 6   Struck tent 5 am. Small piece of beef and bread for breakfast. Black tea for dinner and same for supper. Walk 20 miles. Camped and mosquitoes ate us up almost.

SAT. 7   Camp'd at a little lake after 7 miles over bad trail. Up to our knees in mud and over mountain. Done some washing. Caught fish for breakfast & din.

SUN. 8   Walk 8 miles to the Forks Quesnel. Things bad at this time. Bread 4s. per lb. Shovels 16 dollars. Pick axes $10.

TUES. 10   First trial at gold digging. Found the colors down the creek. Almost broke.

THURS. 12   Got a job to pack 80 lbs. to Antlers Creek 50 miles distant for which I receive 30 cents per lb. from a Mr. Kemble, a Boston man.

FRI. 13   Left the Forks 7 am. with 100 lbs. weight. Paid 1s. for a box of matches. Walked 12 miles. Camped with a packer. Almost broken hearted thinking of wife and boy. God bless them.

SAT. 14   Started 6 am. Could not stop tears from coming thinking of home. Walked 11 miles. Cam'd the bottom of Keithley hill.

SUN. 15   Walked about 4 miles. Raining all day. Rested and read the Bible.

MON. 16   Raining. Only 6d. in my pocket. Walked 13 miles through mud and snow up to my knees—over high mountains. Arrived at Antlers Creek 8 pm. Slept at a restaurant on the floor.

TUES. 17   Stayed at Antlers. Had some beef. Made stew. I am in a little better spirits, having a berth in view for a short time. Got 30 dollars for packing.

THURS. 19   Staked a claim off. I am always thinking of my dear wife and blessed boy.

SAT. 21   Got a job to paper Bar Room at Cushin & Stevenson's Restaurant. Price 20 dollars about 1 1/2 day's work.

FRI. 27   Got acquainted with the Butcher. Lent hand in the slaughter house. Got trimmings. Had a good feed.

SAT. 28   Helping butcher. Flour 5s. per lb. Got first gold.

SUN. 29   Found a deal of pleasure in reading the Bible and wife and boy's portrait by my side and in my mind.

July 1862

TUES. 8   Still at business. Dreaming of wife and boy. Thought wife was unkind to me when I arrived in England. At this time I am $20 in pocket and about 30 dollars out on credit.

SAT. 26   3 men murdered between the Forks and Bridge.

August 1862

FRI. 8   Went over the mountain to see Frank. Slept there.

SAT. 9   Returned to Antler with cattle for butchering. Always thinking of home and wife and boy. Pray God they are doing well.

SUN. 17   Bishop preached.

WED. 20   Bill Hill gambler shot W. Smith at Williams Creek.

September 1862

MON. 8   First snow storm. Driving 20 head cattle on mountain.

TUES. 16   Still mining. Sold 4 lbs. candles at 1s. 2d. per lb.

October 1862

many blank pages ...

SUN. 12   Beaver lake.

FRI. 24   Left staked ground foot of mountain Pavillion near bridge.

SUN. 26   Left the Pavillion House.

(This is the last entry in the diary).

Top: Miners arrive at a wayside house on the Cariboo Road.
Bottom: A wayside house at midnight.

ORIGINAL TOURIST

from *The North-West Passage by Land*
by Viscount Milton and W.B. Cheadle

*Celebrated as the first tourists to the Cariboo, English
physician Walter Butler Cheadle (1835-1910) and Lord Milton
(1839-1877) travelled to the exotic west coast of Canada in the
early 1860s. Their lively account of this adventure,* The North-
West Passage *by Land, went through eight printings in 10
years. After returning to England, Cheadle became dean of
St. Mary's Hospital medical school and Milton became a
member of Parliament for Yorkshire. In this excerpt, Cheadle
and Milton travel into the Cariboo, establish a base at Cusheon's
Hotel and set out to explore the country and its mining
operations. They learn the sad fates of William Dietz and his
partner after their gold strike at Williams Creek. Residents
throw a party for Cheadle and Milton, serving up Cariboo-style
hospitality with a hilarious mixture of the rough, makeshift
conditions of a new frontier and the more delicate sensibilities
of transplanted British culture.*

The accommodation along the road was everywhere miserable enough, but after leaving Clinton it became abominable. The only bed was the floor of the "wayside houses," which occur every ten miles or so, and are named the "Fiftieth" or "Hundredth Mile House," according to the number of the nearest mile-post. Our solitary blankets formed poor padding against the inequalities of the rough-hewn boards, and equally ineffectual to keep out the cold draughts which whistled under the ill-fitting door of the hut. A wayside house on the road to the mines is merely a rough log hut of a single room; at one end a large open chimney, and at the side a bar counter, behind which are shelves with rows of bottles containing the vilest of alcoholic drinks. The miners on their journey up or down, according to the season— men of every nationality—Englishmen, Irishmen, and Scotchmen, Frenchmen, Italians, and Germans, Yankees and niggers, Mexicans and South Sea Islanders—come dropping in towards evening in twos and threes, divest themselves of the roll of blankets slung upon their backs, and depositing them upon the floor, use them as a seat, for the hut possesses few or none. The next thing is to have a "drink," which is proposed by some one of the party less "hard up" than his friends, and the rest of the company present are generally invited to join in.

After supper and pipes, and more "drinks," each unrolls his blankets, and chooses his bed for the night. Some elect to sleep on the counter, and some on the flour sacks piled at one end of the room, whilst the rest stretch themselves on the floor, with their feet to the fire. Occasionally, a few commence gambling, which, with an accompaniment of drinking and blasphemy, goes on for the greater part of the night.

Descending from the high land, we came to the "Hundred Mile House," at Bridge Creek. This is the commencement of a tract of country more fertile than any we met with, except that of the Delta of the Fraser; and yet the amount of good land is [of] but small extent. Here and there a rich bottom, a consolidated marsh, or the lowland on the banks of some stream, had been converted into a productive farm, and the low hills afford plenty of pasturage; but the whole of the rising ground is merely sand and shingle, and nothing but bunch grass flourishes there. On the road we met a small bullock-wagon, escorted by about twenty armed miners on foot. This proved to contain 630 pounds weight of gold, the profits of a Mr. Cameron, the principal shareholder in the noted Cameron claim. This gold, worth about £30,000, had been amassed in the short space of three months, and represented probably less than one-half the actual produce of the mine during that time.

At Soda Creek we took the steamer for Quesnelle. Captain Done, the commander, was a jolly, red-faced, portly fellow, of exceeding hospitality. He invited us to his cabin—the only furnished room on board—and bringing out a box of cigars, and ordering a whole decanter full of "brandy cocktail" to be made at once, desired us to make ourselves happy. Every quarter of an hour we were called out by the nigger "bar-keep" to have a drink with the Captain and the "crowd," as the general company is termed. A refusal would have been considered grossly rude, and we had to exercise great ingenuity in evading the continual invitations. The only excuse allowed is that of having just had a meal, for a Yankee always drinks on an empty stomach, and never after eating; and American manners and customs rule in the mines. The steamer cost no less than 75,000 dollars, or £15,000; the whole of the machinery and boiler-plates having been brought 200 miles on the backs of mules.

At Quesnelle Mouth we slung our roll of blankets on our backs, and started on foot for William's Creek. The road was very rough, a narrow pack-trail cut through the woods; the stumps of the felled trees were left in the ground, and the thick stratum of mud in the spaces between was ploughed into deep holes by the continual trampling of mules. The ground had been frozen, and covered with several inches of snow, but this had partially melted, and rendered the surface greasy and slippery. We stumbled about amongst the hardened mud-holes, and our huge jack-boots soon blistered our feet so dreadfully, that by the second day we were almost disabled. Fortunately we picked up a pair of "gumboots"—long boots of India-rubber, used by the miners for working in the water—which had been cast away by the road-side, and substituting these for our cumbrous riding-boots, struggled on less painfully afterwards. The trail, gradually ascending, passed along the sides of pine-clad hills closely packed together, and separated only by the narrowest ravines; we had indeed entered the same region of mountain and forest which we had formerly encountered on the upper part of the North Thompson. By the road-side lay the dead bodies of horses and mules, some standing as they had died, still stuck fast in the deep, tenacious mud. We passed a score of them in one day in full view; and hundreds, which had turned aside to die, lay hidden in the forest which shut in the trail so closely. Martens and wood-partridges were numerous, and a tall Yankee, from the State of Maine, who had joined our company, greatly distinguished himself, knocking them over with his revolver from the tops of the high pines in a manner which astonished us. As we approached William's Creek, the ascent became more rapid and the snow deeper, for the frost at this height had been unbroken.

On the evening of the third day's march we reached Richfield, sixty-five miles from the Mouth of Quesnelle; but, acting on the advice of our friend from Maine, walked on through Barkerville to Cameron Town, lower down the same creek, where the richest mines were being at this time worked. It was already dark, and we had a rough walk of it—along the bottom of the narrow ravine through which runs William's Creek, scrambling over "flumes," logs, and heaps of rubbish for about two miles, before we doffed our packs at Cusheon's Hotel. We had reached Cariboo at last, although by a much more roundabout way than we originally intended.

William's Creek takes its name from one of its discoverers, William Dietz, a Prussian, who, with his companion, a Scotchman named Rose, were amongst the most adventurous of the pioneers of the Cariboo country. Neither of them ever reaped any reward from the discovery of perhaps the richest creek in the world. When a crowd of miners rushed to the place, they left in search of fresh diggings. The

Scotchman disappeared for months, and his body was found at length by a party of miners in a journey of discovery, far out in the wilds. On the branch of a tree hard by hung his tin cup, and scratched upon it with the point of a knife was his name, and the words, "Dying of starvation." William Dietz returned unsuccessful to Victoria, and, struck down by rheumatic fever, was dependent on charity at the time of our visit.

The district of Cariboo is the richest portion of the British Columbian gold field, and here the geologic disturbance has been the greatest. Cariboo is a sea of mountains and pine-clad hills, the former rising to a height of 7,000 or 8,000 feet, surrounded by a confused congeries of the latter. Everywhere the surface has been disturbed, so that hardly a foot of level ground can be found, except at the bottom of the narrow gullies running between these hills. Strata are tilted on end, and beds of streams heaved up to the tops of hills. Round this centre of wealth poured up from the depths below, the main branch of the Fraser wraps itself in its semi-circular course, and has received from thence, by numerous tributaries, the gold found in its sands.

Gold was first discovered on the sand-bars of the Lower Fraser, in the state of the finest dust. The old miners of California traced it up the river, and followed it as it became of coarser and coarser grain 400 miles along the Fraser, and then up the small of affluents from Cariboo. Here were found nuggets, and lumps of auriferous quartz. The hunted metal was almost run to earth. But the exciting pursuit is not yet quite over. The veins of auriferous quartz have not, so far, been discovered, although conjecture points to their probable position. Lightning, Antler, Keighley's, William's Creek, and many others, all take their rise in a range known as the Bald Mountains, and most of them radiate from one of them, the Snow-Shoe Mountain. Here the matrix is presumed to lie, and although it may have been denuded of its richest portion, carried down as the drift gold of the creeks, fortunes still lie hid in the solid rock; and when the quartz-leads are discovered, British Columbia may emulate California in wealth and stability. The hundreds of mills in that country, crushing thousands of tons of gold and silver quartz per day, have proved that this branch of mining is far more paying and reliable than the uncertain and evanescent surface diggings, which formerly there, as now in Cariboo, furnished all the gold obtained. Several different qualities of gold are found in Cariboo. In William's Creek alone, two distinct "leads" are found; one where the gold is alloyed with a considerable proportion of silver, the other higher coloured and much purer. All the gold of this creek is battered and water-worn, as if it had been carried some distance from the original bed. At Lowhee, only three miles distant, it is found in larger nuggets, less altered by the action of water, and almost pure. On Lightning Creek the gold is smaller, much more water-worn, but of the first quality.

The great drawbacks to the mining in this district are the nature of the country, the mountains and dense forest forming great obstacles to proper investigation, and rendering the transport of provisions and other necessaries exceedingly costly. The long and severe winter, which prevents the working of the mines from October until June; and the great geological disturbances which have taken place, although they doubtless are one cause of its exceeding richness, render the following of the "leads" very difficult and uncertain. The two former disadvantages will be removed ere long by the clearing of the country, the formation of roads, and the employment of steam power to drain the shafts. The difficulties encountered in tracing the course of the gold are more serious; but more accurate knowledge of the geological formation will give greater certainty to the search. At present the changes which have taken place in the face of the country continually upset the most acute calculations. The drift gold carried down the streams settled on the solid "bed rock," or in the blue clay immediately above it, and has been covered by the gravel accumulated in after times. Now, if the streams ran in exactly the same channels as they did when the gold came down, the matter would be simple enough. But great changes have taken place since then. At one point an enormous slide has occurred, covering in the channel, and forcing the stream to find a new course. At another, some convulsion appears to have upheaved a portion of the old bed high and dry. In the first case the "lead" is found to run into the mountain side; in the other it scales the hill. But these eccentricities are only discovered by experiment, and many a miner works for weeks to sink his shaft of thirty or forty feet, to find nothing at the end of his labour. His neighbour above or below may perhaps be making £1,000 a day, but the creek ran not through his claim in these past ages when it washed down the auriferous *débris*. More fortunate men, however, who, in mining phrase, "hit a streak," often make large fortunes in Cariboo in an incredibly short space of time.

The extraordinary yield of the Cariboo mines may be inferred from the fact that in 1861 the whole of the colonies of British Columbia and Vancouver Island were almost entirely supported by the gold obtained from Antler Creek alone; and from that time to the present year, or for four years in succession, William's Creek has also alone sustained more than 16,000 people, some of whom have left the country with large fortunes. And yet William's Creek is a mere narrow ravine, worked for little more than two miles of its length, and that in the roughest manner. The miners are destitute of steam power, and many requisites for efficient mining; and all that has been done hitherto has been mere scratching in the dark.

Out of many instances of the wonderful richness of these diggings it may be mentioned that Cunningham's Claim yielded, on an average, nearly 2,000 dollars, or £400 a day, during the whole season; and another, Dillon's Claim, gave the enormous amount of 102 lbs. of gold, or nearly £4,000 in one day. One hundred feet of the Cameron Claim, held in the name of another man, produced 120,000 dollars.

The wealth thus rapidly obtained is generally dissipated almost as quickly. The lucky miner hastens down to Victoria or San Francisco, and sows his gold broadcast. No luxury is too costly for him, no extravagance too great for the magnitude of his ideas. His love of display leads him into a thousand follies, and he proclaims his disregard for money by numberless eccentricities. One man who, at the end of the season found himself possessed of 30,000 or 40,000 dollars, having filled his pockets with twenty-dollar gold pieces, on his arrival in Victoria proceeded to a "bar-room," and treated "the crowd" to champagne. The company present being unable to consume all the bar-keeper's stock, assistance was obtained from without, and the passers-by compelled to come in. Still the supply held out, and not another "drink" could any one swallow. In this emergency the ingenious giver of the treat ordered every glass belonging to the establishment to be brought out and filled. Then, raising his stick, with one fell swoop he knocked the army of glasses off the counter. One hamper of champagne, however, yet remained, and, determined not to be beaten, he ordered it to be opened and placed upon the floor, and jumping in, stamped the bottles to pieces beneath his heavy boots, severely cutting his shins, it is said, in the operation. But although the champagne was at last finished, he had a handful of gold pieces to dispose of, and walking up to a large mirror, worth several hundred dollars, which adorned one end of the room, dashed a shower of heavy coins against it, and shivered it to pieces. The hero of this story returned to the mines in the following spring without a cent, and was working as a common labourer at the time of our visit. A freak of one of the most successful Californians may be appended as a companion to the story just related. When in the height of his glory, he was in the habit of substituting champagne bottles—full ones, too—for the wooden pins in the bowling alley, smashing batch after batch with infinite satisfaction to himself, amid the applause of his companions and the "bar-keep."

Our quarters at Cusheon's Hotel were vile. A blanket spread on the floor of a loft was our bedroom, but the swarms of lice which infested the place rendered sleep almost impossible, and made us think with regret on the soft turf of the prairie, or a mossy couch in the woods. The fare, limited to beefsteaks, bread, and dried apples, was wretchedly cooked and frightfully expensive. Beef was worth fifty cents or two shillings a pound, flour the same, a "drink" of anything except water was half a dollar, nor could the smallest article, even a box of matches, be bought for less than a "quarter"—one shilling. Before we reached William's Creek we paid a dollar and a quarter, or five shillings, for a single pint bottle of stout.

Coin of any kind is rarely seen, gold-dust being the circulating medium, and each person carries a small bag of it, from which the requisite quantity is weighed out for each payment.

In the mines we visited at Cameron Town the "pay-dirt," as the stratum of clay and gravel above the "bed-rock" in which the gold lies is called, was from thirty to fifty feet below the surface. A shaft is sunk to the required depth, and the "dirt" carried up by a bucket raised by a windlass. This is emptied into a long box, called the dump-box or "long tom," having a false bottom of parallel bars, with narrow spaces between them, raised a few inches above the true bottom, across which several cross pieces are placed. A stream of water, brought in a series of troughs called "flumes," sometimes for a considerable distance, pours into the dump-box at one end, and runs out by another series of troughs at the other. As the dirt is emptied in, a man armed with a large many-pronged fork stirs it up continually, and removes the larger stones. The smaller particles and the clay are carried down the stream, while the gold, from its greater weight, falls through the spaces between the parallel bars of the false bottom, and is arrested by the transverse ones or "riffle" of the true one. The "pay-dirt" is generally not more than from three to five feet thick, and the galleries of the mine are consequently very low, the roof being propped up by upright timbers, and cross beams wedged in above. The water is pumped out of the mines by a water wheel and chain pump, but these are quite useless in winter, and become covered with enormous icicles.

One or two were still kept working, even at this late season, by help of fires and roofing over. The Cameron, Raby, and Caledonian Claims, three of the richest in William's Creek, were, by good luck, still in full swing, and we frequently went down with some of the happy proprietors, and crept about the low dripping galleries, washed for gold, or picked out the rich "pockets" formed under some arresting boulder. In many places we could see the glistening yellow, but generally it was imperceptible, even in the richest dirt. Mr. Steele, of the Cameron Claim, kindly showed us the Company's books, from which it appeared that the yield varied from 40 to 112 oz. a shaft in the day, and there were three shafts, making £2,000 to £5,000 per week altogether. But the expenses were very heavy, averaging 7,000 dollars a week, or about £1,500. Eighty men were employed, at wages ranging from ten to sixteen dollars a day, or £2 to £3, and this alone would reach £1,208.

At noon, each day, the dump-boxes are emptied, and the gold separated from the black sand which is always mixed with it. At the "washing-up" of one shaft of the Raby Claim, which we saw, the gold filled one of the tin cases used for preserved meats, holding nearly a quart, the value of about £1,000 for fifteen hours' work! Amongst the gold were several shillings and quarter dollars, which had dropped out of the men's pockets, and turned up again in the dump-box.

After going through the mines on William's Creek, we walked over the hill to Lowhee, a smaller creek, lying about three miles off in a yet narrower ravine. The workings were very similar, but the gold was richer and brighter, the pieces more jagged and angular, as if they had not been carried very far from the original quartz reef. The Lowhee gold is very pure, being ·920 against ·830 of William's Creek.

Before taking leave of Cariboo, we must not forget to mention glorious "Judge" Cox, magistrate and gold commissioner there, prime favourite of all the miners, and everybody's friend. The "judge," as he is invariably called, after Yankee fashion, decides the cases brought before him by common sense; and, strange to say, both winners and losers, fascinated by the man, appear to be equally delighted with his judgments. We received much kindness from him, and spent many pleasant hours in his genial society.

Nor would it be just to leave unnoticed the sumptuous dinner at which we were entertained on the eve of our departure. The giver of the feast, Dr. B—k, selected the ward of the hospital as an appropriate dining-room, the single unfortunate patient in at the time being veiled from sight by a sheet of green baize suspended from the wall. We had soup, roast beef, boiled mutton, and plum pudding, with abundance of champagne. The company was somewhat mixed, yet all fraternised with easy cordiality. We had Mr. C—, manager of the Cariboo branch of the — Bank, a gentleman of solemn aspect, and with a large bald head, who wore spectacles, dressed in frock-coat, represented respectability, and spoke on all points with authority; Mr. B—, an old Hudson's Bay man, highly convivial, delighting in harmony; Dr. B—l, a medical gentleman, afflicted with the "cacoethes bibendi," as well as "loquendi"— a lean little fellow, with a large mouth, who appeared in the full glory of a swallow-tailed coat, and was perpetually smiling, yet, in reality, taking a gloomy view of things in general; Mr. C—, a young lawyer, Irish and impressionable; Billy Ferren, a successful miner, from his loquacity nicknamed "Billy the Bladge," rough, noisy, breaking forth into shouts and laughter; Dr. B—k's assistant, quiet and generally useful; and lastly, the lady of the party, Mrs. Morris, more generally known by her Christian name of Janet, fair, fat, and forty, and proprietor of a neighbouring house of refreshment. She had kindly come in to cook the dinner, and when that was duly set forth, she yielded to popular clamour, and joined us at the table.

Before the cloth was drawn—metaphorically—i.e., whilst we were still occupied with plum pudding, Dr. B—l, who had shown symptoms of restlessness for some time, could repress the flood of eloquence rising within him no longer, and having succeeded in catching the president's eye, and received a permissive nod in return, rose cautiously on his legs. A vigorous rapping on the table procured silence, and Dr. B—l, steadying himself by the table with one tremulous hand, and waving the other gracefully towards ourselves, while the ever-beaming smile irradiated his countenance, proposed Milton's health in most glowing terms, winding up his panegyric with a request for three-times-three, and "He's a jolly good fellow." These were given uproariously—the Hudson's Bay man leading, and Janet bringing in an effective soprano.

The eloquent Dr. B—l again rose, and proposed the health of the other visitor in similar eulogistic terms, and that was drunk with all the honours. When thanks had been returned by the honoured guests in an appropriate manner, the irrepressible Dr. B—l rose for the third time, and with grave countenance reproached the host for his reprehensible neglect in omitting to propose the health of Her Most Gracious Majesty the Queen. Dr. B—k felt humiliated; and although urging in extenuation the precipitation with which his friend had proposed the other toasts, fully acknowledged the gross disloyalty of which he had been unintentionally guilty. He trusted the circumstance might never come to Her Majesty's knowledge; and he could assure the company that the spark of loyalty never burnt brighter in any breast than his. From his childhood he had been ready—nay, he might say *wishful*—to die for his Queen and country. Animated by that desire, he had gone out with the British army to the Crimea, and now, marching in the van of civilisation in Cariboo, he was ready to die in the cause.

When Her Majesty's health had been drunk amidst hearty applause, we adjourned to the kitchen. More healths were drunk. Janet made a very pretty speech, and presented Milton with a handsome nugget; Billy Ferren followed suit with a second. Then each gave one to Cheadle with similar ceremony. The irrepressible Dr. B—l rose every few minutes to propose anew the health of one or other of the "illustrious travellers," and was remorselessly sung down by the equally indefatigable Hudson's Bay man, who always had "Annie Laurie" ready for the emergency, and all joining in the chorus, the obtrusive speaker was ultimately overpowered. At last his eyes became glassy, his smile disappeared, and he sat in his chair gloomily silent. All at once, however, he got up, and rushing across the room, made ineffectual attempts to force an exit through the mantelpiece, bobbing against it very much after the fashion of a bird trying to escape through a pane of glass; whereupon he was seized by the assistant, and led off into a bedroom. Cards were now introduced, and we were initiated into " High, Low, Jack and the Game," and "Pitch seven up," but were presently disturbed by a tremendous crash in the bedroom adjoining; the assistant ran out, and found Dr. B—l on the floor, having rolled off the bed into a miscellaneous collection of pots, pans, brushes, and etceteras which had been put there out of the way.

After this interruption conviviality reigned again. We played "Pitch seven up" till we were too sleepy to see the cards; the Hudson's Bay man tuned up indiscriminately, Janet sang "Auld Robin Gray" five or six times, "Billy the Bladge" carried on a fierce argument with the manager of the bank on colonial politics, everybody talked at the same time, smoked and drank whisky until far on towards daylight, when we turned out into the cold night with the thermometer standing at five degrees, and made our way back to Cusheon's.

THE CARIBOO ROAD

from *The Cariboo Trail: A Chronicle of the Gold-fields of British Columbia*
by Agnes C. Laut

Agnes Laut was a talented and insightful journalist, teacher, novelist and travel writer. In 1912, she exposed the pervasive racist attitudes of her times with her intelligent reporting on British Columbia's fear of Asian immigration and the union movement. This may surprise readers: in the following excerpt from The Cariboo Trail, *she uses the typical language of the era, revealing the extreme prejudices of the frontier, in her descriptions of some of the amusing characters to be met on the famous Cariboo Road. The Cariboo Road opened the way for permanence-minded settlers to move north with their families and belongings, and Laut's piece acts as a bridge from the era of transitory adventurers, explorers, trappers and gold seekers to the era of agricultural pioneers and community builders. Laut died in 1936.*

The passengers jumped for a seat, the long whip cracked, the horses sprang forward. So began a wild ride on the Cariboo Road.

There was something highly romantic in the stage-coach travel of this halcyon era. The driver was always a crack whip, a man who called himself an "old-timer," though often his years numbered fewer than twenty. Most of the drivers, however, knew the trail from having packed in on shanks's mare and camped under the stars. At the log taverns known as road-houses travellers could sleep for the night and obtain meals.

On the down trip, bags were piled on the roof with a couple of frontiersmen armed with rifles to guard them. Many were the devices of a returning miner for concealing the gold which he had won. A fat hurdy-gurdy girl—or sometimes a squaw—would climb to a place in the stage. And when the stage, with a crack of the whip and a prance of the six horses, came rattling across the bridge and rolling into Yale, the fat girl would be the first to deposit her ample person at the bank or the express office, whence gold could safely be sent on down to Victoria. And when she emerged half an hour later she would have thinned perceptibly. Then the rough miner, who had not addressed a word to her on the way down, for fear of a confidence man aboard, would present "Susy" with a handsome reward in the form of a gaudy dress or a year's provisions.

Start from a road-house was made at dawn, when the clouds still hung heavy on the mountains and the peaks were all reflected in the glacial waters. The passengers tumbled dishevelled from log-walled rooms where the beds were bench berths, and ate breakfast in a dining-hall where the seats were hewn logs. The fare consisted of ham fried in slabs, eggs ancient and transformed to leather in lard, slapjacks, known as "Rocky Mountain dead shot," in maple syrup that never saw a maple tree and was black as a pot, and potatoes in soggy pyramids. Yet so keen was the mountain air, so stimulating the ozone of the resinous hemlock forests, that the most fastidious traveller felt he had fared sumptuously, and gaily paid the two-fifty for the meal. Perhaps there was time to wash in the common tin basin at the door, where the towel always bore evidence of patronage; perhaps not; anyhow, no matter. Washing was only a trivial incident of mountain travel in those days.

The passenger jumped for a place in the coach; the long whip cracked. The horses sprang forward; and away the stage rattled round curves where a hind wheel would try to go over the edge—only the driver didn't let it; down embankments where any normal wagon would have upset, but this one didn't; up sharp grades where no horses ought to be driven at a trot, but where the six persisted in going at a gallop! The passenger didn't mind the jolting that almost dislocated his spine. He didn't mind the negro who sat on one side of him or the fat squaw who sat on the other. He was thankful not to be held up by highwaymen, or dumped into the wild cataract of waters below. Outside was a changing panorama of mountain and canyon, with a world of forests and lakes. Inside was a drama of human nature to outdo any curtain-raiser he had ever witnessed—a baronet who had lost in the game and was going home penniless, perhaps earning his way by helping with the horses; an outworn actress who had been trying her luck at the dance-halls; a gambler pretending that he was a millionaire; a saloon-keeper with a few thousands in his pockets and a diamond in his shirt the size of a pebble; a tenderfoot rigged out as a veteran, with buckskin coat, a belt full of artillery, fearfully and wonderfully made new high-boots, and a devil-may-care air that deceived no one but himself; a few Shuswaps and Siwashes, fat, ill-smelling, insolent, and plainly highly amused in their beady, watchful, black, ferret eyes at the mad ways of this white race; a still more ill-smelling Chinaman; and a taciturn, grizzled, ragged fellow, paying no attention to the fat squaw, keeping his observations and his thoughts inside his high-boots, but likely as not to turn out the man who would conduct the squaw to the bank or the express office at Yale.

If one could get a seat outside with the guards and the driver— one who knew how to unlock the lore of these sons of the hills—he was lucky; for he would learn who made his strike there, who was murdered at another place, how the sneak-thief trailed the tenderfoot somewhere else—all of it romance, much of it fiction, much of it fact, but no fiction half so marvelous as the fact.

Bull-teams of twenty yokes, long lines of pack-horses led by a bell-mare, mule-teams with a tinkling of bells and singing of the drivers, met the stage and passed with happy salute. At nightfall the camp-fires of foot travellers could be seen down at the water's edge. And there was always danger enough to add zest to the journey. Wherever there are hordes of hungry, adventurous men, there will be desperadoes. In spite of Begbie's justice, robberies occurred on the road and not a few murders. The time going in and out varied; but the journey could be made in five days and was often made in four.

The building of the Cariboo Road had an important influence on the camp that its builders could not foresee. The unknown El Dorado is always invested with a fabulous glamour that draws to ruin the reckless and the unfit. Before the road was built, adventurers had arrived in Cariboo expecting to pick up pails of nuggets at the bottom of a rainbow. Their disillusionment came; but there was an easy way back to the world. They did not stay to breed crime and lawlessness in the camp. "The walking"—as Begbie expressed it—"was all down hill and the road was good, especially for thugs." While there were ten thousand men in Cariboo in the winter of '62 and perhaps twenty thousand in the winter of '63, there were less than five thousand in '71.

This does not mean that the camp had collapsed. It had simply changed from a poor man's camp to a camp for a capitalist or a company. It will be remembered that the miners first found the gold in flakes, then farther up in nuggets, then that the nuggets had to be pursued to pay-dirt beneath gravel and clay. This meant shafts, tunnels, hydraulic machinery, stamp-mills. Later, when the pay-dirt showed signs of merging into quartz, there passed away for ever the day of the penniless prospector seeking the golden fleece of the hills as his predecessor, the trapper, had sought the pelt of the little beaver.

All unwittingly, the miner, as well as the trapper, was an instrument in the hands of destiny, an instrument for shaping empire; for it was the inrush of miners which gave birth to the colony of British Columbia. Federation with the Canadian Dominion followed in 1871; the railway and the settler came; and the man with the pick and his eyes on the "float" gave place to the man with the plough.

Nellie Verdier Hance rode sidesaddle 300 miles to become the Chilcotin's first White female settler. Nellie and husband Tom were typical of the hardy pioneers who founded settlements in the Cariboo–Chilcotin.

Portrait of a Pioneer Family

from *Chilcotin: Preserving Pioneer Memories*
by Veera Bonner

Born at Big Creek in the Chilcotin, Veera Bonner, nee Witte,
along with her sisters, Irene and Hazel, embarked on a labour of
devotion, gathering and recording the family histories and stories
of Chilcotin pioneers, many whose names grace the towns, roads,
landmarks and waterways of that country. One such family,
Bonner's maternal grandparents, exemplify the kind of settlers
that were drawn to the region: tough, versatile people with the
intelligence and backbone required to develop the array of skills
their harsh new environment demanded. Tom and Nellie Hance
(the first White woman to settle in the region) were committed
to making a strong contribution to the Chilcotin, their chosen
home. They took on a variety of roles, lending a hand wherever
it was needed. They befriended and helped the Natives with a
mutual exchange of goods and labour. The district of Hanceville
still bears the Hances' name, and their memory. In the following
excerpt from Chilcotin: Preserving Pioneer Memories, *we see*
also the Chinese presence that was integral to the development
of the region.

Nellie Verdier Hance was only in her teens when she rode with her husband on the long saddle horse journey accompanying the pack string to his isolated trading post in the Interior and the log cabin that would be her first home. The cookstove that she used throughout her lifetime was brought in on packhorses. On her arrival in the Chilcotin she was the only white woman in the country, with visits to family and friends in Victoria few and far apart.

What a trip that nearly 300-mile journey from Yale to Hanceville must have been for a young woman unaccustomed to riding—and using a sidesaddle. Each long adventurous day took them deeper into a wilderness she knew little about, fording rivers, braving rough trails, depending only on the capable frontiersman who led the way. At last the home stretch, the 75-mile ride down the narrow canyon trail to the Chilcotin Valley and Hance's pre-emption where neat buildings and fences nestled below the hill. Juniper, fir, and willow clothed the hillsides, while open fields, with clumps of aspen, dropped away to the turquoise river and blue hills rising in the distance.

As the young bride took in the beauty of the wild unsettled land, her husband's words came back to her: "There are no white women, only the natives and they speak little or no English. No doctors, no mail delivery, only rough wagon trails and no bridges. But we are working to change these things. It's a good country, Nellie. I'll build you a fine home there."

Nellie Hance was quick and industrious and took on the task of homemaking cheerfully. As she matured she responded to the challenge of pioneer living with courage and dedication: feeding the hungry, ministering to the sick and injured and, when necessary, laying out the dead. During the years when there was no medical aid in the country, her family remembered that she always kept a bag packed and ready in case she should be called away in a hurry.

As settlement progressed, she delivered many of the babies born in the Chilcotin. When Mike Minton, who homesteaded on the south side of the Chilcotin River, was hurt in an accident, she rode over every day to take care of him, her infant daughter tied on her back in a shawl. This visit meant overcoming her fear of water because she had to ford the river as there was no bridge. On one occasion while in the middle of the ford she felt the bundle on her back slipping. Terror gripped her as she struggled to hold the baby at her back and at the same time keep a grip on the bridle reins as her horse plunged through the deep, swift water. Once safely across she slid from her mount, collapsed on the grassy bank and, hugging her baby to her breast, burst into tears. By the time she had collected herself and proceeded up the steep hill and across the flat to the Irishman's cabin, the anxiety was gone and she could smile again. She entered the room in her usual quick, competent way and Minton never guessed that anything had gone wrong.

Although she never learned their language, her association with the Indians was amiable. In the early years, both in spring and in fall, it was a familiar sight to see a long line of old Indians, the halt and the blind, walking along the dusty road to Hanceville, some coming all the way from Nemiah Valley on foot. On arrival, they sat on the steps of Nellie's house where she affably communicated with them across the language barrier while the natives drank tea and ate a meal. When they left in a day or so these "blind creatures," as the Hance youngsters dubbed them, were loaded with gifts of food and other essentials packed into their big baskets which they carried on their heads. Always generous, Nellie gave to Indians and whites alike wherever there was a need—a fortune in flour, jam, vegetables, butter, cloth, and meals.

At Nellie's funeral a lengthy column of natives followed the crowd of mourners winding their way up the hill to the burial ground to silently show their regard for this small woman who had held the respect and loyalty of the Chilcotin people for nearly 50 years.

As more and more people settled, Tom Hance's application for a post office was granted on October 1, 1889. The post office was located on his TH Ranch and named "Hanceville." The Hanceville Post Office remained on Hances' TH Ranch for 83 years and was manned by the

Hance family for 77 consecutive years. Tom Hance was appointed postmaster in 1889 and Robert Graham took the contract to carry the mail to and from Soda Creek once a week. The *Daily World* newspaper, published in Vancouver, reported on March 11, 1890: "Mr. Graham's remuneration is very meagre and the service accordingly is not as complete as it should be ... " Three months later, in June, 1890, Graham resigned in favour of O. T. Hance, "the energetic and enterprising trader and postmaster at Hanceville," according to the *Daily World*.

Hance carried the mail for many years, first by packhorse over old Bald Mountain Trail and then with a team. In the fall of 1890 he cut out a sleigh road, bypassing the bleak and exposed Bald Mountain trail. He finished the "Hance Timber Road," as it was called, the next year. This route was straightened, widened and ditched in 1922 when the Conservative government was in power and Roderick Mackenzie was member for Cariboo. It was eventually gravelled and is now paved.

Tom Hance was appointed a Provincial Police Constable on August 16, 1895, one of six men so appointed by Superintendent F.S. Hussey in Victoria. He had, however, been acting constable for some time before that, as evidenced by letters dated February 21, 1894, empowering him to seize and hold a stolen calf. A log jail, erected on the TH Ranch in 1898, was described by Government Agent Wm. Stephenson of Quesnel Forks as a "good strong place with two good cells in the back, and a room 10' x 14' in front." Hance was jailer as well. The Government Agent suggested to Superintendent Hussey that two pairs of leg irons be sent to Constable Hance for use in the "Lockup." When an Indian had broken the law and was brought in to the jail, he was usually allowed to do little tasks about the place during the day and only locked at night. On cold nights the prisoners slept on the floor in Hance's warm kitchen.

After the murder of Lewis Elkins in December 1897, the settlers in the upper reaches of the Chilcotin sent a petition to Victoria, asking for a mounted constable to patrol the frontier. Robert Pyper of the North West Mounted Police was dispatched in January 1898 as a full time Provincial Constable. In December of that year Hance, who had been criticized by Edmund Elkins, brother of the murdered man, for not being aggressive enough with the lawbreaking Indians, was suspended from the Police Force. A year later Norman Lee, Charles Crowhurst, and Bidwell (JP) were complaining to the Superintendent of Police that Constable Pyper was too aggressive with both whites and natives. Pyper was, however, generally well liked and credited with doing a good job. Two years later Pyper was transferred to Soda Creek and Hance again appointed Constable for Chilcotin.

On May 2, 1899, papers were sent by the Provincial Secretary in Victoria to O. T. Hance appointing him Coroner for the Province of British Columbia. Hance returned the papers stating: "... I do not feel that I would like to hold a position of that kind ..."

In July, 1905, the Chilcotin Stage was robbed somewhere between Hanceville and 150 Mile House. When the stage arrived at the 150 Mile it was discovered that a large hole was torn in the Hanceville mail sack, which had contained a "considerable amount of registered mail," and the sack was empty. It was thought that the robbery took place at one of the stopping places along the way. The *Ashcroft Journal* reported on August 12, 1905, that "Constable Hance (who was also the postmaster), immediately on receipt of the information, camped on the trail of the thief and has now under arrest an employee on a ranch near Riske Creek. A second party is suspected of being an accomplice and is probably in the hands of the law by now.

"Hanceville has always been considered a post office of importance as the ranchers and other residents of that locality do most of their business through the registered mail, and reliable information is to the effect that this particular week the consignment was a valuable one."

Hance had always maintained fair and honourable dealings with the native people and had no trouble with them. He kept a well-stocked store with reasonable prices and carried on a brisk trade with the local bands. Their high regard for him was reflected in the Chief's actions when a crisis arose after an Englishman named Hewer moved in and applied for the Anaham Meadows, land considered Indian property. This encroachment touched off a council of war among the Indians. They decided to run the intruder out, with a massacre if necessary. Chief Anaham quickly rode down the river to warn Hance to be ready to leave the country in a hurry.

With his lathered horse standing at the hitching rail, Anaham entered the Hanceville Store and in a few words of broken English and Chinook delivered the warning: "My boys start, maybe go crazy," he warned. "Kill 'em all whiteman. Can't help it, me. You go quick." The Chief explained that he would send a runner ahead to tell the trader when to leave. Hance thanked him. They shook hands and the Chief departed.

Realizing the danger, Hance immediately sent a message to Hewer to impress upon him the seriousness of the situation. He then got together a light camp outfit and for many uneasy days and nights kept a team standing harnessed in the stable. Fortunately. Hewer was frightened by the threat of an uprising. He dropped his application and violence was averted.

Tom and Nellie Hance had a family of four sons and one daughter: Grover, Percy, Hattie, Judd, and Rene. Grover Orlando was the first white baby to arrive in the Chilcotin. He was born at 50 Mile House on April 19, 1888, under a doctor's care. The next son, Percy Royal, was the first white child born in the Chilcotin. He, Hattie, Judd and Rene were all born at Hanceville with an Indian midwife in attendance. When the older children were small, their playmates were Indians, children of natives employed on the ranch or those who came to trade at the store. The Hance youngsters sometimes wondered why they were the only kids with white skin while all the rest were brown.

Many natives worked for Hance, living with their families on the place. An Indian named Silpat helped him plant his crops each spring. Another, Sklam, was there for many years and when he died, was buried on the TH. Though Hance hired help for the heavy field work, he liked to put in the vegetable garden himself and always planted his onions on Easter Sunday. Chinese people were also part of the Hances' lives. One of their Chinese helpers was named Hang. He did chores around the house, helping with cooking, gardening, and milking. Hang was good-natured and dependable, and would readily interrupt his work to run to the youngsters' aid if one of them needed help. As a little girl, Hattie took full advantage of this. When frightened she would yell at the top her voice: MAMA, PAPA, HANG!" confident that at least one of them would hear her and come to her rescue. The children learned early to be considerate, courteous, and respectful to those around them regardless of colour or race, and these became lifelong attributes of the Hance family.

A few Chinese men would winter east of the Hanceville Bridge overlooking the river in what was called a China House. This cavelike dwelling was built into the sidehill near the top of the first bench. Tom and Nellie Hance and their family were regularly invited there for Chinese New Year, and the children remembered it as warm and pleasant. The family would share a meal with their Chinese hosts and then be laden with gifts to take home: China nuts, ginger in earthenware jars, China tea and fascinating Chinese matches that fizzled and spit, smelling of sulfur, before bursting into flame. Sometimes there would be a special gift of a small ring or bamboo bracelet for Hattie.

The Hance children were tutored at home through the winter months by an Englishman named Jefferson. The front, or office section of the jail, was used for a classroom. As soon as the weather turned warm in the spring, Jefferson went off prospecting, leaving the youngsters free again. There was a playroom upstairs where Judd spent happy hours carving and painting realistic horses and cows, which the children used in their games. But the great outdoors was their favourite place to play. The eldest four would sometimes all scramble onto their gentle old horse named Tommy and ride over the hillside trails, their dogs, Wozzle and Zena, frolicking beside them. But life wasn't all play; there were chores to do, too. One was bringing in the sheep in the evening. If the flock was hard to find and the children were gone too long, they would see their father's tall form walking out to look for them. He was always anxious for their safety.

Chiwid, a legend of the Chilcotin, tending her fishnets at Fletcher Lake.

Chiwid

from Chiwid
by Sage Birchwater

*Chiwid (pronounced Chee-weet or Chee-Wit) shunned the
comforts of home and human companionship after her jealous
husband beat her with a chain. Although Alec Jack tried to
make amends by raising money to send his beautiful, young wife
to Vancouver for treatment, Chiwid left him to live outdoors,
roaming the Chilcotin from Anahim Lake to Riske Creek.
She was a good shot with her bent rifle and was rumoured to
have spiritual powers that enabled her to hit a squirrel even after
her eyesight failed, and to survive sleeping outside in extreme
cold. Some took advantage of her vulnerability. Many more
assisted her with firewood, transporation, food and clothes.
Old and blind, she spent her last years in the Stone Creek
Reserve home of Katie Quilt, where she died in 1986. Chiwid
captured the imagination of Sage Birchwater, who collected
anecdotal encounters from residents for a book. Birchwater
has worked as a trapper, photographer, environmentalist
educator and oral-history researcher. He served as the Chilcotin
correspondent for two local papers while raising his family south
of Tatla Lake. Birchwater currently works as a staff writer for the
Williams Lake Tribune. What follows is his introduction to his
book* Chiwid, *and selected anecdotes from that book. Together,
they paint a vivid picture of the Chilcotin community and its
response to this strange and mythic woman.*

The country in those times was changing. It was still an unbroken sea of jackpine and spruce forests that rose from the Fraser River and spread westward to the rugged peaks of the Coast Mountain Range, some 320 kilometres away. But it was a time of great hardship and sorrow for the Tsilhqot'in people. Sickness and disease had weakened them and reduced their numbers. Newcomers were making their way into the high Chilcotin Plateau country, a territory the size of Vancouver Island. Some came on foot, others by saddlehorse, others still by covered wagon.

On June 18, 1904, the Oblate priest, Father François Marie Thomas, sprinkled water on the head of a child not quite a year old, and said her name: Lillie Skinner. It was "priest time" at Redstone Flats, deep in the heart of Tsilhqot'in territory.

In those times, the Catholic Church was starting to have its way with the Tsilhqot'in people. Many Tsilhqot'in, too, were eager to learn more of the whiteman's ways, so as not to be at a disadvantage in their dealings with the outside world. Churches were being built at several villages throughout the territory occupied by the nomadic Tsilhqot'in. The annual event known as priest time served the Tsilhqot'in as instruction in whiteman lore.

Father Thomas was making his annual trek through the country. His journey began some three or four weeks earlier in the Blackwater country to the north. Once there was enough green grass for feed, he set out by saddle horse from Quesnel to the Southern Carrier village of Nazko. From there he continued west to Kluskus, then on to Ulkatcho Village. Turning south, he followed the Dean River to Anahim Lake, where he was met by a delegation of Tsilhqot'in who brought him east into their homeland.

At Redstone Flats, the Tsilhqot'in people gathered from distant camps in the surrounding countryside to receive their yearly sacraments from the priest. Marriages were conducted, graves were blessed, and babies were officially welcomed into the Church. This backlog of the previous year's Church business was attended to in less than a week's time.

It was for these reasons that in 1904, the young mother, Loozap, had camped at Redstone with the infant daughter she named Chiwid. The child had been born shortly after the priest's last visit to the country the previous June.

Chiwid was baptized Lillie Skinner on account of two problems the Canadian government and the Church encountered among people whose custom was to own just a single name. The government wanted a register of the Tsilhqot'in people, and it needed a census so that reserve lands could be set aside and the land could be laid open for pre-emption and settlement by the whiteman. The other problem was that the Tsilhqot'in names, spoken in the language of the country, were often unintelligible to non-Tsilhqot'in speakers. In their official record-keeping, then, the Church bestowed English names on their Tsilhqot'in converts. A first and last name, in the manner of the British and European tradition.

This was all new to Loozap as she approached Father Thomas. And to complicate matters further, the young mother was born deaf and could only speak "on her hands."

As she stood before the altar with her child, it was somehow communicated to the priest that the child's father was a whiteman, Charlie Skinner, who ranged herds of horses in the country to the south. He had pre-empted a vast string of meadows in the shadow of the Potato Mountains.

Father Thomas filled out the baptismal record as follows: "Lillie (Skinner), age 11 months, Redstone Flat, B.C., June 18, 1904."

Beside "father's name," the record was left blank. Beside "mother's name," the record reads: "Lausap (Rosa)." Loozap received the comfort of an English name as well.

As for the infant girl, she would go on to a life that confounded both Tsilhqot'in and whiteman. Many people called her "half crazy and half coyote." Others felt that at some point in her life, her human spirit had departed and that the spirit of an animal had taken its place ...

Stories about Chiwid became a story about the Chilcotin, of events experienced by the people who lived there. It was a story about the transformation of a country, the clash and integration of cultures, and the strength of individuals.

—*Sage Birchwater*

ALICE ENGEBRETSON, born in 1916, is the oldest child of Andy and Ada Holte who arrived in the Chilcotin in a covered wagon from Washington State in 1922. The Holte family, which also included Tommy (born in 1918) and Illa (born in 1920), took six years to work their way across the Chilcotin. They arrived at the Engebretson ranch house in Towdystan in 1927 and stayed there five years. This is where Alice first met Chiwid, her husband Alec Jack, and their two daughters Cecilia and Julianna. Chiwid's daughters were only slightly younger than the Holte children.

Chiwid's father was a white man by the name of Charlie Skinner. I never knew him, but heard he was responsible for a lot of wild horses in the country. In Nemiah Valley. He acknowledged Chiwid as being his daughter, which is more than a lot of white men would do.

Chiwid's mother, Loozap, was deaf and dumb. She had lots of kids: Scotty Gregg, Ollie Nukalow, Madeline Palmantier, and a kid called Coyote Dag. All from different white fathers.

I was about 10 years old when I first met Chiwid. We lived at the Engebretson ranch house at Towdystan. Chiwid and Alec Jack were living at the Nimpo Meadow. They had two daughters, Cecilia and Julianna, who were a bit younger than us. But I remember them well.

Chiwid was a very sweet person. Nice looking and very kind. She was kind of tall, with a nice figure. She looked very good to me. She was good to all the children. She used to stay with my parents, while her husband Alec Jack was off chasing coyotes and wild horses with my dad ...

Alec Jack was very violent. Especially with horses. Scotty [Gregg] said he was the meanest man he had ever seen. He said he especially didn't like anything that was female.

Scotty tells about him tying up a mare one time, and beating it with a logging chain. The horse retaliated and kicked him right in the stomach. Every time that horse saw Alec Jack, she took after him. Scotty said he sure thought that was a smart horse.

I saw some other tricks Alec Jack pulled. He was mean for no reason.

One time he and my dad ran some bear cubs up a tree. Then they got some sticks and poked the bears down and sicked the dogs on them. The bears were just screaming. I was 12 years old at the time, and went behind a tree to cry. I never got over that ...

Alec Jack made homebrew, then the beatings would start.

—*Alice Engebretson*

HANK LAW *lived in the Chilcotin on two different occasions. In 1931 he arrived on his bicycle from Vancouver. When he got to Riske Creek he traded his bike for a saddle horse. "Not many Indians had seen a bicycle in those days." He got married in Tatlayoko, then left the country to serve in World War II. In 1960 he returned to Puntzi to work at the air base. He then bought the old Pyper place at Pyper Lake.*

I first met Chiwid the year she got in that mixup with her man. He beat her up with a logging chain and cut her with a knife.

I was building an annex on the Red Cross outpost hospital at Alexis Creek in 1932-33 when Dr. Knipthal called me into the hospital to show off his stitching job of sewing her back up. He was taking off the bandages and she was sitting on a high stool.

She looked young, maybe 18 or 20 years old, and the doctor was very proud of his work.

I saw her on and off, pretty near every year after that. She used to travel with a couple of pack horses and a saddle horse from Chezacut way. She went from Tatla Lake on out to Stone. She never went in a house, and that always upset the do-gooders. They always said, "She can't do this," and "She can't do that." But she outlived most of these can't-doers.

Eventually she got rid of her horses, and travelled by foot. She'd shoot a moose with a bent up old .22, and camp right there until she and the bears and the coyotes had eaten it all up.

I got married in Tatlayoko in 1935, and didn't see Chiwid again until we moved back to Alexis Creek in 1937. Then I went to war for five years, and didn't move back to the Chilcotin until 1960. We went to Puntzi, and I worked at the air force base there. Then we got the old Pyper place at Pyper Lake. That's where I saw Chiwid again.

She had got rid of her horses by the time I moved to Pyper Lake. When she wanted to move camp, she had quite a way of doing it. She had all her stuff tied in several bundles. When she moved these bundles, she did it so she could always keep an eye on them. I guess Indian kids used to steal stuff from her. She threatened to shoot them with her .22 if they didn't quit.

Lillie Skinner got her name from the chickadee. It's said that Chiwid is the Indian name for chickadee.

The name comes from the sound the bird makes. In January, it goes "chee-wit." In February, "chee-chee-wit," and in March it goes "chee-chee-chee-wit."

Chiwid used to be on my place at Pyper Lake when the suckers were running in the spring. When you saw the eagles sitting in the trees above the creek, you knew Chiwid was there. She'd be camped along the creek, catching the suckers in her net.

She spent several winters at Pyper Lake while we were there. It could be 60 below out there. And the bloody lake would be cracking. And the timbers cracking. And the northern lights shimmering in your face. And she'd be quite comfortable. Well I don't know how comfortable, but she'd be breathing the next morning. And that's what it's all about. It's surprising what you can stand if you have to ...

She'd talk to me, or to anybody else she knew. Just the odd word. But any man she had never seen, she'd just ignore them. Just turn around and walk the other way. She took to me okay. She was quite normal. But she was still quite aloof. She had this thing in her mind to live away from other people.

One time at Pyper Lake, this young fellow and I had some cows we wanted to find. We took off from my place early in the morning, and were going by the swimming hole, when my friend said he could smell smoke. Well, it was fall time ... hunting time, and since it was my range, I decided to take a look around. Then I saw a wisp of smoke, and saw what looked like a bedroll right up close to the fire.

So I barrelled down there, and this other fellow with me. We had a dog with us. As soon as I got close, I could see who it was. It was Chiwid. She had a bunch of rags over her and a few old cans and a frying pan, and that was it.

So I'm standing there. I got off my horse, and had the horse on one side and the dog on the other. She reared up and threw the clothes off her, and spit out a big gob of tobacco juice. Then she stood up and talked to me. We were standing there talking, and all of a sudden she froze. Just froze, and she's listening. And you know it must have been two minutes later that my horse looked, and my dog looked. Two minutes after she could hear whatever it was moving in the bush.

That's how she was. She was way ahead of the animals to hear anything or smell anything.

One time she was heading up to my place, and I was coming up the trail behind her on a saddle horse. She kind of stopped when she heard me coming, and waited for me to go by. When she saw it was me, she stopped and said: "Howdy."

I asked her what the problem was, and she said: "I smell'em skunk." Then she pointed up the hill. That's where I was going, so I left her there and took off. You know, two days later there was a skunk in there. But she bloody well knew way before it happened. This is how she was.

I've seen her take her moccasin rubber off, and have no moccasins on. Just bare feet. And empty the snow out. You know how cold it is when you can empty the snow out, and it's just like sugar? Anybody else would freeze, but not the old lady. She wasn't all bundled up in clothes. She had no sleeping bag. It was just a pile of old clothes and rags.

I was giving her a ride one time from the store to her camp at Pyper Lake. I picked up this bag of stuff to take to her camp, and felt the bag bust. So I quickly put it down before anything could spill out. It was the sugar sack that had busted, and some of the sugar spilled on the ground.

You know, she went and got an old can, and was on her hands and knees. I think she picked up every grain of sugar there was. She wasn't going to waste it, that's for sure.

—*Hank Law*

GERRY BRACEWELL came to Tatlayoko Valley from Alberta in 1940 to work for K.B. Moore, her future father-in-law. She took over the ranch after K.B. died in the 1950s. She is a registered big game guide and is well known for her knowledge of the outdoors and wilderness.

Chiwid was a very beautiful woman when I first came into this country in 1940. I remember seeing her camped in a little grove of poplar trees at Graveyard Springs, along the old road into the West Branch. I remember how beautiful she was. All by herself, with very beautiful, long black hair, as shiny as a raven's wing. She was just there in the wilderness.

That's when I started becoming interested in her activities, because nobody knew much about her. There were stories that went around that her husband mistreated her, that she was a bit demented as a result of the mistreatment. Because he was jealous.

She had a saddle horse, but the last one she had died at Barr Hill. Fred Linder saw Lillie walking with a tobacco can of water, trying to revive her dead horse. Fred told her that the horse was dead. That she couldn't bring it back to life.

She was known as the Cattle Queen to the Graham family. Eventually she lost all her cattle.

One time Fred and Betty [Linder] heard a weird sound up in the hills on a very cold winter night. It was 40 below and Fred and Betty went to investigate it. They found Lillie's camp. She had a very small fire, and was camped there with just one miserable little blanket. They felt sorry for her, and Betty managed to get a small pension for her, so she could have food. She wouldn't even use it to benefit herself by it. Her family used it.

People were totally amazed at her endurance. She was very wise as far as wilderness goes ...

I remember her catching fish on the north end of Potato Mountain. There's a little pond up there and a little creek trickles through it and there's a swamp lake. She had a little rock dam on the creek, then she'd let the water out. The fish would get stranded in the dry creek bed and she'd go along and pick them up.

Marvin Baptiste tells a story about Chiwid when she was camped at Choelquoit Lake one time. She caught a bunch of fish and cooked them in the big pot she used to pack around. She set the pot off the campfire to cool down, then decided to take a little nap. Asleep on her blanket she was awakened by this old smacking and slopping going on. She opened her eyes and there was a big black bear with his head in the pot, eating all her trout. She leaped up over the fire and kicked the bear in the butt. The bear took off without looking back to see what was chasing it.

Lillie had a lot of guts. She wasn't afraid of anything.

—*Gerry Bracewell*

RITA LULUA MELDRUM is the second-oldest daughter of Mary Jane Lulua, Chiwid's youngest daughter. While Rita was growing up near Henry's Crossing, her grandmother often camped nearby.

Chiwid was my favorite grandmother, and I was her favorite grand-daughter. She was unique because she used to live outside. Nobody else did at 50 below. She stayed quite close to our house.

When she lived outside she just had a little campfire. But when she came to live with us inside the house, the house would be boiling.

She always thought it was cold. For some reason, she always got it reversed. She could never get it hot enough. If we had the windows open, she'd close them. If we tried to open the door, she'd close it again.

Granny used to tell stories, but I can't remember them much now.

My dad [Henry Lulua] didn't really trust her. We were told not to go and see her. But we used to sneak to go see her anyway.

She just drank out of little tin cans, and I loved it. I thought it was really neat. We had cups in the house and Granma had tin cans to drink out of. We used to drink out of her tin cans and our parents used to get mad at us. But I thought it was neat.

Granny travelled around. She just packed her stuff from one place to another on foot. My parents thought she was crazy, but I didn't think she was crazy at all. I thought she was really spiritual. Everybody else thought she was just nuts.

Every time Dad would go out hunting or something, all of a sudden Granny would sniff the air: "Oh your dad just shot a deer today."

And I'd say: "Really?" And I'd run back to the camp and tell my mom and my aunt Jenny.

And she'd go: "Ah! That's just lies. She's filling your head with lies."

And you know, dad would come back home half an hour later with a deer or something.

She was always right on, I thought. I knew she made sense, but everybody told me: "Don't listen to her. Don't listen to her."

I used to remember Granny moving away and coming back again. I don't know how often she spent time with us. I always remember the times she was around, which wasn't very often.

Granny didn't like my dad. She always thought my dad was wrong for my mom. I always thought she was a sweet lady.

I don't remember Granny using a gun to hunt. She always used little strings to catch animals. She lived outside and survived.

The elders told us kids to stay away from Granny. They said she was really bad because she got spiritual powers. Even my Aunt Jenny said she had bad spiritual powers.

—*Rita Lulua Meldrum*

JOY GRAHAM came to the Chilcotin in 1935 to take a job house-
keeping and never left. She married Bill Graham, the oldest son
of Tatla Lake Ranch owner Bob Graham, and brother of Betty
Linder, owner of the store at Tatla Lake. Among her many duties
around the ranch, Joy also worked in the store.

Chiwid was a strange woman. She didn't mix with the Indians hardly at all. They thought she was strange and they sort of shunned her because of it. We'd see her at the store in Tatla Lake once in a while.

She didn't have much meat on her. She was pretty skinny. You might say she just existed.

She had squirrels and she'd bring the pelts into the store and trade them for groceries. Betty always gave her more for them than their value. She tried to give her all the necessities.

In winter time she'd come into the store and it was cold. She had every stitch of clothes she owned on. What really got me was her feet. They'd be in moccasins and they were frozen stiff. And she'd walk into the store and these frozen moccasins would go "clack, clack, clack" across the floor.

It didn't seem to bother her feet any. As far as I know she never froze her feet. But she had those moccasins on and they were just as stiff as boards.

—Joy Graham

PHIL ROBERTSON first went to Tatla Lake in 1946 to feed
cattle for his cousin Alex Graham. Then he went to work for Bill
Graham driving his bulldozer. Bill offered Phil a job to work the
machine on the highway to Anahim Lake, and in 1953 Phil and
his wife JOYCE decided to move to Tatla Lake.

Joyce: When we first went to Tatla Lake, Chiwid had a horse. Maybe a couple of years later, something happened to her horse. It was so old and everything.

Fred Linder was coming up the old Bear Head Hill Road that used to come from Chilanko along the edge of the hill. It used to cross at the bottom of Tatla Lake and go up through the draw there. Bear Head Gulch we called it.

Lillie was camped out at the bottom there when Fred came along and she was in a great fuss. Oh, so upset. There was a bear stalking her horse, but the horse had died and the bear wanted to eat on it. But she didn't want the bear eating on that horse. She had this old .22 and she was going to shoot this bear.

So Fred got the .22 and lined it up on the bear, and pulled the trigger. Nothing happened, just "click." So I guess that was the end of that. He didn't shoot any bear. Not with a gun like that ...

The government used to give Lillie an allotment every month for groceries. Betty Linder was to look after it for her, and make sure she got food. We used to take groceries to her. A little box of everything. There was a certain amount of money and Betty would put in what she thought she'd use. One time she put in a bar of Lifebuoy soap.

The next time we went, I found her Lifebuoy soap lying on the ground. She must have chucked it. The paper was ripped off, and there were teeth marks on it. I guess she didn't know what it was. I don't think she washed very much.

She didn't use all the groceries Betty sent out. I know she had to have her tea, sugar and flour. She liked lots of sugar. She made tea with no milk, but lots of sugar. Maybe two or three teaspoons.

Phil: One time, Lillie was camped over by Hook Lake. Late 1953 or early 1954. It was terribly cold that winter, about 55 or maybe 60 below, and lots of snow. I think she had a tent that time.

Alex Graham was riding over that way and he came upon her camp. She had a deer strung up in quarters, hanging from the limb of a jackpine tree, and he says, "You catch'em mowich, Lillie?"

"No," she says, "I no catch him."

He said: "How you get him then?"

"Well," she says, "Coyote kill him. Me, I take him from coyote."

That's how she got her deer. The coyotes run it down on the lake.

—*Phil Robertson*

HENRY SOLOMON is a respected Tsilhqot'in elder. He lives in Nemiah Valley with Mabel, his wife. Note that Solomon often refers to Chiwid as "he." The Tsilhqot'in language has no gender pronouns, and older-generation Tsilhqot'ins, when speaking English, tend to use "he" and "she" interchangeably.

I guess one year it was 50 below. Chiwid still camp outside at Stone Reserve. Every time, somebody told him he's going to freeze outside. Chiwid, he don't want to stay inside. He say: "It's good to stay outside. More better. Cold wind. North wind."

Chiwid was kind of a witchdoctor. He dreamed of coyote. Coyote, he won't freeze. Chiwid, he dream about something like that. Kind of a witchdoctor. Suppose you not like that, you're going to freeze.

He don't have much blanket. Just sleep right under the blanket. Maybe put a little tarp over him. Every place he go, he don't put up no tent, nothing. So he do that all the time.

You know, when Chiwid sleep you don't know which way his head is. Just curl up like a coyote. Like a dog put his head under him like that. Just curl up like that. Chiwid sleep like that. I seen him. Just sleep there right out, open place. Maybe put a little tarp over. Sleep like that all winter. Snow on top. He don't care. Seem like he don't feel the cold at all. Got a little camp fire, that's all. Sit beside. About 20 below wind. Must be tough.

Sometime, Chiwid go way down to Riske Creek. Way down through the pass. Way down along the river. Pick them blackberries down there. Saskatoon trees grow real long, down along the river.

Chiwid he come from Tatla Lake, that country. He used to live all over. Anahim Lake.

So he go down there to Riske Greek. He just have a pack horse and one more horse. Chiwid and his daughter, Mary Jane, that was married to Henry Lulua. That little girl, that's the only one that ride a horse that time. Chiwid he don't want to ride a horse. Just lead him. Pack the little girl. Chiwid, he just walked.

I was about eight years old when I first see Chiwid. I was raised at Toosey reserve by my grandmother.

Long time ago, lots of people they go pick berries at Riske Creek. They come from Redstone and Anaham. They go down with a wagon. Before there were hardly any cars. That time, Chiwid go down with a pack horse and pick some berries along the river down there. He camp by himself all the time. Seem he don't like to camp around pretty close to anybody. Seem like just that little girl go with him, and he camp some place. But he don't want to camp around a bunch of people.

That first time I see Chiwid, he looked pretty good. Strong. When he go down the river, it's a long ways down there. Maybe three miles. Real hot down there. Kind of rocks all over. The last time we went down there, me and my wife and her mother and old man Sammy, Mabel's dad. That time we see Chiwid picking some berries down there too. That must have been 30 years ago.

Once we were going to Anahim Lake. We go by the wagon through Tsuniah. Then we come out at Tatla Lake. Then, just on the other side of Tatla Lake, we found a junk pile there. We got no spare tire for our wagon, so we stopped to look for a tire. My wife, he look way over there and see somebody sitting over there. So we went over there. Chiwid was sitting right there. Got a bunch of stuff all over. Camp right there. He don't want no tent. He sleep under a tree.

His mind not very good, Chiwid. He told us somebody kill somebody. Somebody got knocked over the head. He said they take him back to Anahim Lake. We went over to Anahim Lake. Nobody got killed. Guess he just say that way.

One year, we see Chiwid coming along the road, way down by the bridge at Taseko River. See her coming this way. We were on our way home. Pick up our kids from the school bus at Stone Reserve. We see Chiwid packing her stuff alongside the road. So we stop.

We tell him: "We take your stuff to Tommy Lulua's place at Henry's Crossing?" He said: "Just past Tommy's place and then camp."

So we bring his stuff right out. Piled up his stuff before we left.

Pretty soon, Tommy, I guess he go and see Chiwid. Tommy Lulua, he told Chiwid: "We stay together?"

Old Chiwid, he say he don't want no more man no more. He told Tommy he don't like no man like you anyway. So, Chiwid don't want to go with him.

"Suppose you stay with me," Tommy Lulua tell him. "You not going to stay under the tree no more. You stay in good house."

He say he got lots of grub and stuff like that. He say he got lots of cattle.

Still, Chiwid, he don't want him Tommy. He told Tommy he don't want no more man. Can't stay with you. That's what he do. So Tommy, he don't bother Chiwid no more.

One time, I stay with Chiwid in the hospital. He was blind already. Got cold sick from staying outside. I got sick, too. So I stay in the hospital. I guess Chiwid got no Tsilhqot'in to talk to in the hospital, so that nurse want me to talk to him. I talk to him for a long time.

I ask him: "Which way you leave Alec Jack?" I told him.

He say: "One fellow, he fool me pretty bad."

So I tell him: "What you do?"

He tell me: "One fella just look like Alec Jack. He got his hair combed just like Alec Jack. He look like same as Alec Jack. That's the fellow that fool me."

Chiwid tell me he start to stay with that fellow for quite a while. Pretty soon, some way, he find out. He figured that fellow wasn't Alec Jack. So he said he left him again.

That's what he said. I guess he kind of went cuckoo. He said he don't want to get fooled anymore.

Alec Jack, he talk to you really good. Tell you lots of oldtimer story. He stay with me eight months. Every day he tell you different story. About a long time ago before any white people around here. Long time ago there's a bunch of Chinamen along the Fraser River.

Chiwid get pretty blind when he stay at Stone. One time we watch him shoot ducks. He can really shoot good. Every shot he got something. Right in front of Stone, way out in the field. We watch him. Pretty soon, he go way out there. Pick up the ducks and bring back to his camp. Pretty good shot.

Sometime, a witchdoctor can shoot. He can't miss nothing. Witchdoctor used to be like that before. Don't matter where he shoot, he kill them. I think Chiwid like that some way. That's why every shot he get something. Some kind of witchdoctor. Can't miss anything.

Seem like Chiwid don't stay with people. Long time ago, witchdoctor don't like to stay around with a bunch of people. Don't stay in a group. Some people like that before.

Dream like coyote all the time. Then you make some noise like a coyote.

—Henry Solomon

Riding up the Road

from *Cariboo Cowboy*
by Harry Marriott

*Born in England in 1891, Harry Marriott immigrated to
British Columbia in 1907. He made his way by Canadian
Pacific rail to Ashcroft, gateway to the great ranching country
of the Cariboo, and up the Cariboo Road to the Gang Ranch,
at that time the largest spread in North America. Marriott,
like many young cowboys who lost their greenhorn status at
the Gang, was soon busting broncs and driving cattle. In this
excerpt from his memoir,* Cariboo Cowboy, *Marriott takes us on
a tour of the country that parallels Cheadle's earlier frontier tour,
showing us a Cariboo now firmly established in farming and
ranching. For young Marriott, the gold rush of Cheadle's time
is a story told by old-timers. Marriott embodies the romantic
view of the cowboy in his majestic landscape. Humble and
stoic, he is simple in his tastes and grateful for small pleasures
like the beauty of nature and the good fellowship of people he
meets along his solitary way. His cheerful view of life is perhaps
naive. For example, his theories on mixed marriage stand out
in sharp contrast to the actual experience of Native women, as
seen earlier in* Chiwid. *But Marrriott's optimism is contagious
as he displays a deep and genuine affection for the Cariboo and
its people: cowboys, Natives, homesteaders and ranchers alike.
Harry Marriott died in 1969.*

Along in early June of 1914—the annual bunch of scrubby yearling heifers having been all spayed and picking up again after operations—I rode up the river on my old Pinto and asked my boss, Andy Stobie, if I could get a couple of weeks or so off. I wanted to ride "Up Country" as far as Barkerville which lay about sixty miles in a north-easterly direction from the little town of Quesnel on the far stretches of the Cariboo Road. I wanted to take a look around and see if I could find some more cow country. I'd had a pretty fair run on the grindstone, so I figured a couple of weeks change would be as good as a rest.

Stobie told me that it would be all right for not more than three weeks at the most—and I told him I'd be back under that time. So back down the river I rode, and in the next day or so I started out, with a clean shirt and underwear, a good ten-gallon Stetson and a good black silk handkerchief around my neck, good rigging in the line of a good saddle, bridle, boots and spurs and a real raw-hide lasso rope, and a good chunk of a saddle horse I called Pilot. I knew he'd carry me thirty-five miles a day without trouble as long as he had a bite of feed and a drink of water—kind of often and regular.

I rode up the river as far as the Gang in my first day, and of course stayed there overnight, and my old friend, Jack MacIntyre, unlimbered his usual silent tongue to wise me up to the short cut on the trail to the Chilcotin River. In the morning I stepped up on old Pilot, and headed him over the trail up the river.

The trail spun its way along the higher benches of the river and along about two o'clock in the afternoon I rode on up through a timbered slope and when I reached the top of the ridge I could see a river tearing along from the west. To me it looked like it joined up with the Fraser about four miles east of this ridge and I knew at once that I had come on to the Chilcotin River.

I got off my horse, Pilot, and let him feed for awhile on a little open spot, reached into the gunny sack I had tied behind my saddle and fished out a little bite of lunch that I had talked out of old Fungo—the cook at the Gang—and while I was eating this bread and beef sandwich I was turning my head around just like it was on a swivel and sizing up my bearings.

On the north side of the Chilcotin were at least ten miles of bunch-grass flats and slopes running down to the river—so I knew that they were the Gang Ranch steer range pastures. If I rode on far enough I'd finally get in sight of the company cabin on the Chilcotin—and I felt kind of sure I'd find Jim Ragan there. He was in charge of the Chilcotin range for the Gang.

I caught Pilot and started on the trail up the river, and after riding for about eight miles the trail took a turn down a long ridge and I came to a bridge on the Chilcotin—which I crossed. The river was sure aboiling down through that canyon, just arunning like the mill tails of Hell, and looking at it, I figured a man would never have a Chinaman's chance of ever getting out alive, if he ever got in there.

About a mile and a half up the trail from the bridge, I could see a log cabin and a log barn and a small green patch, and I knew this must be the cabin so I let Pilot take his time climbing up the hog's back trail. I rode up to the barn and saw Jim just turn his saddle horse loose. He looked up when I hollered out, "Howdy old-timer." Jim looked real surprised and said, "Well, you old son of a ... ! Where do you think you're going to?" So I told him I was heading my horse for Barkerville to have a look around a day or two.

I hadn't seen him for around two years—since we were breaking horses and haying at the Gang—so we had lots to talk about. I turned Pilot loose in the saddle horse pasture and after a darned good supper of salt pork and beans, and fried buckaroo spuds and hot coffee and hot biscuit, and a couple of cigarettes, I rolled into some extra blankets Jim had there, figuring I'd had a hell of a good day. I sure didn't need any rocking in the cradle to get a real sound sleep that night.

Morning came rolling in with the old sun just ashining through the cabin window, and I heard Jim fussing around the stove and mixing up a batch of hotcakes which soon enough we tied into with some bacon, syrup and coffee.

Jim was sure glad to see me, and I was tickled to see him again. We talked the usual cow range gossip that all cowboys enjoy and he suggested I'd better rest up my horse for a day or so before going on and he'd show me around, which sounded good to me.

It didn't take me very long to see that Jim was looking after a much bigger spread on the north side of the Chilcotin than I had down at the old Crow's Bar. The Gang had 1,400 steers on that north side which Jim was responsible for while I had only around 550 spayed heifers on the Crow's Bar end. Of course I knew that the company put about five hundred heifers each year into their cow herd for replacement stock so that, to my mind, accounted for a lot of the difference—but that Chilcotin steer pasture sure looked like a grass paradise to me.

Jim said to me we'd saddle up and take a little ride to see some friends of his and have noon with them, so we caught up a little sorrel mare called Dollie out of the pasture for me to ride, while Pilot really filled his belly with grass.

We rode on down the hog's back to the bridge, which he told me was called Chilcotin Falls, and up the river about half a mile was a little ranch right alongside the river which was owned by two young English fellows, named Farwell and Gerald Blenkinsop, these boys owning a small bunch of cows and growing real good alfalfa hay, and looked like they made a good living there.

After we'd had a good dinner and a smoke, Jim and I started back for the cabin. After we'd crossed over the bridge we noticed some fresh wheel tracks and saddle horse tracks just below the bridge, so we followed up the tracks and a few minutes later came on to a little tent, and a campfire outside the tent, and an Indian "klootch" with three kids playing around the tent, and a fair-sized white man with them.

Jim knew the outfit real well and we had a half hour's talk with them. The white man was an educated Englishman who spoke English with a very high Oxford accent, and was a remittance man who had five hundred dollars allowance sent to him every three months from old England by his folks back there. The Indian queen who was called "Crazy Jennie" seemed to be just what "His Lordship" needed out here in the wild and woolly Chilcotin country. It seemed like she was a good cook and a good worker and probably a good bed partner—so it was just made to order all around.

This Indian gal must have been real smart to learn and observe things because she spoke somewhat with an Oxford accent too—which I guess must have sounded like home to the high-class Englishman.

Crazy Jennie had these three kids, each one from a different pappy—one little girl had real brown hair and a lot of freckles, and Jim said this bright little girl's pappy was a pretty good Scotchman who had ranged around the Chilcotin some in previous years. The oldest of the two boys with her was a full-blooded Indian boy who might have had a pretty good dad by the look of him. The second boy had real kinky black hair and Jim told me he was the son of a coloured gentleman who had lived down the river and had died a few years previously.

All in all, they presented quite a picture there on the bank of the Chilcotin and Jim and I climbed up on our horses and started up the long hog's back trail to the cabin and when we stopped awhile to give our horses a little breather, Jim turned in his saddle and said to me, "Harry, if I can just put a Californian in that little bunch down there I'll sure as hell be able to start a show." I told him I figured it was a very worthwhile objective.

I don't know how this Cariboo Country would ever have got going unless these old-timers—some of them afoot, others with some sort of a horse or a team—had not started with an Indian gal, or klootch as they were called, and as they settled on creeks and flats along the rivers, and by endless hard work and effort, carved themselves out a little home and ranch, and raised up a family of half-breed kids.

I have noticed that these Indian gals never had very much at any time and when one of them took up with a white man she lived a lot better than in an Indian Reserve. They always looked up to the man as being the boss at all times, and few if any white girls would take the rugged life, and having to get along with very little, like the Indian gals did. There were little or no legal troubles because very few actually were ever legally married to any white man they lived with, so if any trouble came along and a "split the blankets" situation arose, there were no divorce cases or pocket-book breaking alimony business in that deal.

The Indian gal shopped around and probably picked up another fellow and the white boy generally rustled himself up another partner.

A great friend of mine, and a real top number one figuring hound, once told me that it was his "idee" that an Indian gal lived with a white man for his money and better grub and clothes and that she lived with an Indian for straight love of him. Once in a while she'd live with a Chinaman out of plumb curiosity but, by and large, I've seen a lot of darned good handy Indian gals in my time, and in those days white gals were as scarce as hen's teeth and awful hard to get, and what few there were, were scattered over the ranges and had more beaux after them than would patch old Hell a mile, and then some.

Jim and I got back up to the cabin and after awhile he cooked supper while I split some firewood and packed some water to the cabin. When we had finished supper, the days and the daylight being long, Jim said, "Harry, we'll take a ride over to Beecher's." Beecher's was near Riske Creek which was only about seven or eight miles away, and not far to ride on a long summer's evening.

So we rode over to Beecher's, which was a general store, a hotel with a bar in it, and a little ranch operation with it. However, Beecher's was quite a trading spot for the ranchers around and the Indians from the reserve. It was also a post office and on the main road from the Cariboo Road to the Chilcotin district, so there were sometimes quite a few travellers stayed at Beecher's, on the weekly stage line which ran through the Chilcotin as far as Kleena Kleene. Beecher himself was an old-timer who had originally come from England and had settled there, and had started his trading store and did considerable trade with the Indians in furs and sold a lot of booze over his bar.

Jim made me known to all and sundry in the bar, and I had several rounds of "O-B-Joyful" with the boys and looking around I failed to see Jim. However, I met up with a very agreeable man called Tommy Armstrong, who had been running a little bunch of cows about forty miles to the west of Beecher's. Tommy told me he was going to ride over to the company cabin that night, so we decided we'd ride back together as I couldn't find hide nor hair of Jim Ragan when it came time to go. So after I had ginned up the boys for another round of booze or two, Tommy and I started back on the trail to the cabin with a bottle of hootch apiece tied behind our saddles and feeling no pain at all. We started out just as the last string of daylight was fading out into the darkness and rode along the trail to the cabin, talking about this and that, and every so often we'd take a little nip out of the bottle tied on behind our saddles, and it was not very long before it was pitch dark and I noticed, or thought I did anyway, that we had ridden off the trail someway, so I tied my bridle lines together and let them hang loose, figuring that this Dollie mare I was riding would find her way straight to the gate on the trail, at the steer range pasture—but it didn't turn out that way. As we came in the darkness to a small lake Dollie walked eight times around that lake followed, of course, by Tommy on his horse. So after the eighth time around I said to Tommy, "That's enough, we'll just tie up our horses to these cottonwood trees and wait a few hours till daylight." This we did, and I groped around in the dark and found some dead cottonwood twigs and made a little fire, and we sat down and talked and catnapped a little by the fire, taking a little jolt of booze every so often to keep up the circulation and our bellies warm. After some considerable time the daylight began peeping its way in and that grand old haymaker, a nice warm sun, rose up over the mountains to the east of us.

Sure enough, the gate going in to the Gang Ranch steer range was only about half a mile from this lake we camped out at, so my little Dollie mare must have figured she was pretty near home when she went round and round that lake so often as she did with me. It didn't take us very long to get through that gate and down to the cabin, where we found Jim Ragan in bed, so I made a fire in the stove as I was a little chilly. What with getting thawed out by the hot fire, and nicely woozy with all those snorts I'd been having and not being used to it, I got higher than a hoot owl, and staggered off to bed and slept like a dead man.

The next day early I started out on Pilot to ride out towards Soda Creek, and I made around thirty miles that day, and stayed at a ranch on Meldrum Creek, close to the Fraser, which was owned by a gentleman called Major Richards, who sure made me very welcome, and the day following I rode in to Soda Creek, having crossed the Fraser on a ferry at that place.

Next day I rode Pilot right along the Cariboo Road up towards the little town of Quesnel. It was about sixty miles from Soda Creek to Quesnel and that was two easy days' ride for me and Pilot—there being different ranches and stopping places every five to fifteen miles along that Cariboo Road.

I was beginning to get more or less convinced as I went along that the country along the Cariboo from Soda Creek north was not much of a "cow country" as I knew cow ranges—so I rode on up ten miles on the Barkerville road from Quesnel, and stayed overnight with an old French Canadian named Jerry Gravelle who was a very old-timer in that area. He gave me a whole pile of good information in regards to this Upper Cariboo—it was a country of mines and timber and no signs of any worthwhile cow range. Anyone running cows in that thick jungle of timber would pretty near need a bell on every hoof of them to find them, except when the snow was laying on the ground. After meditating on this matter, I figured I'd start south again in the morning and get back again to Crow's Bar which was around one hundred and ninety miles away.

So in the morning I bid good luck to this kindly old French Canadian voyageur and his pretty little half-breed daughter, and I headed old Pilot for Crow's Bar—stopping at Quesnel overnight. That evening I was sitting outside the hotel on the verandah and I noticed a very old man with a long white beard sitting there. He said his name was MacClean and that in the gold rush around 1860, on a place called Lightning Creek near Barkerville, he had shovelled out thirty-six bucks worth of gold nuggets for days on end.

Next morning I was all ready to light out for Soda Creek when a young fellow stepped up to me and asked me if I would sell my horse Pilot. He said he would give me $200 for that saddle horse. Of course I told him that Pilot was a Gang Ranch horse and I had no right to sell him, even for such a fancy price.

This young fellow turned out to be the famous Dr. Baker, who was afterwards a real household word in that upper Cariboo. I heard several different stories of Dr. Baker operating on guys' appendixes on the kitchen table—miles away from any sort of help—so I'll bet the doctor was just the ticket for that sort of scattered country.

I did notice half a dozen pretty good layouts between Quesnel and Soda Creek but they looked like good mixed farms to me, not cattle ranches, and I was glad when I crossed back over on the ferry at Soda Creek and headed my horse to the Chilcotin pasture where once again I stayed overnight with Jim Ragan. In the morning, wishing him "So long," I crossed the Chilcotin and over the trail to the Gang and next day down the river to Crow's Bar and home. I'd had a good trip and a change of scenery and seeing different folks, so I was ready to go to work.

I had just got back from my trip about a couple of weeks when Tommy Derbe—who had his ranch on the north end of the Crow's Bar pasture—sold out the ranch and cattle to a man named Henry Koster and a young man named Joe Smith who was the second son of the old pioneer, Joe Smith, who started and owned the Clinton Hotel in around 1864.

Henry Koster was the son of a German aristocratic family who emigrated to this Cariboo Country in the days of the Barkerville gold rush—and afterwards took up the Alkali Lake Ranch. He was married to an English lady, and was a man of great ability and had a very far-seeing head on him. Not only was he a good cattleman, but he was what the experts call "a man of good executive ability." The ranch he purchased from Tom Derbe was just a stepping stone from which in after years he built up and owned the Canoe Creek Company's ranch and the Empire Valley holdings.

Henry and young Joe Smith, as he was affectionately called, and myself all formed a permanent and lasting respect and friendship for each other for many years—until both Henry and Joe crossed over on that "One Way Trail."

I was not anyways sorry at all to see Tom Derbe sell out his ranch because I had never even got a thank you out of him for the many odds and ends of things I had done for him at different times. It was a good thing for him that he did sell out because if a man owns a ranch and doesn't ride around his cows kind of regular, and lets his calves run around unbranded, sooner or later someone else may brand them for him—not with his brand at all but their brand, which will soon run a man out of cows.

Summertime was in full swing in 1914 when I was sitting on a little bit of a porch on the Crow's Bar cabin after supper, smoking and watching the sun spreading his evening rays on the mountains, when I saw a rider coming down the trail and as he got closer I saw it was my boss, Andy Stobie. Of course I jumped up and started the fire going to get him a bite of supper. He stayed overnight with me and I proceeded to give him a detailed account of the progress I had made at Crow's Bar.

I told the boss of a lot of things I'd done—how I'd put up a saddle horse pasture, and another log cabin to hold supplies and extra equipment, which was very badly needed. I had rebuilt and renovated the barn, and had increased my horse hay from five to fifteen tons, and had made a ditch about a mile and a half long to turn a rush of snow water each spring down into a fair-sized lake which in turn freshened up the water for the cattle to drink, and on top of that, I had faithfully looked after the cattle with very few losses.

Andy listened to me very closely and said, "Aye mon Harry, ye've done very well," so I was pleased and glad to hear he was satisfied with my work.

It appeared that Andy Stobie had been notified to appear as a juryman at the Clinton Cariboo Assizes, which at that time were held once a year in Clinton, and he asked me if I would like to come to Clinton with him for a few days. I at once agreed that I'd like to go on the trip. Next day Stobie and I rode to Clinton, getting there around five o'clock in the afternoon and I stabled both saddle horses in the big old barn across the street from the Clinton Hotel—Andy getting a room for us in the hotel with two beds in it. The town was very full of people during those few days of the Assizes, as a considerable number had been notified for jury service—which was imperative for them to attend—and I met many folks from all over the Cariboo.

There was a great deal of hitting the bottle every day in the hotel and Andy Stobie was generosity itself with his own money—far too generous for his own good—and his cry, "Everybody up," several times a day and night was replied to by all and sundry at the bar. I didn't drink much booze in those years, and I took it on myself to be Stobie's "Man Friday." When he would finally get pretty full I'd always be sticking around close to help him up to bed, and to be sure I had a pretty stout eye-opener for him first thing in the morning.

I took care of our saddle horses every day and would sometimes get an hour or two listening to the court cases—which were many and varied—ranging all the way from cow stealing to murder trials, and a rape case.

The Clinton Hotel certainly did a roaring business in those years with its never-ending string of travellers and freight teams up and down the road. The bar did a big business in selling liquor, many of the boys waking up in the morning after the night before with big hang-overs, a sick stomach and a flattened-out pocket book.

The Assizes got wound up and, after several days in Clinton, Stobie and I stepped up on our horses and headed for home. After riding 25 miles as far as Meadow Lake, Andy rode on to the Gang and I turned off on a trail leading on down to Upper Big Bar Creek and from there on to Big Bar Mountain and the Crow's Bar pasture. I was pleased to get back to the cabin after the few days of different folks I'd met from many points in the Cariboo. After I'd turned my horse out in the saddle horse pasture and had cooked my supper, I sat down on the porch and watched the golden sun settling down behind the high mountains away west of the river. I never did get tired of looking at those sunsets—the whole country looked like it really was a peaceful, quiet and grand picture of natural beauty.

"Hot-stove" bachelors and cold-blooded murderers met their match in city girl Olive Spencer Loggins, a Cariboo homesteader.

Danger Comes Calling

from *Tenderfoot Trail: Greenhorns in the Cariboo*
by Olive Spencer Loggins

In the opening chapter of her homesteading account,
Tenderfoot Trail, *Olive Spencer Loggins writes that in 1926*
the B.C. government assisted poverty-stricken Vancouver families
in the early grip of the Depression by offering land pre-emptions
in undersettled areas of the province. Loggins and husband,
Arthur, expectant parents facing an uncertain future, leapt at
the opportunity. When Loggins stepped off the train in a small
Cariboo town the following year with her husband and baby, her
dreamy, Hollywood-manufactured view of the western cowboy
mystique was deflated by the prick of first-hand experience.
Loggins, a practical, modern woman, quickly oriented herself
to the harsh reality of her new home, a still half-wild land.
The following excerpt displays the capable, determined spirit of
Loggins, and women like her, as she coped with the difficulties
and dangers of isolation—another hallmark theme of settlement
in the Cariboo–Chilcotin.

The clear light of a sparkling cold morning revealed the first glimpse I had of Lone Butte. Courtesy called it a town, but hamlet was the correct name for this tiny whistle-stop railroad place which consisted of one hotel, a small station house beside the tracks, a large general store, a one-roomed schoolhouse and a community hall which answered all social requirements. Church services were held there whenever a minister could make the trip to this lonely backwoods town. There were about sixteen homes in all and every one of the buildings were built of logs.

Straight lodge-pole pines were stripped of bark and the ends of the logs cut out in such a way that the log set upon it fitted tightly. Then when all the logs were up and a roof added, the logs' spaces were filled with moss and plastered with clay to fill any crevices that could permit freezing draughts to blow inside. Some white-painted corrals stood next to the railway tracks, a reminder that this was cattle country and Lone Butte known as a "cow town."

About one quarter of a mile north stood a solitary square rock sparsely covered with scrawny jack pines. There were no other rock formations in sight; snow-covered land surrounded it on all sides. It was for this large, square rock that the town was named. Months later we saw luxurious summer verdure where fine Hereford cattle grazed and even saw two cute bear cubs playing on top of the butte with mother bear well hidden, but no doubt carefully watching her family.

We entered the general store and found that it already had a "hot-stove" conference in progress. Several of the bachelors we had met at breakfast at Horns' Hotel, plus a few other local residents, sat around a huge iron heater which had a heavy steel rail around it, on which rugged, wet winter footgear was steaming. I was informed that this was called "thawing their feet out." The men all stopped talking and gave me, the only female present and a complete stranger to boot, a very thorough scrutiny. I did the same for them and must confess that my first acquaintance with the male inhabitants of this district was extremely disappointing.

Having seen many "Westerns" in the moving picture theatres, I had my own preconceived ideas of what cowboys should look like, all garbed in fancy buckskin jackets, wide leather chaps and possessing dashing ten-gallon hats. What I now saw was the most nondescript group of men in patched blue-jeans, badly cured moosehide coats and a general air of personal neglect, unwashed and unkempt. Nothing there to remind a young city woman of galloping horses ridden by dashing cowboys, speeding into the wide open spaces; another dream gone west!

We had to stock up on groceries for the next three or four months, because with thirty-five miles of snow-drifted land between the ranch at Deka Lake and the store at Lone Butte, I could no longer run to the corner store for groceries for forgotten items of food, as I had been accustomed to do in the city. I consulted my tentative list from which Arthur had economically deleted all meats excepting for one roast of beef and some bacon. He plainly expected to hunt and supply our table with all such necessities from now on.

One of the hot-stove league left the group and joined us at the counter, bent upon offering some unsolicited advice.

"What you folks need is plenty of beans!" he told us. "Don' matter if'n you can't get meat as long as you've got lots of beans. Spuds, too, gotta have spuds and they're cheap. Prunes is good, too, if you can afford 'em. Most folks up here can't afford canned goods, but mebbee some dried fruit's what you'd ought to get."

I shuddered at the prospect of his unappetizing, starchy list of foods and asked him cautiously, "What do you mean 'can't get meat'? We have heard that all one has to do for a meat supply is to shoot game, that this is the best game section in British Columbia."

"Ha-ha-ha! Somebody's been foolin' you, missus. All the dang moose and deer leave this high country in the late fall and the biggest piece of game you're likely to shoot is a jack-rabbit."

I looked at him anxiously, then let my eyes range over some sides of beef that hung in a cold storage addition to the main part of the store. But I knew we were operating on a shoestring so I stuck resolutely to flour, beans, rice, macaroni, coffee, tea and sugar. For luxury foods I had my canned cherries and peaches in the quart preserving jars. I bought some dried prunes, facetiously called C.P.R. strawberries by people whose pocketbooks would not allow them to buy the fruit that honestly bore the name. Prunes were inexpensive at that time, but I was to find them indispensible during the winter months in the Cariboo country. The storekeeper was totalling my purchases when the unkempt man spoke to us again. His manner and his information were not designed to encourage newcomers to the region.

"I hear you're goin' to pre-empt land in the 'Isch-ka-bibble'?" he positively jeered, "there's a no-man's land if ever there was one! Nobody lives up there 'ceptin' mebbee a few Indians. Guess sometimes the game warden'll poke around when you least expect him. Your wife'll go plumb crazy up in them woods all by herself. Couldn't get my wife to live up there for all the free land in Canada! No Sirree!" he punctuated his words with a successfully aimed bullseye of tobacco juice into the spittoon at the far corner of the store.

"Oh, come off it, George! The Isch-ka-bibble's not that bad," protested the storekeeper uneasily. He probably was afraid we'd take the next train back to Vancouver.

"Do you mean we won't have any neighbours where we're going?" I asked him, already afraid of his response. Before the man could answer, George was ready with a comeback. He delivered it after once more aiming at the spittoon.

"Wouldn't say no neighbours 'xactly. Matter of fact Ed Martin's got him a woman up there, a housekeeper he calls her. Then there's always the Indians snoopin' around and a few old bachelors livin' alone and prob'ly climbin' the walls for lonesomeness!"

My husband paid for the groceries and herded me away from the vicinity of George and his spiteful tongue. The unkempt fellow sent a baleful glance after us, which I took the trouble to return in full measure. Of all my choices for neighbours in the backwoods he was the one I could do without. He was a knocker, of no use to himself or likely to his family either. George did nothing to boost the country where he was earning his living. I decided that the fewer men of his kind that we met, the better for our morale. There was to be no turning back, from now on, my husband and I were pioneers.

One September day Randy approached me and asked, "Will you make out your grocery order, Olive? Tomorrow I'm going to take Johnny's old wagon to Lone Butte to pick up supplies. We are expecting some of the building materials for the new cabin to arrive on today's freight shipment, and I plan to start early."

When I had milked Beauty next morning, Randy had located the team and driven away to Lone Butte. I had a full day ahead and decided to make a batch of cheese, and also planned to process some venison that Hank West had brought to me. I was frying the pieces of meat to pack into the jars for processing, when I heard horses approaching. I went outside and saw two R.C.M.P. officers dismounting. Their mounts were the finest I'd ever seen in a country that specialized in fine riding stock. The men were virile and handsome, I thought, and wouldn't have any difficulty in getting their women. Their reputation for always getting their man was well known.

The sergeant in a business-like manner jerked me back to reality with his first question as he eyed me speculatively, "Is your husband around here, ma'am?" I replied that Arthur was working at the Martin ranch on Drewry Lake and that Randy Jackson, who stayed with us, was also away. Both policemen were studying the woods behind the clearing on which the cabin was built, and scrutinizing carefully the shores of Dragonfly. The sergeant frowned and turned to me once more. "Tell me, ma'am, have you seen any strangers around your place in the past two days, I mean men who have never called at your house before?"

I said no one had been here except old Hank West and English Deka. I asked if anything was wrong. "Well, yes, we are looking for two men, they are most likely mounted and armed." The officer looked at me appraisingly and said further, "They are wanted for murder and are from the Babine River country further north. They're very tough men and I think your husband had better come back here and stay until we find these men. We will call in at Martin's ranch and send him back. Under ordinary circumstances this is no place for a woman to be alone, but especially now!"

My heart began to pound as I looked at the sergeant. "Yes, please ask him to come home. Randy Jackson may be away overnight, he went into Lone Butte just a short time ago, so I'd appreciate it if my husband can get this message as soon as possible." I spoke quickly, and watched them mount and ride off in the direction of Martin's ranch with growing apprehension.

I went indoors and was working again on canning the meat when I heard horses' hoofs close to the cabin once more. Could the officers be returning for some reason? But when I glanced out of the window, my heart gave a furious frightened lurch. Jumping from their saddles were two of the roughest and most savage-looking men I had ever seen. I didn't need anyone to tell me that here on my doorstep were the two wanted desperadoes hunted by the R.C.M.P. Without a doubt they had been hidden close by while the officers were questioning me; their immediate arrival after the departure of the policemen testified to that. They now felt certain that a lone woman could do nothing to prevent them from doing what they wished. I was soon to learn that I was in for trouble, if not in actual danger of being killed.

The leader of the two was a vicious-looking white man and his companion was a half-breed. They dismounted confidently and tied their sorry-looking mounts to the porch rail. Apparently they had had the cabin under surveillance for some time, perhaps since before Randy had driven away with the team. As they came towards the door I grasped the .22-calibre rifle from the gun rack, and how I wished that it were the heavy .303. But Arthur usually carried that in his saddle boot now that the hunting season was here, in the hopes of shooting some game while en route to or from Martin's place. The .22 offered little or no protection against such tough-looking antagonists, and they proved to be as brutal as their appearance.

With no hesitation, the white man took a quick step towards me and pulled the gun from my hands with an evil grin. "Give me shells for this rifle! If you've got any other guns I want them, too!" he growled. He turned to the native and muttered something to him. This man went out towards the barn. These criminals were taking no chances. I guessed that if they found fresh horses on the place they would take them; their own mounts had been ridden hard and looked exhausted where they stood, heads drooping, beside the porch. I knew that it was useless to refuse and silently handed the ruffian the shells he had requested. His keen eyes detected the box that held cartridges for our .303 gun. "Where's the big rifle?" he demanded harshly. "I'll take that, too!"

I managed to jerk out the words, "My husband takes the rifle to hunt moose. It's not here now!" I was trying desperately to estimate how long it would be until I could expect help. The R.C.M.P. officers would have reached Martin's ranch quickly, I figured. But if Arthur happened to be out on the range, the message would have to be relayed on to him; I could only hope and pray that he would arrive in time.

The renegade discounted my answer and began searching for the large rifle, which he thought was hidden somewhere in the cabin. He yanked the bedding from our bed and pulled the mattress off. Then he caught sight of my baby in his crib. Roughly pulling the sleeping child from his bed, he carelessly tossed the tiny body at me. I gasped, but luckily managed to catch Roland, while the man rummaged through the blankets in the crib. The rough awakening had frightened my son and his loud, startled cries filled the room.

The half-breed returned to the cabin and whispered something to the leader. The two men started to thoroughly ransack our cabin. They took four loaves of bread, several cans of vegetables, some pound prints of butter and whatever else was edible from my cupboard shelves. They did not discover my cache of preserved meats and fish in the root cellar for the simple reason that the trap door to the cellar was hidden by a strip of carpet, but they made sure of taking whatever there was in my cupboards. Now they looked about for something in which to carry the loot and, lacking suitable sacks, these ruffians simply spread two blankets upon the floor and started to throw everything into them. We were to lose everything, even our bed coverings; my anxiety was evident to the thieves and they studied me maliciously.

This started a new fear; these men had murdered once and could suffer no more for subsequent killings should they be apprehended. Perhaps these evil glances they were now giving me meant that they had decided to do something to my son and myself! Their plans for escape and to obliterate signs of their presence here could well include disposing of the one witness to this. After I was dead and my baby with me, they could set fire to the cabin and destroy the evidence of murder in it.

These terrible thoughts were running through my mind as I crouched in a corner of the cabin with my son clutched tightly against my breast. The food was now collected and my .22 rifle thrown on top. One fellow went outside and came in with a lariat which he cut into lengths and secured the blanket bundles with them. They were muttering together now and still sending sinister glances at me. Then they discovered the pot of cooked meat on the stove, and carried it to the table with pleased grunts. They pulled pieces of meat from the pot with filthy hands and crammed them into their mouths and gulped them down half chewed, as voraciously as any starving dogs. I watched their gluttony and was thankful there was such a lot of meat in the pot; this pause to eat a meal, which undoubtedly they really needed, might delay them long enough for Arthur to yet come in time. I could do nothing but pray and try to keep hoping for aid.

The renegades were still gobbling food when the door was thrust open violently and my husband stood there with his rifle levelled, covering the intruders. He shouted, "Get your hands up! Reach!" The men, stunned, had no choice, and of course they obeyed. Without taking his eyes from them, Arthur spoke to me. "I'll need your help, dear. Put the baby down and bring those pieces of rope outside after I go out with these men. They left their rifles by the door. Take them indoors first of all, then help me truss up these fellows, they're the ones the R.C.M.P. are after!"

Arthur herded his prisoners out onto the porch and indicated one of the posts. "Tie that fellow up first, while I keep them both covered!" I looked at the half-breed fearfully, he returned a stolid gaze out of dark penetrating eyes. Dare I approach him with the rope? If he made a bid to escape and jumped me, could my husband shoot him down with me standing in the line of fire? But I decided that I hadn't much choice and, taking the rope, I went up to him as he stood with his arms still raised. I wound the rope around the man's shoulders and the porch post and made a good, tight knot. "Now make another firm tie around his knees, and then fasten his hands together behind the post!" My husband gave me orders as he kept a steady eye upon both prisoners.

I did better than that, starting at the neck I wound more rope about the body of the half-breed, stopping occasionally to add an improvised knot of my own such as could never have passed scrutiny in the Boy Scouts' manual. When I was finished the native looked like a mummy swathed in rope and the effect was so comical that in spite of the tenseness of the situation, or perhaps because of it, my husband burst out laughing. "Good heavens, even Houdini couldn't get himself out of that bind!"

"If Houdini went around killing people, nobody would want him to get loose, either. At least, this man won't get free!" I retorted, and turned to help Arthur with the other prisoner.

"Here, take the rifle and keep this man covered, I'll tie him up myself," my husband said, but that proved to be an almost fatal mistake. In the split second that elapsed while the rifle was transferred to my hands, the prisoner seized the one chance for escape that he was likely to get. He dived headfirst over the porch rail and landed in a sprawling heap on the ground. Taken by surprise, Arthur yelled frantically at me, "Shoot! Shoot! Don't let that man get away!"

Without even thinking about it I swung the rifle to cover the fellow who had jumped to his feet and was gathering himself for a leap towards the nearby woods. The fact that his escape was soon to be realized moved me to an almost involuntary action. As if hypnotized I pulled the trigger and fired. The man sprawled once more on the ground and it dawned on me that I had wounded him, perhaps even killed the man! I looked at my hands unable to believe that they could have been responsible for such a deed! The kickback from the heavy rifle caused me to stagger backwards. I was still staring at the fallen figure when my husband grasped the rifle and said, "Pull yourself together, dear! These men are murderers and wouldn't have thought twice about killing you to cover their tracks and escape the law!"

With his rifle ready he went cautiously over to examine the fallen man. Arthur straightened up and said, "It's just a leg wound, he'll live to face trial and, I suppose, cost the taxpayers a lot more money."

I couldn't feel too sorry for the taxpayers at that moment, I was so thankful that I had not killed the renegade. Still a tender heart inside, in spite of the efficient manner in which I had handled this crisis, I thought. Then Arthur called me to lend a hand with my victim. "Come and help me get him onto the porch. I will have to apply a tourniquet to stop the bleeding. If I don't he's liable to bleed to death anyway!" This matter-of-fact approach was like a cold dash of reality and I forced myself to go over and help Arthur. We each got a shoulder beneath the wounded man's arms and assisted him up the steps to the porch. He was indeed losing a lot of blood, so my husband set the gun beside the porch rail and told me to bring some strips of sheet material with which he could staunch the thigh wound. He started to cut away the buckskin pants the man was wearing.

I went inside and started to tear up a clean cotton sheet when I heard a heavy thud and a big commotion on the porch. I dashed outside and there a terrible sight met my eyes. The wounded man had somehow managed to surprise my husband and was now straddled over him. He was exerting every ounce of strength he possessed to choke Arthur to death! My husband was gasping and trying vainly to break the death-grip which the murderer had upon his throat and his face was a terrible colour. No one needed to tell me that I had to act quickly!

I grasped the heavy rifle by the barrel and jumped into the melee. Wielding the weapon like a club I brought it down on the head of the killer with all the strength I possessed. I believe at that particular moment it must have been, as in the case of Sir Galahad in Tennyson's poem, the strength of ten. The man crumpled under my savage blow and released his grip on Arthur's throat. I hurled the inert body off that of my husband, and lifted Arthur's head. Gradually the horrible colour receded from his face and he managed to gasp hoarsely, "That was too close for comfort. Thank God you kept your head, dear! I'd have been a goner in another minute!" I helped him into the cabin and onto the bed. I was shaking terribly by this time, but thankful that my nerve had held up at the crucial moment.

"Will you be all right, Arthur?" I anxiously asked my husband. "You look terrible, but I must say, not as bad as that fellow, I may really have finished him this time! But in case he comes around, I'll go out and tie him up and get the gun, it's lying right where it fell when I stunned him. But I wouldn't trust that man even in that condition!"

With no namby-pamby pretense of handling the still-unconscious man with care, I grasped his arms and trussed him firmly to the porch post in the same manner that his companion was fastened. I wanted no further harrowing attacks from either of these renegades; I finally realized it was their lives or ours! I looked at the prisoner, propped in a sitting position against the post, and saw that his leg wound was still bleeding. Something would have to be done to stop it. I went inside and told Arthur what I had done and he felt that we could attempt first aid together. "But he'll have to remain tied, I'm afraid to trust him," I asserted as I gathered bandages again.

Then I heard a team approaching the cabin, followed by an amazed shout from Randy. "Whoa there! What in the world's been going on here?" Our friend rushed inside with an agility surprising for his sixty-seven years. "Looks like a scene from one of those westerns! Blood and all! Those two fellows are the ones the R.C.M.P. men want?" he queried. Then he looked at Arthur more closely. "Say, just what did happen? When I got into town the news was everywhere about these men that the R.C.M.P. were chasing. I got a few things together and drove right back. Didn't figure this young lady should be alone here with murderers in the vicinity!"

"It's been a sort of graduation day for greenhorns around here today. We both got in on the act, but the bloodiest of the two men is my wife's trophy. If she hadn't kept her head and been able to act quickly, I'd have been a goner, myself!" Arthur related proudly.

I disclaimed all the credit. "Indeed, Randy, if Arthur had not arrived when he did, those desperadoes would likely have finished both Roland and me. The story would have ended much differently I fear."

Arthur and Randy took the bandages, which I had started to prepare before all the excitement started, and went out to inspect our victim. I set about restoring the room to some kind of order. I placed all the food back in the cupboards and the blankets back on the bed. I looked at our son, who had gone back to sleep in the crib where I had hurriedly set him down while I went to assist his father with the capture of the criminals. I gave silent thanks for our safety.

Randy came in for hot water. "Will you fix me a quick meal, girlie? We're going to make that fellow as comfortable as possible, but naturally we'll leave them tied up. Arthur says you insist upon that and I don't blame you. They are tough hombres! Then I'll ride up towards

Canim Lake, the officers told Arthur and Ed Martin that they would continue their hunt in that locality. The sooner we contact the officers the sooner we'll get rid of our prisoners, eh?"

Our friend rode away and I prepared a meal for ourselves. The renegades had eaten all the meat brought by old Hank West, but that fact had made all the difference in the day's happenings. When my husband remarked that he supposed we should feed our prisoners, I replied somewhat edgily, "They shouldn't need another ounce of food, they ate a whole pot of venison before you came to the rescue. Somehow I don't feel the least bit sorry for those men!"

I just didn't relish the idea of having those murderers attached to the supports of our porch even for one night, but we had no choice. My husband slept the sleep of the just, but all night long I imagined I heard suspect sounds on the porch and I kept popping in and out of bed. I kept up this watchdog act all the dragging hours of darkness; the prisoners, also wide awake, would turn their eyes keenly upon me whenever I went near them. But somehow the night ended and I eagerly looked forward to the arrival of the R.C.M.P. officers and Randy Jackson later in the day.

In mid-afternoon the R.C.M.P. men arrived and confirmed our belief that these were the wanted criminals. "Congratulations! It took courage to tackle these fellows," the sergeant told us, then smiling to me, "The 'Mounties' aren't the only ones to get their man. You didn't do so badly in that department yourself, ma'am."

I served the officers an early supper and, carefully guarded by the policemen, the prisoners were untied and provided with a meal before leaving Dragonfly. Then the officers arranged a sling between two of the horses in which to transport the wounded prisoner. The other was mounted and his hands securely fastened. "By the way," the sergeant said as he bade us farewell, "there's a reward posted for the capture of these men. I think the amount is two thousand dollars. You will be notified by the commissioner's office and they will be mailing you a cheque."

"A cheque for two thousand dollars! You must be kidding?" I gasped incredulously. "Why, that's a fortune!" and I looked at the prisoners almost kindly as they rode away.

Rookie Cop at Soda Creek

from *History and Events of the Early 1920s*
by Bill Riley and Laura Leake

With increasing settlement came the need for community infrastructures such as a police force. In its early stages, the introduction of law and order was conciliatory: it was a law of compromise that endeavoured to keep the peace while respecting the need to blow off steam. Bill Riley joined the B.C. Provincial Police after fighting overseas in the First World War. Sent with his family to the Cariboo, not far from Lone Butte, without instruction or training, he coped with the make-do conditions of Cariboo life as he learned the art of compromise with hellraising railroad gangs and illegal liquor vendors. Here is an excerpt from his self-published book about that time, History and Events of the Early 1920s, *co-authored by Laura Leake. Note once more the reference to the gold-rush days of the past, now the stuff of legend.*

After a short time in Ashcroft and Clinton, I was transferred to Soda Creek where there had been no constable for over fourteen years. The reason was that it was a small six- or eight-family village since the freight teams had been operating—quite peaceful, quiet, and happy, but progress was beginning to extend to the outback.

Such was the case for the few inhabitants of Soda Creek; they were scared to sally forth after dark, and the settlement had reverted overnight into something like the old Gold Rush days—wine, women, song, gambling, bootlegging, and brawling in the streets. The one-street, one-horse town had suddenly gotten tough. The steel gang had suddenly descended on this wee settlement and pulled the rug from under the feet of those living there. They were hard, boisterous, and irresponsible, and their motto was to live for today and to hell with tomorrow. Such were the gangs of workers employed by the contractors who were building the P.G.E.

There were usually three gangs in a situation of this kind—one working, one quitting, and one moving in. The steel gangs had landed, and I alone was chosen to be stationed there to keep the peace, a consignment I welcomed in my ignorance, not knowing what I was getting into. It was a job where I learned the hard way that discretion was much better than valor. It was to be one of the most exciting and interesting experiences of my career as a policeman to date. I left Ashcroft with my wife, Winnie, and family of two—Kathleen Patricia, five years, and Charles Burton (Chuck), five months, on the twentieth of December 1920 for Soda Creek. We boarded the P.G.E. passenger train at Clinton, and in 1920, this train only went as far as Lone Butte, the end of the line for passengers. Being with the government permitted us to transfer to the work train to the end of the line at Deep Creek, first stopping at what was called Williams Lake. Williams Lake was then only a few old shacks and a few new ones and a marquee tent that was the Wainberg Hotel, pitched in a sea of mud about 400 feet from the train station. This was about daylight and I expected a short stop, but was told we would be here unloading goods for an hour or two and to go to the hotel and get breakfast. So we plowed through the mud—Winnie carrying Chuck—I carrying Pat to the hotel. Tent or not, it was a happy occasion; we were tired and hungry—all but Chuck, who was amply supplied by his mother's milk. So we ordered ham and eggs, which were served in due course, exactly at the same time that we were informed that the work train was leaving for Deep Creek. We hadn't time to swallow a bite. We couldn't afford to be left behind under any circumstances, so I folded the paper tablecloth over the ham and eggs. We picked up the kids and plodded back through the mud to the train, which didn't pull out for another two hours.

Two Chinese had pre-empted the seats, but were persuaded to move when Chuck began wailing and Pat commenced to sit on the floor and cry. Finally, we reached Deep Creek and were driven to Soda Creek by stagecoach.

Deep Creek is between 300 and 400 feet deep and probably that far across, and was the only gap so far encountered on the P.G.E. right of way, from the starting point at Squamish, that could not be spanned by the usual wooden trestle. It was the end of the line until a modem steel bridge could be erected; however, work north of the gap was going ahead; the grading and steel-laying continued and would be ready for traffic when it was needed, and all was accomplished and complete by 1921.

Entering Soda Creek from the south, the road angled off the highway coming to a dead end where the post and telegraph office had the honor of being the last building on the one street, about half a mile or so. First there were a few nondescript log shacks, a barn or two, a general store, owned by a very fine Chinese named Louie, attached to this was a cafe run by Louie's brother Bow, a few yards further on, my humble home, office, and lock-up that I previously described. Beyond that, about a half acre of fenced-in garden, the old ramshackle hotel, the little red schoolhouse, some more modest log residences and finally at the end of the street, the post office.

I was passing the hotel a few weeks after arriving in Soda Creek when I noticed a truck parked at the door with no licence plates on it. I went in and found the driver, who certainly wouldn't have passed the present-day breathalizer test. He told me he had the plates, but had forgotten to put them on, but that he would do it right away, so I kept on going to the telegraph office to play Grant Grinder some cribbage. On the way back, I checked the truck again and found that the plates had been bolted on, but upside down!

Above the town was the Cariboo road, above that again about a half mile was the P.G.E. right of way, which was at this time being graded for laying the steel. This was where the steel gang was camped—200 men, more or less, many of whom descended on the town every chance they got to spend their money and live it up.

Our arrival at Deep Creek was quite inglorious. It was a Mr. Watt who drove us into Soda Creek who had a Maxwell car. He dropped us off at an old dilapidated log cabin, built about 1890. It was twenty-five by twenty-five with a wee kitchen, or living room, containing a dark windowless, wooden cell, and a small bedroom. A provincial police station, originally built for a single man, was about to be invaded by a family of four.

It contained an old, small, rusty wood-burner stove, no sink drain, no toilet (just a one-hole job outside), and no water. The bit of household goods we owned could not arrive for a week or so, and there we were with nothing but pioneer spirit and a sense of humor. My wife, Winnie, was an English city girl, and she enjoyed every minute of it as I attempted to take the kinks out of what many people would have viewed as an outrage.

We had a few problems in those early days with the stove. One cold day, an Indian knocked on the door and said there's smoke coming out of our chimney. Well, I wondered, where else would he expect it to come out of, so I went to look-see, and found that the tin stovepipe was on fire and belching flames and ashes four feet into the air. The old tin wood-burning heater was in the corner of the room, six-foot stovepipe up three or four feet, then parallel with the ceiling and up through a tin plate and through the roof. I was not used to this type of heating and had neglected to check for faulty stove pipes. Everything was red hot and we had very little water, so we threw salt on the burning wood, tore down the pipes up to the ceiling, and threw what water we had up through the ceiling and luckily got the fire checked, more good luck than management, but Chuck's buggy, which also served as a bed, was underneath that elbow and black creosoted water drenched it from stem to stern while Chuck was chuckling away in the corner. Winnie managed to clean it up some way while I installed new pipes.

Night came, we slept, hunger came, we ate, cold came, we fired up, but whatever else came, so did friends. Folks we had never met before came to help with bed clothes, friendship, and smiles. Hell; we were anything but discouraged; it was the twenty-first of December and our salary check was due in a week or so, a monthly $110. So here we were in a strange place, crowded out with strangers, with men of a type that made me wonder. I was here in an official capacity and actually lost as to how to act or what to do, but I couldn't have cared less. We had a few dollars and a short way down the street was a Chinese store with an attached cafe. We had just sized up our few blessings when hunger pangs became audible, So we packed up the kids again and went to the cafe for the first meal in twenty-four hours.

I wore no uniform, and no one knew me from a bale of hay. No uniforms were issued to the provincial police until 1926. All I wore at that time was a little silver badge that read British Columbia Provincial Police, so though I felt like a stool pigeon, I just kept my mouth shut and ears open. There we sat, Winnie and I and the two kids in a bevy of railroad workers—tough and motley, but men of good heart and backbone, good honest working men from whom I found later that if they were treated with respect, respect was forthcoming. After filling our stomachs, things immediately warmed up even before our meal was over.

Far be it for me to invite trouble. To dodge it suited me fine. My lack of police experience made me wonder what I was doing here anyway. My nearest colleague was thirty miles away. I knew no one in Soda Creek, and the department hadn't primed me or given me anything to work on, just dumped me here without instructions, advice, or sympathy. My next-door neighbor, 100 yards away, was widow Houston, whose husband Wayne had been one of the most prominent stage drivers of former days and her son Douglas lived with her. Even before we went to eat shortly after our arrival, she ran over to the police office and asked me to shoot a chicken hawk that was bothering her flock. She said her son Doug was out someplace, and it was he that informed me in an indirect way that liquor could be purchased without hesitation at the one and only hotel.

Referring back to the cafe where we were having dinner, some Joe burst in and yelled, "Doug—where can I get a bottle?" and a fellow at the far corner yelled back, "At the hotel," just as he spotted me for the first time and wished he had kept his mouth shut. He told me about it later when we became acquainted and good friends, saying what a damned fool he felt at the time and so I got my first lead, followed up on that and others as they tumbled into my lap, and decided on a procedure that worked real good.

It is amazing how fast the grapevine-type communication travels. Almost immediately, the cry went out, "There's a cop in town." I got nasty looks, dirty looks, pleasant looks, and welcome looks. All were not bootleggers, gamblers, or bawdy-house keepers and many were soon friends, happy to see that their plea for law and order had been heard, which made things more pleasant for me. The impression I got in the following few days was that they were certainly justified in asking for help. Hundreds of men and few women. My wife soon learned to prefer indoors to outdoors when dusk fell upon these mid-north banks of the Fraser River where such boisterous times were unknown since the Gold-Rush days in the early 1900s and late 1890s.

I had no phone for the first few months. Any message I would get was through the postmaster and telegrapher, Grant Grinder, whose office was at the far end of the street. Grant was a swell person, born and raised in the Cariboo, had a dry sense of humor, and the best cheat at cribbage I ever encountered. He got along just fine because the only way I could win was to peg a few extra too, but he caught me oftener than I him, so I would go down to defeat. When I was not out on patrol, once a day he would walk a few hundred yards to my office, play a two-out-of-three game of cribbage and, once a day, I would repay the visit to his office.

By this time, I was well known by the fraternity of bootleggers and gamblers, and they were more than surprised when I walked in on them in their individual dives and requested a short, private interview that was in each case promptly forthcoming. One by one, I informed them that I came with friendly advice, to which they were very attentive, though curious. I simply told them to carry on, providing past rowdiness and disturbances of the peace ceased immediately, that they were to police their own operations in a quiet manner. Otherwise, I would chase them out, even if I had to call in the whole provincial police department and their bonanza would end.

This was the last thing they wanted, of course. From then on, all was rosy. Sure there was the odd fight in the street, but all I had to do in such a case was to ask those involved to fight it out in the timbers above town. They listened well; I am proud to say, I did not have one court case during my period of duty there. The permanent residents moved around freely and were happy. The department was happy, no complaints, sitting back, playing cribbage, and going fishing.

Lillian Collier learned all the skills to make her family's homesteading life at Meldrum Creek comfortable.

International best-selling author Eric Collier enjoyed quiet hours reading in the log house he built with Lillian.

TO HEAL THE LAND

from *Three Against the Wilderness*
by Eric Collier

An international bestseller, Eric Collier's Three Against the
Wilderness *is a classic account of homesteading in British
Columbia. Born in England in 1903, Collier was sent as a
teenager to the Cariboo country to learn about ranching from
his cousin, Harry Marriott, author of* Cariboo Cowboy. *In the
early 1930s, Collier, his wife, Lillian, and their baby son, Veasy,
moved to Meldrum Creek, where the couple built their own cabin
and learned to live off the land. Collier had been to Meldrum
Creek years before and witnessed a forest fire that devastated a
droughty meadow. He recognized that the land was sick because
there was no water, and there was no water because the beaver
had been trapped out. He made a promise to Lillian's 97-year-
old grandmother, Lala, that he would bring the beavers back to
the area that she knew as a child before the White man came.
The following excerpt shows Collier taking the first step toward
healing the land. Collier died in 1966, and Lillian followed in
1992. Veasy remains in the Cariboo. The Collier homestead
at Meldrum Creek was slated for demolition in 1989, but,
after local protests, Canadian Army Engineers restored the
deteriorated log buildings. A rough road leads 40 kilometres off
Highway 20 to one of the few literary historical sites to have
been preserved in the province.*

It was so hot that sweat drenched our skin when we were just stretched out in the shade of the cottonwoods, busy with nothing but our thoughts. It wasn't a sticky heat so often dispelled by a thunderstorm, but an arid, molten heat that withered the pea vines and timber vetch, sucked the sap from the slough grass, turning its green a jaundiced yellow, and shriveled the blueberries on their bushes as quickly as they formed. To Lillian the loss of the blueberries was a tragedy indeed. They'd flowered out nicely in June, promising a bumper crop, and given a shower or two of rain in July, their bushes would be loaded with plump purple berries that she looked forward to picking and preserving as fruit and jam for the winter. But there was no rain in July, and not a drop in August. There was day after endless day, and week after endless week of pitiless, searing sun, which meant we'd have no fruit or jam for the winter unless it came in tins from the trading post.

But the loss of the blueberries was only one of the calamities to strike Meldrum Creek in that summer of 1931, when prairie became desert, alfalfa fields rusted before they were in bloom, and when even the pines and spruces seemed unable to find enough moisture in the ground to freshen their needles.

From source to mouth Meldrum Creek's bed was as parched and dry as the game trails leading to it, as were most of the lesser lakes about it too. And in the oozing black mud that soon crusted hard we saw the webbed track of many a duck or goose, too young to fly, too clumsy to run, and without wisdom enough to strike out overland and seek water elsewhere. For them there was no hope at all. Taking full advantage of a profitable situation when they saw it, the coyotes moved down on the watershed in packs to hunt where the hunting was easy. Many a scattering of duck and goose feathers littered the creek bed during that summer of frightening drought.

Waterfowl were not the only form of life to be snuffed out in the mud. With the creek channel and all lesser lakes in the timber dry, cattle wandered along the banks with tongues hanging from their jaws, all seeking water. In front of the old beaver dams there was an inch or two of foul water that was as much mud as liquid, but between this and dry ground was several yards of deep and sticky bog. Goaded on by their thirst, the cattle wallowed out through the mud, trying to reach the puddles beyond. Many never got there but instead mired to the belly, unable to go back, unable to go on. And there in the mud they died though the process of dying might take all of four or five days.

And come roundup time in the fall, many a rancher would be shaking his head at the wasteful loss of it all, and thinking that if things didn't change, the day wasn't far off when maybe his cattle would have to go all the way to the river to find themselves a drink.

But the stinking slime of Meldrum Creek was not the only mire laying claim to a victim. Other creeks were in like condition, and on open range land where water supply consisted mostly of shallow depressions in the ground that collected and held the spring runoff of the snows, the situation became so hazardous to livestock that the Grazing Rights Branch, Department of Lands and Forests, built fences around many of the potholes so that cattle could not try to get out to what little water might be left in them, and so bog down.

If fencing was a temporary safeguard, it was not a permanent cure. In time, posts supporting wire or rail would rot in the ground and have to be reset. And of what use to stock was the surrounding range if their only available water supply was fenced off and denied them?

The only permanent solution to the trouble was to conserve enough water in the kind years so that there would be plenty in the lean. That's what had to be done, and maybe it could be too. Anyway, an idea began shaping in my mind, vague at first but becoming clearer the longer I thought it over. And when all was crystal clear, I told Lillian about it.

"The Water Rights Branch," I suddenly announced. "We'll write to them about it."

"About what, the blueberries?" With a laugh Lillian said, "I've got blueberries on the brain."

"It's a good thing you've got some somewhere, 'cause there's not a one in the woods." And after she'd wrinkled her nose up at me for this, I went on, "About Meldrum Creek and the beaver dams."

Lillian's face showed her skepticism. "What would the Water Rights Branch know about beavers?"

"Darned little, maybe. But they should know something about dams."

"Such as?"

"Well," I replied, "the more dams there are on a creek the more water there'll be in it."

Lillian sniffed and the sniff spoke for itself. "Then why don't they build some dams on our creek?"

"Haven't the time or inclination."

"Then why bother writing them?" Lillian was in a mood for arguing.

"Because," I began to explain slowly, "we'll do the job ourselves if they'll give us the go-ahead."

"I see." Lillian sat very quiet and still for a moment, hands folded in her lap. Then: "Sit down and write them about it," she said. "But I think it will only be a waste of time."

And so to the Water Rights Branch, Department of Lands and Forests, I penned a lengthy letter, explaining the situation as I saw it on Meldrum Creek, and emphasizing my belief that the only permanent solution to the water problem lay in repairing the beaver dams scattered over the upper reaches of the watershed, and reflooding the marshes. We were willing to do that work ourselves without asking help or payment from anyone. Would the Water Rights Branch give the project their official blessing, and provide us with some protection for the dams after they were repaired? It would be silly of us to begin the job if, before it had been given a fair trial, the dams were tapped of their water by the ranchers below.

And the letter went off and in due time was answered. "We are of the opinion that your plan would be of no benefit whatsoever to the annual flow of Meldrum Creek—" There it was, polite, concise, chilly, the drab phraseology of officialdom wherever it might be encountered. There it was, the encouragement given us by the Water Rights Branch;

but if it dampened our spirits for the moment it couldn't douse them altogether. There was still another source we could turn to for encouragement and it was Lillian who reminded me of it.

"Why don't you put the whole project before Mr. Moon?" she suggested, after the opinion of Water Rights had been digested and forgotten.

"Charlie Moon?" I lifted my eyebrows. "Darn it, yes, Charlie Moon." Then heaving up from the chair and walking to the door and back again: "Why not?"

Charles Moon was the largest landowner in the valley. His Meldrum Creek ranch was only one of a half dozen other such holdings scattered about the cattle ranges of the lower Chilcotin. He walked with a slight stoop as men nearing the three score years and ten mark are likely to walk, especially when fifty of those years have been given to hard but honest labor. An Englishman by birth, Moon came to the Chilcotin near the close of the nineteenth century and went to work for one of the cattle outfits of the day for a wage of thirty dollars a month and board. From such a modest beginning he lived to carve himself a miniature cattle empire that in 1931 ran some three thousand head of Hereford cattle, and had thousands of acres of deeded land under fence. This achievement was not a matter of luck at all, but of hard work, sound reasoning, and good management.

His Meldrum Creek irrigation licence had first right on the creek for water and until its requirements were met all others must go without. It was to the rancher Moon then that we now turned for encouragement that the Water Rights Branch would not or could not give us.

And with vastly different results. "Anything you do up there," wrote Moon in reply, "can't make matters much worse down here. I always have believed that the extermination of Meldrum Creek's beavers is largely responsible for the fix we are all in now. As far as I am concerned, go ahead with what you have in mind and let's see how it works."

This reply was all we wanted at the moment. If the largest landowner on the creek gave our plan his blessing, what more could we ask? Nothing, save that perhaps the Almighty Himself would send us a winter of heavy snows or a summer or two of prolonged rainfall. We were to get all the snows we wanted before many more winters had gone. In the meantime we had to live. We had to live off the woods, and, if they hadn't much to offer, they were generous with what they had. Improvisation became the keynote of existence itself. Nothing was wasted that could be put to any use. Deer were not only to furnish us meat but clothing too of sorts. The hide of the buck I'd shot at the water hole was still hanging on the limb of the tree where I'd thrown it, well out of reach of the coyotes. It was a bedraggled and smelly hide too, what with the blood caked on it, and the maggots crawling over it. But the maggots wouldn't hurt it any, there'd been precious little meat left on the hide when Lillian and I got through skinning the deer out. Anyway not enough to keep a maggot healthy.

Lillian had been eyeing the hide for quite some time, in a contemplative sort of a way, before reminding me that: "Veasy needs some footwear." And guessing that there was more to come I said nothing, just studying her face.

It wasn't slow in coming. "I'm going to try my hand at tanning the deer hide." The way Lillian said it, tanning a deer hide was simple. "And make Veasy a pair of buckskin moccasins." That sounded simple too.

Skeptically I asked, "You ever tan a deer hide before?" guessing that she hadn't.

"No, but I've watched Lala tan them."

"Oh yes, Lala." And the way I said that fetched a glint of stubbornness into her eyes, and thrust her jaw out a little.

I half closed my eyes and ruminated, "Lala set out snares for blue grouse and caught them too. And she dug up wild sunflower roots with a sharpened stick, and roasted them in the campfire ashes like we'd roast a spud." An eyelid lifted. "Think you could snare a blue grouse?"

"Could if I had to," she snapped.

So I called a truce by saying, "Of course you could, but there aren't any blue grouse around here. Just willow grouse and fool hens. And I can shoot them with the .22 rifle."

"Lala never had a .22, all she had was snares." After firing that one at me Lillian softened a little and smiled. And to keep things that way

I said, "We'll start tanning the hide tomorrow, just like Lala tanned them. But you'll have to tell me what to do because I wasn't around when Lala was fixing buckskin."

It wasn't so hard after all. First we soaked the hide in a tub of lukewarm water for all of three days, then threw it over a peeled cottonwood pole, and with a draw knife made from the blade of an old scythe, scraped it of all hair, flesh, and grime until it was almost snow-white. Following this, the hide was soaked for another two days in a solution of heavy soapsuds, and then wrung dry. Now the skin was ready for the greasing. Lala had always used the rendered grease of a bear for this, but we had no bear grease just then and had to use precious lard instead.

After another immersion in soapsuds to rid it of all grease, the skin was now ready to be stretched. Lacing the hide to a stout pole frame and taking up the slack in the laces until they were as taut as a fiddle string, we next devoted an entire day to probing the skin methodically with a flat, U-shaped bevel-edged stone inserted and bound into a cleft stick. Following this mauling the hide was now as soft and as pliable as the finest velvet, and ready for the final operation of smoking. To obtain just the right amount and quality of smoke, I dug a shallow pit, kindled a fire in it, and then smothered the fire with fir cones. Over the pit we built a tepeelike structure, and wrapped the skin around its poles and covered it with saddle blankets. After several hours of smoking, the hide took on a golden brownish hue and was ready for processing into gloves, moccasins, or a coat.

It took Lillian a couple of days to make Veasy his moccasins, but they were a success from the very first stitch. "My turn next," I said. "When are you going to make me a pair?" Lillian took careful appraisal of what was left of the buckskin.

"I want to make him a pair of gauntlet gloves too," she explained, "and after that there won't be enough left to make any more moccasins."

"I'll go shoot another buck."

Her eyes went to her stone meat crocks and she shook her head. "There's plenty of meat left in them yet. We don't need a buck now. Wait a while until we really need meat. Then you hunt a deer, and I'll fix you some moccasins too."

It was Lillian's scheming mind that found profitable use for the squawfish. The three of us were sitting at the shore of the lake, watching them turn flip-flops in the water. It seemed as though there was a squawfish around for every square foot of space on top of the water.

"We must grow all our own vegetables," she suddenly decided.

"Vegetables?" I scuffed the ground with the toe of my boot. "In that, and without fertilizer? Maybe it will grow hay of sorts, but vegetables, never."

"I'm going to have a flower garden too," she blithely rattled on. "No home is home without a flower garden."

At that I burst out laughing. "Sure, we'll have roses and orchids, and gladiolas and every other what not. See here, apart from the matter of altitude—we're somewhere around the thirty-five-hundred-foot level here and it freezes almost every month of the year—this soil is so shallow that I doubt you'd even grow a spud in it, at least it wouldn't be much bigger than a marble if you did."

She stamped her foot. "We'll grow potatoes and good ones too. And carrots and beets, and peas and cabbages—don't you see, it's just a matter of fertilizer."

"Just a matter of fertilizer," I mimicked. Then went on: "In the first place we're a long way from any commercial fertilizer, and in the second, it would come sort of high for our pocketbook even if there was any around to be bought. Of course there'll be some horse manure from the barn next spring but—"

"Not nearly enough," she cut in. Then pointing to the lake; "There's all the fertilizer we need, and the very best too."

"Lake—fertilizer?" It all sounded crazy to me.

But Lillian just nodded. "The squawfish."

"Squawfish!" It wasn't at all crazy now. "Well I'll be damned. Who'd ever think of that. Maybe you've got something."

Lillian said nothing for a moment, but just sat there, as if savoring her triumph. But after a bit she went on, "In the spring, when they leave the lake and begin moving up the creek to spawn, we can dip them out by the sackful. And spread them in layers on the ground and plow them under. Now can we grow 'most all of our own vegetables?"

I'd never thought of the squawfish as a possible source of fertilizer. Lillian had already tried her hand at frying them but the experiment was a dismal culinary failure. There was nothing wrong about their taste, but they had so many little barb-shaped bones you'd starve to death separating bone from meat.

The following spring Lillian made a large dip net out of twine, and when the squawfish began moving up the creek to spawn we built rock dams in the channel, leaving a gap in their middle. Lillian held the net in the gap while Veasy and I went upstream a short distance, then waded down toward her, beating the water with sticks, shouting, falling over the slippery rocks but forever driving swarms of fish into the mouth of the net. When piles of them flapped and squirmed on the bank, we loaded them into gunny sacks, and toted them on our backs to the quarter acre of ground already cleared of its brush, and plastered it with fish and then plowed them under. Though that patch of ground stank to high heaven for three weeks after the sowing of the seed, by the time the smell was gone, young plants began thrusting up through the warm, gravelly soil and by midsummer we had a vegetable garden that might have evoked the admiration and envy of any professional market gardener.

Lala never had mentioned the squawfish, perhaps because in her day on the creek there had been few if any there. But then there were plenty of trout. She explained to me how the Indians laid their gill nets across the narrow waist of Meldrum Lake and hauled them in next morning heavy with plump, red-fleshed trout. At a later date, when exploring the shore line ourselves looking for mink or other signs, we discovered the water-logged remains of many a pole raft used by those earlier Indians in their fishing. But all that lay with the heyday of the beaver, when every lake was kept at a constant level, and a swift cold stream of water flowed over the dams all summer, ensuring a continuous well-oxygenized water from source to mouth of the creek.

With the extermination of the beavers and subsequent loss of precious water impounded by their dams, the creek became shallow and in the summer much of its bed was dry. There was no longer a clear, cool flow moving between its banks, and without that flow, no trout could survive for very long. And as the trout perished, squawfish began multiplying, no doubt to fill a vacuum that was caused by the passing of the trout.

One evening, when squatted upon a block of wood at the cabin door, turning such matters over in my mind, I absentmindedly remarked to Lillian, "Think we'll ever see the day when you and I will be able to sneak down to the creek, sink a baited hook into the water and catch us a mess of trout?"

Lillian was brushing her hair, fixing it tidy like for the night. Not until that chore was done to her complete satisfaction did she give me any reply. Then, "If the beavers come back, yes." And there was something in her voice that made me glance sharply at her and say, "You really think there will be beavers here again, someday?" Her face was deadly serious as she retorted, "Of course I do. Don't you?"

UNEXPLORED TERRITORY

from *Grass Beyond the Mountains*
by Richmond P. Hobson Jr.

Born in Washington, D.C., in 1907, Richmond Pearson Hobson Jr. attended Stanford University and saved toward his dream of owning a cattle ranch. After losing his savings in the stock market crash of 1929, he made his way into British Columbia with the legendary Panhandle (Pan) Phillips in the early 1930s to investigate ranching prospects. Together they formed the Frontier Cattle Company. Hobson's partnership with Phillips lasted until the 1940s. He resumed ranching in the Vanderhoof area with his wife, Gloria, and published his enduring trilogy about ranch life that inspired a 1990s TV series named for his second book, Nothing Too Good For a Cowboy. *Hobson died in 1966. This excerpt from Hobson's first book,* Grass Beyond the Mountains, *evokes the eerie grandeur of the untamed northwest Chilcotin wilderness and captures the flavour of cowboy humour and camaraderie as the duo pushes through established boundaries to explore uncharted land. Their yearning for virgin territory recalls the earliest days of exploration in the region, and the drive for unclaimed resources. Rich and Pan are accompanied by a young wrangler and his father, a seasoned rancher who, in the spirit of neighbourliness and self-sacrifice, goes out of his way to see the boys safely over dangerous country, but forgets to tell his wife he'll be a few days late for dinner.*

A weird reddish light shone dully through a leaden sky on the long, snakelike line of horses picking their way along the edge of an ugly expanse of dead gray muskeg that dipped into space beyond the northern horizon.

Somewhere here—under the dark jungles of the unknown Algak Mountains, and on the southern edge of a fantastic world of muskeg and black stinking ooze—our bays, blacks, buckskins and grays passed into the big white blank space, shown on the map as "Unexplored Territory."

North of Anahim, the character of the land had changed so gradually that it wasn't until now, after we had trailed miles beyond the Holte meadows, that it suddenly dawned on me that this unexplored country we were penetrating resembled nothing I had ever seen or heard of.

A barren, grayish brown muskeg spread octopus-like before us; its huge body and tentacles vanished in dull dead space north and west of us.

Andy Holte knew muskeg country. Up ahead of the line of loose horses, Pan and I saw him pull his horse to a stop, and motion Tommy to drop back towards the middle of the string.

We saw him gaze a moment out at the great opening, then turn abruptly to study the wet, green, moss-hung spruce that rose abruptly from the muskeg edge to jut, sheer and impenetrable, hundreds of feet towards a misty haze, hanging low at the base of red rocky buttes, strangely incandescent and unreal.

The horses had all stopped. It seemed as though they waited in grave suspense for Andy's decision. Tommy's cayuse picked his way like a cat across a short piece of shaking surface to the centre of the line.

"This bog sure looks bad to me," remarked Pan, without taking his eyes off the Teamster. "Look, he's took his cap off."

Looking from Pan to Andy, I saw Andy Holte, cap in hand, scratching the fringe of hair over his ear. This act usually denoted intense concentration on the part of the Teamster. It was as if he subconsciously thought the weight of the cap interfered with his thinking. Then he seemed to have made up his mind. He dropped the golf cap on the exact centre of his head, swung the brindle about, and rode on into the north. He pressed his horse close into the trees and roots between the jungle and the ooze.

Andy's skill and judgment in picking safe crossings around and through floating, moss-covered arms of bottomless muck, his knowledge of the colors, the shape, the appearance of the muskeg, and what lay beneath its deadly surface, enabled him to lead the train without mishap for several miles over a terrain where ignorance or bad judgment would have resulted in horses and men dropping through the surface to possible death in the sucking mud.

The horses followed in Andy's tracks. Pan called to me over his shoulder, "This is the biggest break this trail outfit will ever get. I'm tellin' you, friend, not one of us savvies this bog country; and if you or me or Tommy'd been the lead, some of us would have swallowed mud by now."

"What about Mrs. Holte?" I called back. "She didn't even know Andy left the barn."

Pan grinned. "If I know Mrs. Holte, she'll never blame anyone, not even her Andrew for what he does. She probably figured Andy would miss his dinner anyway. We won't say a word to him about it. Let's see how long he stays with us."

Miles up the muskeg, Andy stopped the horses. Here, where a narrow slough extended back into the mountains from the muskeg edge, green wide-bladed slough grass grew lush and rank.

"A good place to camp," said Pan. "You must be able to smell your way over the mud and moss, Andy." He dragged out his lariat, and jumped down off Big George. "Rope corral," he said.

I was the official camp cook. All I had to do was catch and unpack the kitchen horse, start the fire, find and haul a bucket of water, split the cooking firewood, and cook up the meal, and then set up the tent.

When it came to the trail duties of each man on a trip, the Top Hand was a perfectionist. He took each camp job seriously, particularly the cook's. Pan made an immaculate camp, and as I had unanimously elected him trail boss at the start of the trip, I had no kick coming when he barked at me and snorted down my back about some little detail I didn't think mattered.

It was our custom to relax and drink coffee for fifteen minutes before the fire immediately after the horses were disposed of. I had become a ten-minute-coffee expert. The Top Hand, who had given me inside tips, took a kind of personal pride out of the surprised look on the Teamster's face when, ten minutes or less from arrival time in camp, I yelled, "Coffee time, you tramps—come on the run, you miserable trailmongers, before I drink it down myself."

My system was as follows. Upon arrival in camp, I jumped off my horse, completely ignored the rest of the outfit and their routine camp-arrival conversation, caught and unpacked the kitchen horse —average time two and a half minutes. Now get this trick, you packers and campers, if you haven't already learned it. Here is where the big secret of ten-minute "coffee time, you tramps" comes in.

I reach into one pack box and produce two handfuls of finely cut pitch-pine shavings, and a few small pitchy sticks, cut the day before. Setting this incendiary material in a small pile within five feet of kitchen, I strike a match, and collect limbs from under nearby trees. By the time I run back to the fire with a lard pail full of water, the fire is going full blast. Average time for bringing java pail to boil—four to five minutes. Thus ten-minute coffee.

Unpacking ten horses and bathing their backs usually took the two packers two to three minutes per horse. I was usually able to let go my loud ugly blast before the boys were unpacked.

Tommy was wrangler. He kept two horses staked out close to camp. An hour before dark, he jumped on one of these camp horses and rode out bareback in the direction of horse bells to round up and drive the cayuses back to the rope corral. Here the Top Hand assisted in putting rope hobbles on all the horses, with the exception of the two animals kept at the end of the picket rope.

Usually I had the tent strung up, the firewood in, and the evening meal ready an hour and a half after reaching camp.

I repeat, "evening meal," for the benefit of minority groups who have unmercifully snubbed, and finally cowed me into inventing a new term for the nightly six-to-eight-o'clock repast. Friends of mine have taken definite sides on this dominant issue. I have been torn from one side to another, and often forget which team my immediate acquaintance is on.

Consequently I have been soundly reprimanded for blurting out "dinner," when I should have called it "supper," these friends insisting that only people who don't work use the expression "dinner" for the "evening meal." On the other hand, I know well-meaning people, many of them still lurking about the New York countryside, who appear to be badly shaken up when I've called the noon meal "dinner."

So there you are, you serious-minded friends of mine, not "lunch," not "dinner," not "supper," but "evening meal."

Andy was much impressed by our speedy and efficient camp routine. He squatted on his heels in front of the fire and told us yarns of long trails and horse trades and horse runs. Never once did he bring up the fact that he'd forgotten to tell his wife about going along with us.

The dull dead sky had been gradually replaced by clear blue. After dinner, I filled my tobacco pouch, and while there was still light enough to see, struck out for a quick walk up the pothole. It was just about dark when I rounded a bend, and I was surprised to see the pothole widen to almost a valley that seemed to wind back into the heart of the Algaks. However, it was too dark to make sure of this.

I hurried back to camp, and standing before the fire, told my discovery to the relaxing bogtrotters.

Andy took off his golf cap. He fumbled for a minute with the bushy growth of blond hair over his ear, and then started to scratch it. The Top Hand looked at Andy and then at the campfire.

Andy replaced his cap and spoke in a high voice to Pan, "I'll tell you what I'll do with ya, Pan. I'll bet my ground-gainin' brindle saddler against your petrified-boned black hesitator that we find a trail startin' into the mountains from the end of this slough.

"I remember," continued Andy, "a Kluskus Indian called Alexis telling me about a swamp meadow running into the mountains from the edge of a big muskeg. He told me that, years ago, Ulkatcho Indians cut a trail into the mountains from the upper end of the meadow. They used to hunt the cariboo herds between the Algaks and the Itchas and pack out meat in the fall. Chances are this is the route."

Before dawn Andy froze out of the saddle blanket we had given him and started a fire. As soon as it was light enough to see, we had a cup of coffee, and Andy jumped on his horse and rode up the pothole to look for the trail.

It was a lucky day. Andy found an ancient trail that wound its way gradually up through the heavy jungle. Before sundown our horses broke out onto a parky grass land. From here on Andy picked the trail through the scattered bullpines, climbing always higher and higher towards the red buttes above us.

We began to get an occasional glimpse through the openings at the jungle we had outwitted, and the dead gray muskeg in the distance. The sun dipped behind fluffy white clouds on the horizon, throwing a pinkish light on the parklike land through which the pack train moved; and slowly, almost before we were fully aware of approaching night, darkness fell like a blanket around us.

On a high grass-covered bench Andy stopped his horse. I was sure that, had it still been daylight, we could have looked north into the unknown land we had travelled so far to reach. In the morning we would look down into the no-know land, and perhaps look upon our future home. We made camp. The flames bit into the darkness.

High up on the bench, at the base of the red cone-shaped buttes, dawn broke early. The mountain air was sharp and cold. A thin white lacing of frost covered the ground.

Sitting in front of the fire, Andy, Pan, Tommy and I drank steaming coffee, looked out into the north, and watched pale dawn lift like a magic curtain before us. Gradually distant shapes and shadows took form.

We gazed in awe down at the panorama of a silent, lonely jack-pine land, so vast, so immense in scope that its monotonous green boundary faded in hazy space at the base of a high, snow-capped mountain range that looked to be at least seventy-five miles north and east of us. Andy was sure that the distant snow mountains were the Fawnies.

I have seen great sweeps of arid desert wastes and burning bad-lands, and enormous stretches of prairie, but none of these sights affected me like this first view of the dull green jackpine world that stretches more than a thousand miles north from the Fifty-second Parallel into the Arctic.

A strange hollow loneliness seemed to reach up out of the vastness of the jackpines, and caught me for the first time in its grip. An eerie, empty, lifeless land of monotonous sameness; uninspiring, unspectacular, colorless, exuding a sinister feeling of complete isolation from the living. A land that breathes no spirit of a past life, and gives little hope of a future one.

We caught up the horses, packed and herded the train east through the snow brush at the edge of timberline. As the day wore on, Andy led us higher and higher towards the Algak summits, and a great open gap in the country ahead, where a deep canyon split the range. The northern tip of the gray muskeg gradually became visible as we climbed higher. One arm swung around in front of our mountain range.

At this height we could see a scattering of small yellowish dots and lines, tiny, green-rimmed, pothole lakes, occasional brown splotches, and a few reddish-colored areas. These were the only marks that broke the monotony of the ten thousand-odd square miles of jackpine immediately visible to the naked eye.

As the day progressed, a thin mist rose up out of the bottoms and obscured any further view of what lay beneath the Algaks. For the rest of the day, as we travelled east, the ominous spell of the jackpines under the mist held us in its silence and gloom.

We made camp above timberline on the edge of a glacial lake surrounded by snow brush, alpine grass and rocks. It grew dark. The fire blazed up. Echoes of the horse bells clanged hollowly. Miles away, from down in the land of pines, floated a low moaning call, long-drawn-out and melancholy. I shuddered. Nobody commented.

Pan got to his feet and stepped out beyond the light of the fire. He reappeared a moment later dragging the scraggly roots of a dead snow brush tree and, after throwing it on the fire, walked to a pack box, and reappeared, this time tightly clutching a bottle of whiskey. He flourished it above his head. Andy stared up unbelievingly at the unopened bottle.

Pan said, "Men—it's country north—new country. A range beyond the stamping grounds of saner men. An empire where we can run stock without interference—and live our own lives."

He stopped for a moment. I wondered what was coming next. Pan lifted out the cork from the bottle, tilted it to his lips. The bottle gurgled for an instant. He replaced the cork, carried the bottle back to the pack box, then returned empty-handed to the fire.

He continued, "We've found our country—a green country as big as a quarter of the United States—a place that will be all our own—nobody else will want it. Nobody can get into it, and we're lucky if we can get out of it.

"Our neighbors will be the wolves. Our music the call of the loon. Our beds will be the earth. Our books and movie shows will be the look on the other guy's face. Our roads will be the muskegs. Our cars the cayuses. Our playmates will be the whiskey jacks and the squirrels—and, friends, our cattle feed will be the jackpines and the snowballs."

The Top Hand breathed a long sigh, looked sadly at the three of us sitting by the fire, and stepped to the pack box, lifted out the bottle, returned, took another long gurgle, shuddered, shook his head, and carried it back to its resting place. Pan resumed his eulogy on the country as he walked back to us.

"Gentlemen of the jackpines, this is sure one proud day of our lives. It's a moment for prayer and thanksgiving. After a year of careful exploration, my top-heavy, foot-heavy friend, Mr. R. Peterson Hoopson, and myself have found it. We are now noted explorers—noted for our discovery of a great jackpine cattle range."

Before he finished this, the Top Hand whirled on his heel and made two jumps towards the pack box. But before he got one gurgle, Andy had him by the legs, and I bowled him over. Tommy arrived late and sat on his head, while the Teamster put the cork back in the bottle, leaned it against a box and fumbled for a rope. The Top Hand offered no resistance as we half hitched his wrists and ankles, and dragged him over to the fire. I found the bottle and passed it to Andy, as Pan continued talking.

That evening in May near the summits of the Algaks might have been a sad and gloomy one for us all. Pan's disappointment at the sight of the jackpine waste country north, and his realization that our thoughts, dreams and efforts of the past year had been dashed to pieces in our first view of the unexplored country, was probably greater than mine. But Pan had a certain way about him, and so had Andy. They had a terrific sense of the ridiculous and, being born showmen, neither of them would show his keen disappointment by any outward sign.

Pan and Andy put on a regular show with Tommy and me as their audience. In accordance with the would-be civilized standards, we should have been a sad and broken-looking crew, but to all outward appearances, we were exactly the opposite.

We demolished the bottle of whiskey before the fire. Andy, leaning back against a rock, with his feet towards the fire, told us legends and stories and bits of history about the little known country below us.

He told us what he knew about the Ulkatcho Indians. They were the only inhabitants of the country, a wild, uncivilized, once-warlike tribe of Indians. Legend had it that they were part Sioux, that a band of forty buck Sioux had travelled west beyond the Rockies several generations before on a raiding trip. The band had kept coming until they reached the headwaters of the Blackwater at Ulkatcho Lake. There the Sioux were astonished to find a village whose only inhabitants were women, children and decrepit old men. All the young bucks had been ambushed and killed on a recent raiding trip by the warlike Chilcotins.

The original Ulkatchos were supposedly an isolated band of Carrier Indians, a widely scattered tribe, who still occupy a large section of country in the general vicinity of Stuart Lake in the northern interior of B.C.

The Sioux believed that the Great Spirit had guided them to this happy hunting land of Ulkatcho, and had ordered them to guard the country with their lives. They went through the Sioux marriage ceremony with the widowed Carrier women, and so the legends of the wild country have it that the Ulkatchos of today are the descendants of that strange mixture of adventurous and warlike Carriers and renegade Sioux.

Andy told us that there were supposed to be between three hundred and four hundred Ulkatchos wandering through the bush. Nine tenths of them had never seen a town, and the other tenth had only been to Bella Coola, where they journeyed in small groups during the fishing season in the summer. Some of the Indians had horses, a few owned a cow or two, and the rest were foot-travelling hunters and trappers.

"I've heard," said Andy, "that a white trader from Quesnel, a moose of a man named Paul Krestenuk, a real honest-to-God Russian frontiersman, travels more than two hundred miles into Ulkatcho once a year with a string of wagons, and trades the Indians grub and clothes for fur. So if that story is true, he must have cut some kind of a trail to Quesnel. That's a town at the end of steel on the Pacific Great Eastern Railroad, several hundred miles east of here. That would be a big help to you boys if ya moved into the country."

The Teamster rolled himself a smoke, chewed off the end of it, fumbled for his cigarette lighter, and then putting the mangled butt in his mouth, removed his cap and scratched his ear.

Pan reached into the fire, and pulled forth a burning log about three feet long which he handed over to Andy.

"A light for your smoke," explained Pan.

The Teamster gingerly gripped the non-burning end of the stick, and with some difficulty held it to his smoke. I thought for a moment I smelt burning hair, and saw Andy suddenly throw the log to the ground, bend over it an instant, and then straighten up with a satisfied grunt to blow a cloud of smoke in the air. I noticed one eyebrow was missing. The Teamster reached for his cap and placed it back on the centre of his head and continued:

"Boys, before daylight tomorrow morning we're gonna have coffee, and then climb up that pinnacle to the highest point in the Algaks, and when daylight breaks, we'll see country no white man has looked at before, and we'll see the Itcha Mountains, and what lays at its bottom. I don't know, but I have a hunch there's a surprise in store. To bed, you night owls—we'll need sleep and strength to get up on that pinnacle."

Long before daylight Andy had us out of our beds and drinking our morning coffee. The air was cold. When it was just light enough to see, Pan took the lead, and we strung out behind him, climbing one behind the other up onto the cracked walls of the shadowy peak, giant of the Algak Range.

The pale sky turned to brilliant blue, and below us Ulkatcho Indian land unfolded. A few miles east of us, the snow-capped Itchas dropped abruptly some four thousand feet to a yellowish opening that stood out in bold contrast against the jackpine green. More yellow arms, necks and islands were scattered along the base of the mountains.

I had my father's set of high-powered Navy glasses strung over a shoulder. Andy borrowed them for a quick look. He held the binoculars to his eyes.

"Yellow patches down there are grass," he commented. "Highland meadow grass."

He swept the glasses in an arc to the east, held them there a moment, then continued the movement. Suddenly he stopped. "Just a minute," he said.

Using his knees and elbows as a tripod, he squatted against a rock, and remained motionless for a minute, staring fixedly at a vague blur on the distant horizon—a blur that to the naked eye had a dirty yellowish appearance.

"Hurry up, Andy," I said. "Let loose of those glasses. You haven't the savvy to know what you're looking at, anyway."

"Hold on a minute," said Andy. "Wow!"

He sucked in his breath and took off his golf cap and laid it down on the rocks without taking his eyes away from the glasses. Pan stared silently into the distance. Andy cleared his throat.

"I'll tell ya what I'll do with ya," he drawled. "I'll trade you boys ranches straight across—and I'll throw in the brindle pony—and what's more I'll throw in the halter he's wearin' and the set of number two horseshoes he's got on. It's a clear-cut swap," continued Andy. "I'll ride down onto your spread, and you boys ride back to mine. How about it? Ranches straight across."

Pan started across for Andy.

"Give me them oprey glasses—ya miserable hog!"

He grabbed the Teamster and the two of them rolled over onto the rocks. Pan came up with the glasses and began adjusting the focus to his eyes.

"Make it snappy!" I yelled at Pan. "One quarter minute and you've had it." Now I started for the Top Hand, who was still trying to adjust the glasses.

"How the hell do ya work these fancy things? I can't see as good with 'em as I can without 'em."

"Turn them around," Andy advised him. "You're lookin' through 'em backwards."

Pan snorted and hurriedly reversed the glasses. He pushed me away.

"Ranches straight across, Pan!" snapped Andy. "What say, Pan? Layout for layout. No questions asked."

Now Pan swung the glasses and I could tell when he saw the blur. His sweeping movement stopped abruptly. I watched him closely and saw him swallow. I could tell he was excited. He started to say something but stopped suddenly. Then he appeared to pull himself together.

Andy hissed at Pan, almost in his ear. "Ranches! Ranches! Shake hands!"

Pan answered slowly, "Andy, if ya throw in Andy Christenson's, Cyrus Bryan's, and Jim Holt's ranches to boot, I might be interested— but then that layout would be too cut up. I guess we'll have to ride down onto ours, and you backtrack to yours."

I touched the Top Hand on the back of his shoulder as I reached to get a neckhold on him. He swung around and shoved the glasses into my hands.

"Country north," he said simply. "The gold mine—we've found her."

Quickly I adjusted the glasses to my eyes. I was tense. I guess I was about as excited as an excitable person can get. I couldn't hold the glasses steady to my eyes. I sat down and rested my elbows on my knees the way Andy had done.

Pan was saying, "Nothin' to it. Nothin' to it at all. Any man, any boy can want to do something and any one of them can do it if they want to bad enough. All they got to do is go ahead and do it. There's nothin' to it at all. And ya don't even need any brains. Just enough to keep ya in that straight line you've set your mind to."

"Shut up," I cracked at the Top Hand. "I can't concentrate with all that stupid babble going on."

Tommy laughed. This was the first noise that had come from him this day.

"Pan's all excited up!" said Tommy happily. "He's talkin' like he's makin' a speech."

What I saw through the field glasses was a wide open sweep of grass land. This opening was many miles north of the Algaks and the Itchas, but it was a whale of a big opening. Its northeastern boundary could not be seen, even through the glasses. It just kept going into the distance.

The main body of the opening was yellow. Andy knew that this yellow color was made by the old bottom, or last year's dead grass. He knew that, where the dead grass was heavy enough to overshadow the new growth of green, it was a lush grass country. Brown arms and necks were scattered here and there, and reached into the jackpines from the main opening. Andy told us this was willow brush.

It was hard for me to realize what we, the first white men, gazed upon. A cattle-ranch proposition that could be the granddaddy of cattle ranches. An empire of grass, just sitting there waiting for some outfit to take over; an almost tax-free chunk of grassy acres that could eventually be surveyed and bought for from one dollar and fifty cents to two dollars and fifty cents per acre from the B.C. government. What a proposition this was! What an opportunity lay ahead of us now!

Pan brought my daydreaming to an end.

"Hand those glasses over to Tommy—ya self-centred society man—so he can have a look."

I knew the Top Hand wanted the glasses again himself; he'd talk Tommy out of them before the kid had had even one good look. I handed the glasses over to Tommy.

Back at camp, Andy caught his horse, and then turned to Pan.

"Jumping bullfrogs!" he said. "I forgot to tell the missus I wouldn't be back for dinner."

Tommy said, "Haw—haw!"

A sheepish grin spread slowly over the Teamster's face. He removed his cap and began scratching the hair over his ear. Pan began to choke.

"I just can't figure it out," explained Andy. "It seems like we just left the barn, and then again it's like a lifetime."

Pan was laughing so hard he had to sit down. I broke down myself, and Andy stood there holding his horse, his face split from ear to ear with that shy grin of his. Andy coughed and pointed at Tommy.

"Say, Tommy, just how long have we been gone? The hours have moved faster than I could keep up with them. I guess my dinner's got cold."

Tommy sadly shook his head at his father.

"Andy," he said, "we've been gone three long days and three short nights. Alice is goin' to be worried about her brindle pony you swiped on her."

"I've got to hurry," said the Teamster. "Time's movin' on. Can you guys spare me a little tobacco and a chunk of jerky?"

Pan got out a box of tobacco, some papers, and Andy filled his pocket, and then stuffed a chunk of dried moose meat in his hip pocket. The Teamster was now prepared to hit the back trail, but he squatted on his heels a moment to give us some advice—advice which we later wished we'd followed.

"Boys," he said, "you're all ready to go down there among the Ulkatchos, and throw your ropes on a grass country that has the earmarks of bein' a big layout and a good one; and I'm hopin' you bogtrotters lots of luck—but I'm gonna warn ya on a few points of what to do and what not to do.

"I've been meadow huntin' through these backlands for seven years, and have learned a few things. I don't claim to know very much about what goes on outside of the sticks, but in these muskegs and jungles I've learned a bit, and found out the hard way.

"You kids are pullin' north into a country so far back and so hard to get into, or out of, that ya don't have to make but a few of the same mistakes I made, and you won't come out. Nobody will drop into a country as big as the State of Washington to find out why you didn't come out for your winter's grub. Not this comin' winter. Ya can bet on that. Next spring some police boys with Indian guides might get into Ulkatcho. By then the coyotes will have picked your bones clean, and the wolves broke 'em up in pieces small enough to swallow.

"First, before ya leave this mountain, get yourselves out paper, and draw a map of what lays before you. Put down all landmarks you can, like the pinnacle we was up on. Spot your yellow openings on your map where there'll be feed for the cayuses, and where you can get far enough away from the trees to spot high landmarks.

"Never leave your camp without packin' a gun, whether you're afoot or horseback. That means each one of you knotheads. Pack your gun along whether it's trouble or not. When ya see a grizzly bear or a moose, stay a long way aways. If a cow moose or a bull takes after ya, shoot over their heads a couple of times. It may turn 'em, but don't potshot and wound one. If ya hit a bull in the horns ya might have a still better chance. A moose can't see very good. You can usually duck into the brush and crawl around out of view till ya get the wind blowin' from them to you. The front feet of a moose can reach out a long ways and slash a horse to ribbons."

The Teamster paused to reach into my pocket for my tobacco pouch. He was saving his own. Then he started to roll a smoke.

Pan was flat on his back pretending to be asleep. Loud plaintive snores issued from his throat. The Teamster picked up a chunk of charcoal from the fire, carefully aimed, and tossed it into his mouth. Pan sputtered and rose to a sitting position.

"You're petrified-boned like your black horse," snorted Andy, "and those wolves are going to make a meal of you, I'll bet."

"Whatcha talkin' about?" asked Pan, wiping the charcoal off his face with the back of his hand.

The Teamster ignored him and continued with his advice. "When you boys meet up with Indians, it will usually be in your camp. Yell 'hello' at them and make them sit down and drink coffee with ya. If they want a little sugar or flour, give it to them— tell 'em it's a present. But don't give everything away. Pan here, he knows; he's got a pack-horse load of Indian stuff. Don't be mean or cheap, act real happy when you're around them, don't ever tell one of them a lie, and I don't have to tell ya, don't play around with their women. Remember they are your only neighbors closer than seventy-five muskeg-and-bush miles to our place. Talk on the same level with them, and pick out one or two good ones for friends.

"All three of you empty-headed walruses has got to know one thing, and know it right. That is that it's mighty easy to get turned around and lost down in those jackpines. When ya establish your headquarters, there will always be the loose horses around camp. Hobble or corral them when you leave camp. The cayuses you're ridin' will take ya back to that bunch of horses nine times out of ten. These swamp-eaters know where camp is and you guys don't. Remember, when the horse wants to go one way and you the other, ya want to let the feller have his head, and you'll land back with the other horses; and, boys, never cross a swamp or a muskeg even if you have to go miles around it. Take to the bush.

"That dinner is gettin' colder all the time, and Hard Grass here is gettin' jittery, so I'll just lope along down the mountain to the muskeg, up the muskeg and into the yard. So long, you mountain bums."

Andy rose to his feet, hopped onto the back of his brindle horse, and without saying another word, trotted off through the rocks on the back trail.

As he passed out of sight, I wondered if he'd make it back the long distance in one day—and if he'd get around the deadly muskeg without trouble.

What a country, I thought. There goes Andy, headed for home, riding over dangerous terrain. His wife and nobody else knows where he went in the first place, or how long he was planning to be gone. If his horse slipped into the muskeg, or stuck his foot in a hole, or got snagged in a windfall, there would be nobody out to look for him. The coyotes, wolves and grizzly bears would take charge of him so fast that after a couple of good rains, Andy's disappearance would remain a mystery for keeps.

There were places in the muskeg where both he and his horse could drop out of sight, and the ooze close over the top of them to hide forever what had happened. The Ulkatcho Indians, disliking and distrusting the white man, who considered country beyond the Algaks a rightful Indian heritage, would think nothing of murdering Andy from the bush, should they find him alone along the trail. Spooky stories were rumored about the disappearance of certain white men who ventured alone beyond the Algaks and never returned.

Although Andy didn't mention it, I realized that, when he left home that day, he had only intended to see us a few miles safely on our way. Later when we came to the big muskeg, Andy stayed on with us to see the train safely through. It wasn't his nature to turn back at that point.

He had then stayed on with us until he saw the big opening where we were headed. Now he was trotting home satisfied that we would carry on okay from here, and that, now we had a definite piece of country in mind, somebody would know approximately where we were headed.

Good old Andy! This world doesn't produce many men with a heart of gold like that comical bald-headed Teamster.

Nine-year-old Davey Anderson made a man's promise
to work for his keep, and he kept it.

Davey Anderson

from *Dog Creek: A Place in the Cariboo*
by Hilary Place

Although born in England in 1920, Hilary Place belonged to one of the earliest generations of White children to grow up in the Cariboo–Chilcotin. History often overlooks the stories of children, but Place's story collection, Dog Creek, *is about his experiences from childhood onwards in the small town perched high above a spectacular canyon chiselled by the Fraser River. The townsite's incarnations mirror the history of the region: it was originally a Native village marked by pictographs, then a wayside hotel for miners on their way to the goldfields before the Cariboo Road was even imagined, then headquarters of the first licensed stagecoach line, and, finally, ranchland. Hilary Place grew up on the ranch and stayed in Dog Creek for 40 years, marrying the Stampede Queen of 1935. He died in 2004. When Place was still a boy on the Place ranch, down the road came another boy, a crippled refugee from an abusive father at the Gang Ranch. That boy, Davey Anderson, made a man's promise to work for his keep, and he kept that promise to the Place family, who took him under their roof as one of their own.*

When we looked down the road from the house, we could hardly believe our eyes. Up the road came a small boy carrying a pack on his shoulder. He was a skinny little fellow with pointed features, big jug ears, and wearing glasses. Each step was an effort for the little guy, for when he got closer we could see that he had been cursed with club feet. Not one but both of them. He lumbered along with both arms swinging, lurching from side to side. His feet were wrapped in canvas and tied up with string. When he got closer we could see that he was a white boy and we wondered where he came from.

It turned out he was the son of Mr. and Mrs. Bill Anderson of the Gang Ranch. His dad was the bookkeeper and storekeeper there. His name was David Anderson and he had run away from home. He said it was because his father had beaten up on him and he showed us the scars and bruises to prove it. Up close you could also see the stains on his pinched face, left there by tears that had flowed. He said he was not looking for charity but that if my dad would give him a job he would show that he could earn a living. He looked you right in the eye when he was talking and you had to believe him. He said he was nine years old.

My dad could see he was just a child but he spoke to him like he was a man and surprised me by saying, "Alright Davey, you can stay here and feed the chickens and look after them, but there is one thing you will have to do and that is go to school and behave yourself."

Davey stuck out his hand and they solemnly shook on the deal.

Davey came into our house and my mother gave him the other bed in the twin bedroom that my brother and I had shared. The first night he almost scared the daylights out of me by screaming and carrying on in his sleep. He apparently was reliving the horrors he had experienced at home. These episodes lasted for three months or so until he finally settled down.

In time we learned the story of his life according to his mother, Mrs. Anderson. He was an adopted boy who really belonged to Mrs. Anderson's brother. This brother had fathered the child by some unknown girl and then gone off to fight in the Spanish Civil War. He never returned. Davey had a few mementos of this shadowy character and that was all. We only partially believed the story as there was a rumour that Davey actually belonged to Mrs. Anderson and that the father was the man lost in the civil war. There was always this kind of rumour running around the country. Some you believed and some you didn't. In this care, God knows Mrs. Anderson and Davey were dead ringers for one another. They had the same looks exactly and the same poor eyesight. Davey certainly was not Bill Anderson's kid as there was no resemblance there at all.

Bill Anderson was a merchant of some considerable skill. He had opened the first Safeway store in Vancouver in Kerrisdale and was a successful businessman until the booze caught up to him and he worked himself down the ladder of success until he reached the bottom at the Gang, drunk and violent. Davey was the object of most, if not all, of his frustration and anger and he beat the kid regularly and often and hard.

We contacted his family at the Gang Ranch immediately after he turned up at Dog Creek. Of course they wanted him to go back home. My mother and dad talked it over with Davey and he absolutely refused to go back to the Gang under any circumstances. He said he would sooner die than go back. An RCMP officer came out from Williams Lake to investigate the matter. Fortunately he was a sensible man with a heart and he recommended that the boy stay where he was in Dog Creek as he was being treated well and was attending school. There was no school at the Gang Ranch at the time.

The chickens never had it so good. They were fed regularly and the henhouse was kept clean, with the nests full of fresh straw. Davey attended school, where he was a good scholar and behaved himself. My dad gave him a few dollars each month, as if he was on the payroll, and he stayed in the room with me for a year. Then one day he asked if he could have one of the rooms up the old staircase where Ed Hillman stayed. I guess he felt more like a working man there. His request was granted and he moved.

A few years went by and Bill Anderson lost his job at the Gang Ranch because of his drinking problem. Mr. and Mrs. Anderson moved over to Dog Creek with their two small boys, Kenny and Gerald, and stayed in our old house, Casey. Davey did not join them but stayed put where he was. Bill got a job in Wells, B.C., as a store manager, but he soon lost it due to his drinking. The family stayed at Dog Creek.

I will digress here and tell you a couple of stories about Mrs. Anderson, Davey's mother, who was a remarkable woman in many ways. She had gained some measure of fame and notoriety back where she used to live north of Edmonton. It seems that the settlement she was in was snowbound when one of the neighbours became very sick. The man's wife called Mrs. Anderson in to look at him and see what was the matter. Mrs. Anderson, who was a nurse, took one look and immediately knew his problem was an infected appendix. She was able to phone a doctor she knew in Edmonton, and after describing the symptoms to him, had her diagnosis confirmed. There was no hope of getting the man out to a hospital, so the decision was made that Mrs. Anderson would operate on the man where he was, under direction of the doctor in Edmonton, who would be in contact on the telephone. There was a small emergency clinic in the town that had enough drugs to put the man out while the operation went on, so he was prepped as soon as possible. Mrs. Anderson said it was a routine operation, there were no complications and she had seen dozens of them done, so she was quite familiar with the procedure, but she said she almost didn't do it at the last minute. It was only after the man said "Please go ahead" that she was able to start the incision. Once she started she said it was easy from then on. The whole thing was written up in the *Edmonton Journal* and she was quite famous for awhile.

The adventure that I personally know about took place when Mrs. Anderson was at the Gang Ranch. She hadn't been there long before she was looking after the ranch help and any of the local Indians who required attention. The first winter they were there, there was an epidemic of flu that was a killer. Word came down to the ranch that the Kalelse family was in deep trouble. Could Mrs. Anderson come and help them out? She immediately threw some clothes in a sack and got in the sleigh with the young Indian who had come with the message, and they headed out to the Kalelse home. It was a full day's travel on the snowdrifted road and it was dark when they got to their destination.

The cabin was a single room with a low-pitched roof. In front there was an overhang that covered a porch about six feet wide. When Mrs. Anderson entered the cabin, the interior was lit by a single coal-oil lamp that barely broke the gloom. She had brought a flashlight and with that took stock of the situation. There were two beds in the room. She went around to look at the people in the cabin and found that there were five children under ten years old, two women, and one man, all terribly sick. As well, there were two people lying dead on the floor.

She and the young man who had fetched her dragged the bodies of the dead people out onto the porch. It was 20 degrees below zero, so she made sure they were properly laid out before they froze stiff. Then she set to work to try to save the living. It was a tremendous task. There was practically nothing to eat in the house—just some rice, some frozen potatoes, and the carcass of a deer, frozen stiff, hanging from a tree outside. First she had to try to clean the place up and clean up her patients. It wasn't easy but she did the best she could. She bossed the young man who had brought her and made him get wood and water and keep the fires going. She boiled the deer meat into a soup and fed it to her patients.

This went on for two weeks with not one contact with the outside world. When finally a cowboy from the Gang Ranch arrived, he found that Mrs. Anderson had not lost one of her patients and that they were all getting well and were being properly cared for. She was proud of that and she had every right to that pride. She had shown a remarkable amount of courage and dedication.

When she lived at Dog Creek, Mrs. Anderson was given a medicine cabinet by the Indian Department. Her duties were to look after the Indians. I was her driver and took her around to fulfill these duties. My experiences on these safaris are a whole separate story but not for now. Eventually Mrs. Anderson got a job as Red Cross nurse at the Alexis Creek Hospital and the family moved there.

Davey stayed with us. In fact, he stayed with us until my dad died and then for two more years after that, 21 years in all. He quit school as soon as it was legally possible and went to work full time for my dad on the ranch. He milked the cows night and morning every day, and despite the fact he had those terrible feet to deal with, he grew incredibly strong, especially in his arms.

I remember one time when we were digging spuds and sacking them up and hauling them to the root cellar by the old mill. Among the sacks was an old peanut sack that was three times the size of an ordinary gunnysack. We filled it up with potatoes and left it there just for laughs for Davey to pick up and throw on the truck. Sure enough, he came along, grabbed it, and threw the 300-pound sack up on the truck like it was nothing.

He was as weak in the eyes as he was strong in the arms and back. I don't know what his eyesight problem was, but I know he couldn't see a darn thing without glasses. I do know what his glasses problem was. They were broken and twisted, wired and glued and soldered and taped and stuck together with chewing gum and God knows what else, and the glass part was cracked.

One time when Davey was about eighteen years old he was breaking a horse for riding. It was one of those animals that you could never be sure when it was going to buck. It generally chose the most inopportune moment in which to indulge itself in the pleasure of dumping Davey in the dirt. Davey had decided to ride this horse up to the top of Canoe Creek Mountain, where the Indians were holding a jackpot stampede (where all the contestants pay entry fees into a jackpot and the winner takes the pot). He was halfway up the mountain when he stopped and dismounted to give the horse a breather. When he got back on, as soon as his rear end hit the saddle, the horse decided it was time to buck. Davey wasn't settled in the saddle yet, so on about the second jump he went flying off and landed in a clump of fir trees. No great harm had been done except the darned glasses had fallen off. He couldn't find them anywhere. Of course he couldn't see anything without them, so he was having a hell of a time. He searched for awhile and then gave up and went on to the stampede. On his way back he looked again for a couple of hours, then returned the next day and for two days more, but to no avail. Finally one of the young Indian boys joined him in the search and was successful. The glasses were found not on the ground, where Davey had spent the last four days on his hands and knees looking for them, but hanging from one of the top branches of the fir tree where Davey had landed. More tape and chewing gum and solder and he was back in the land of the sighted again.

When he had got the horse straightened out after the glasses were lost, Davey decided to continue on to the stampede even if he couldn't see what was going on very well. There was a dance that night in one of the cabins, and Davey managed to get into a fight with one of the Tressierra boys from Clinton. Davey was smaller than his adversary and that, coupled with the fact that all Davey could see was a blur, meant he wasn't doing well. In fact he was getting the daylights pounded out of him. Tressierra was doing great as long as he stayed out of Davey's clutches, but it was inevitable that Davey would grab him and the game would be over. Sure enough, Davey finally grabbed him by the shirtfront and the crotch, lifted this 200-pound man like a doll over his head, and brought him down flat on his back on the floor with a bang that could be heard for a mile. Davey was going to give him another one the same as the last one, but a few of the boys grabbed him and persuaded him to stop. Tressierra came to about noon the next day. I heard that Tressierra was slightly cross-eyed after this and spoke with a stutter, but that is just hearsay and only very probably true!

We used to have dances at Dog Creek every once in awhile, and it was natural that Davey was chosen as the bouncer. We never had any serious trouble after the first dance. At that one, two of the young bucks decided to have a fight in the middle of the dance hall. Davey went over and grabbed them and tucked one under each arm and marched them outside where he proceeded to knock their two heads together until he got a solemn promise from them that they wouldn't do that again. End of trouble.

When Davey was nineteen he moved into a tarpaper shack that was between the powerhouse and the store. He had a dog called Useless that stayed with him there, and also on occasion he would have a visit from one of the local Indian girls named Nora Rosette. Davey was a guy with strong convictions. He didn't believe in living with a girl and so he made arrangements to get married, which they did the first time there was a priest around to perform the ceremony. Nora was a quiet, soft-spoken girl who really loved Davey, and she made him a good wife. They had two children, a boy and a girl, and spent most of their lives around Lac la Hache and 100 Mile House. Nora got some kind of flu one day that attacked her lungs, and she slipped away before anyone realized how ill she was. It was a terrible loss for Davey, but with his remarkable spirit and resilience he weathered the blow and carried on.

I never think of Davey without thinking of his epic walk from the Gang Ranch over to Dog Creek when he ran away from home. He was only a child, just nine years old, and it was a ten-mile journey: down the twisty road in Dismal Gulch and across the Fraser River on the old suspension bridge; up the five-mile mountain to the top where there was an abandoned Indian cabin or two; then down the Dog Creek Valley side to our place. What was going through his head as he trudged along on those twisted feet? He had never been on the road before and there was not a living thing along the way, just the wind swishing through the grass and the hiss of the mighty river. What sort of determination did it take to keep going, mile after mile? What sort of guts did it take for him to stand in front of my dad without a tear and ask not for charity or help, but for a job? All he had in the world was a skinny little body with twisted feet and eyes that could barely see without his broken glasses, and a flour-sack pack containing one parched pair of pants and a faded jacket.

Wet Summer

from *The Ranch on the Cariboo*
by Alan Fry

*Another boy raised to ranching, Alan Fry's primary concern
in* The Ranch on the Cariboo, *his memoir about becoming a
man on the family ranch near Lac la Hache in the early 1940s,
was to grow up as quickly as possible so he could better help his
father, the "Old Man," battle the elements. Born on a Cariboo
ranch in 1931, Fry worked alongside men contending with the
adversities of nature that forged strong ties of admiration through
shared suffering. Fry displays in his stories a great sympathy
and tenderness toward his father, Julian, an English immigrant
and son of Roger Fry, a member of the legendary literary circle,
the Bloomsbury Group. Perhaps the Old Man wasn't cut out
for ranching, or maybe he'd simply hit a string of bad-luck years
that would put a better rancher under; either way, young Alan,
who along with his brother, Roger, took every opportunity to
miss school and pitch in at the ranch, stood by his father during
one wet summer that characterized the unforgiving extremes of
weather testing every rancher in the Cariboo–Chilcotin.*

The Old Man, Julian Fry, with his son Alan. As Alan grew, he battled the elements with his father as they tried to make a go of a failing ranch.

Christmas went and Easter came. The Old Man had saved some necessary riding so we could help him. After Easter we were out to the ranch most weekends. We left school for the summer a month early on a war measure applicable to students with farm work to go to. We joined in a roundup for branding the new calf crop and turnout onto the summer range. There were long days in the saddle and good weather to go with them.

Only days after turnout, we had bear trouble on the range about halfway to the meadow. Riding enough to watch for just such grief, the Old Man came on a calf that had been clawed by a bear but escaped, presumably when the bear turned to kill another animal in the herd. We suspected, in fact, that once a bear had become a killer he wouldn't necessarily want food to do damage but would ravage through the herd, maiming to left and right of him out of the sheer savagery of his nature.

The Old Man brought the calf to the Milk Ranch to try some doctoring. Milking a brindle with plenty to spare after providing for her own calf and ourselves, we had milk enough to give him. But the brindle's milk and the Old Man's doctoring weren't enough. The open wound, which appeared to be draining successfully at the top of the shoulder, infected badly, and soon there was a seam of putrid matter throughout the flesh below the shoulder blade. The calf grew less active and finally would only stand in a corner of the corral, head down, back humped up, the eyes lifeless. The Old Man fetched the carbine and shot him.

The losses continued, with several animals missing. It was hard to be sure of course, unless you found a carcass, that an animal had been killed, the entire herd scattered as it was over many square miles of summer range. Still the situation was critical and would remain so until later in the season when, other food more plentiful, the bears might lay off the livestock.

"What you gonna do, Dad?" I asked.

The Old Man groaned at my abuse of the language but said nothing, having long since given up. "I'm going to kill a horse for bait and offer a reward for bear."

Picking a scrubby horse out of the bunch, the kind of animal that would never bring the price of raising him no matter who you saw coming, he led him onto the infested territory and shot him. Then he passed word around that bears shot on his range were now worth ten dollars a piece and we went back to other tasks.

A couple of the local men with a yen for bear hunting went out to lie by the bait. One bear was soon shot and another wounded. This reported to the Old Man, he paid for the dead one but not the wounded, preferring to have one more attempt made to finish the beast off.

I begged to go out with the hunters on an expedition to track the wounded bear, but apart from finding a place where the brute had lain for several hours and bled, we came on no traceable spoor. Evidently he had lain still long enough for the bleeding to stop, then moved far back into the timber.

The trouble was by no means over. Several more bears were killed during the month, but the signs of damage persisted. Bordy Felker, the owner of the Lazy R Ranch, the biggest outfit in the valley, reported calf-killing on his range several miles to the east.

But nothing more could be done. It was June and the spring growing weather had been good: just enough rain, plenty of sunshine. The Old Man got to walking around in the hay, trying to decide what he needed most: ten days more of growth or a ten-day head start on the harvest. His mind made up, bears were forgotten for lack of time to worry about them.

He gathered crew for which he had earlier made tentative arrangements. Olie Karlander, a hard-working, one-legged Swede who lived down the Eagle Lake road from us, came to work, his wife to cook. Her daughter by a previous marriage, Sylvia Ogden, two years older than I and as good a hand, joined the crew in the field. With Bill Wilson, that made the crew.

Olie was a good man. He'd immigrated years ago, working in the bush as a logger in other parts of Canada. He lost a leg in an industrial accident which put him out of logging, but didn't by a long ways prevent him from making a living. Fitted with a wooden limb, he took to carpentering mainly, but he'd turned his hand at many things, even hacking railroad ties with a broad axe to see himself through the Depression.

A slight man but strong, not tall, quick to laugh, he was strongly principled. Conscientious, he was the sort of man who would work extra time at the end of the day to make up if you gave him coffee in the middle of the morning. And a jug was a yug and a "yug was a damn good ting" but it never interfered with getting on with the job come Monday morning.

Gussy Haller, his family for crew, contracted, taking the Blaze and the Alfie meadows. "It's no use you working under me," the Old Man told him. "You know more about this haying business than I do. Two separate crews running, we'll be through quicker."

Contracting was Gussy's meat, bone and sinew. He was one of that breed of men who are thoroughly competent and hard working in the day to day business of getting the job done. No man, given the same equipment, could get more hay up in a day or take more pride in making the best hay possible in the available weather. If he built you a fence, why, you could count on it to be the best fence you'd ever had built.

But Gussy never successfully got into the cow business on his own. The management end of things just wasn't his cup of tea.

For one thing he thought too much of horses and too little of cows. When he should have been buying heifers, he was dickering for cayuses or grub-staking himself to a winter chasing unbranded wild horses off the Big Bar Mountains along the Fraser River.

Still, he'd found a way to make a living in ranch work, notwithstanding that he never built an outfit of his own. He built instead an unassailable reputation for hard work, dependability, and good faith: a man whose word was worth more than many a written contract any day. If he said he'd cut and stack your meadow at seven dollars a ton, why, count on it man, he'd stack your meadow and give you the best hay he could, no drying it out and fluffing it up to stretch the tape at measuring time.

No, the Old Man made a good decision, putting Gussy on contract and hiring other crew himself to try to be done more quickly if he could. And he'd have done all right, too, except for the weather.

The rains came without mercy. They began with the first mowing; they were still coming with cruel regularity in the fall.

Not once all summer did we put up a stack from hay which had not been rained on once, or several times, and dried out in between. This fussing about, raking it up only to get it wet, scattering it out again afterwards to dry, ruins the hay while it doubles the costs. There was no chance of the beef shipment that fall paying for the kind of harvest we were having.

The intervals of sunshine were always long enough to let us start something, never to finish it. We'd rake some hay, planning to top the bunches into watertight cocks by hand. With the hay half in the windrow and half in the bunch, the cocking only started, the clouds would blow up from nowhere and rain would be there.

Or the Old Man would have a stack half finished. He'd wait until the weather looked settled, then send us out to load our sloops while he'd open up the stack, spreading the emergency top he'd built at the onset of the last storm. Maybe he'd pile a few loads in and maybe he wouldn't, but sure as he had the top of the stack flat to spread out a few more tons, a savage wind would tear through the valley and before he could close up again, it would be raining.

At the Milk Ranch for a month doing two weeks' work, we then moved to the Morton meadow. It rained so much we forgot what a jack pine tree looked like without water dripping off its needles.

Just camping a crew that size in a wet summer at the Morton was bad enough, let alone try to hay as well. Olie and his family took the only cabin, an old one, where his wife could care properly for the two small children. But it was a small cabin and to have no other refuge in a spell of wet weather was no easy matter. It didn't leak but it grew dismal and depressing under the eternally sunless sky.

The Old Man and Bill slept in a fair-sized tent with a fly, an extra piece of canvas the size of the tent roof, stretched over it to be sure it didn't leak. But everything in a tent dampens in wet weather and soon the Old Man was walking half sideways, twisted painfully with rheumatism. He rustled up an old heater from somewhere, setting it up in the tent, and gained some relief from that.

Roger and I shared a badly built pole shack with room in it for two narrow pole bunks, nothing more. It would have been suicide to put a stove in it. Nonetheless it seemed to shed the rain, though damp clothes and bedroll were a constant discomfort. The shortage, too, of hay dry enough for bedding became so acute at one point that we worked down to the knots on the pine poles in the bunks and had nothing with which to replenish the padding.

One night the sky exploded. Torn from sleep by the sheer pain in my ears, I was instantly blinded by a flash of lightning that poured through the cracks between the poles as though the shack weren't there.

I twisted on my bed, burying my face in the blankets, grasping my ears, frantic to shut out the next searing crash of thunder. Before the light was gone it was there, drowning out everything in one's consciousness save the trembling of the bed and the terrifying conviction that the shack would get it next.

After an eternity of ripping crescendos, the echoes died away, leaving a silence so complete one could well wonder if this wasn't eternity itself.

"Roger. Are you there?" It was an exploratory question.

"I ain't nowhere else on a night like this. Sufferin' cats! Here it comes again!" In the brilliant light I caught a glimpse of him then, propped on an elbow, staring into the violence of the night. But only a glimpse, for I threw my face down and covered my ears once more.

Practically no interval before the first clap, we knew the bolt had come to earth within feet of the camp, perhaps in the yard itself. Again we endured those seconds of unholy fury as though we heard the sky itself ripped to shreds, cast into a wild, cosmic confusion. Still, the very fact we heard it assured our safety until the next bolt.

A horse whinnied a scream-like cry of panic and then the bunch raced by, running the yard from fence to fence, pounding hooves close together, in terror, bewildered, running aimlessly but running, for it was all they knew to do.

"You think they'll try to go over the fence?" I wondered aloud.

"Nah. They're scared so bad, you couldn't fence 'em out of camp right now."

Another bolt came but we didn't flinch this time. The brightness was noticeably less and I counted four before the blast of sound.

"Gone over," I observed.

"Yep. Listen, there's the rain."

Down it came, in great solid sheets, splashing on the ground, splashing against the shack, the sound of it running everywhere. I thought of the Old Man and knew how he'd be lying awake thinking of it, thinking of his hay, of how the meadow was wet enough now without all this, of how if something didn't happen to change the weather there wouldn't be hay to winter half the cows, suppose he sold everything but breeding stock at sacrifice prices.

"Dammit, the shack's leaking!" Roger brought me back to our own problems.

"Where? Hell, it never leaked before."

"It's leaking now! Right over my bunk."

"My gosh. Well, there isn't much we can do about that till morning. Roll your bedding to a dry place and climb in here."

"You got room?"

"No, but you gotta squeeze in anyway."

He did have to squeeze in. His bedding was drenched by the time he got out of it. We huddled together on a bunk I reckoned was too small for me alone and there we toughed it out till morning, listening to the rain fall without letup into daybreak.

Fortunately for all hands, the rest of the camp came through dry. One spot leaked in the tent but was out of the way of bed or gear. The cabin took it. The big bonfire we kept burning in the yard had drowned out and as soon as there was the least break in the rain we fetched dry wood from the shed behind the cabin to nurse it to a blaze again.

Roger brought his bedding and we held it against the fire to dry in the lulls, dashing with it to shelter whenever the rain started up afresh. The shack quit leaking and by the time his bedroll was as dry as we could make it he was able to take it back. His meagre supply of hay shot of course, I split what remained of mine. That put us both on the pine knots but good.

Life in camp went on. We all crowded into the cabin three times daily for meals but beyond that there simply wasn't room. Mainly we kept the big fire burning and stood around it, drying the rain off one side, soaking it up on the other.

Sometimes we built fence or slashed brush to extend the yard. At first we went out only in the lulls, but after a while we went out regularly, preferring to be wet and occupied as against just wet. Olie started making logs for a new cabin and then we all helped with that until the logs were gathered and the slow, more skilled task of raising the walls began. At that point the Old Man left Olie one helper, usually Roger, while the rest of us turned back to brush and fencing.

I worried about the Old Man, watching his face grow more weary daily. It seemed one man alone couldn't stand it and yet he plodded on, looking westward at the sky more frequently as time went by, waiting for the break that would show there, had to show there eventually.

"Pretty tough ain't it ... I mean, isn't it, Dad?"

The Old Man looked at me thoughtfully a moment, in an oddly affectionate way. "Do you think you'll stand it?" he asked.

Puzzled, I replied: "Sure, I'll stand it. I was thinking about the hay and all this rain."

"Oh yes, that," he said, and suddenly I knew just what a great big man my old father was. The rain seriously threatening to force a sacrifice of half the herd he'd been years putting together and by the Lord Harry what ate him was the lot of us having to put up with some weather, nothing more important on our minds than three squares a day and keeping dry at night.

The water began to rise in the meadow. This was worst of all for now even if the rains stopped, we could hardly mow hay that stood in several inches of water.

"I think," the Old Man decided, "I'm going to dig a ditch, a damned great long ditch, and get rid of some water."

I pictured a mammoth canal, cut across the vast Cariboo plateau, draining the sky itself. Maybe the weather was really driving him around the bend, more than we knew. "How," I asked, "do you figure to do that?"

"With shovels. How else?"

He called Bill. The three of us trudged down to the far end of the meadow, carrying shovels, a fork, a scythe, and a hay knife, a contraption like a straight-ended shovel only jagged and sharp which one uses by thrusting it downward into the stack to cut the hay when one wishes to use one end of a stack and leave the remainder untouched.

"Now," he explained, "there's a piece of low ground here at the end of the meadow. We dig a ditch, not a big one, starting here in the bush. Then we dig back into the meadow. If water runs in our ditch, we keep on digging. We dig as long as there's water. Got it?"

I could see us going through a powerful lot of shovels before we ran out of water. But we began. Soon our ditch was into the meadow and a current was running, carrying water into the bush and away on a gentle drop of land beyond; such a pitiful trickle though when you compared it to the acres of water sitting on the meadow, it was hard to believe in what we were doing.

We scythed the grass out of the way and with the hay knife we cut the sod into square chunks in a strip two feet wide. Coming behind the knife with a pitchfork, we lifted each square of sod out, tearing it loose at the bottom. We worked in water over our ankles, our feet sodden. As each piece of sedge root sod came out of the ditch, water replaced it.

We'd go home at night after a day of this and peel dead, white skin from our feet. Our boots were ruined. Nonetheless we stayed at it if for no other reason than that we could no longer stand to watch rain pour out of the sky. Our ditch grew longer and longer, farther into the meadow than the Old Man had planned, and we were encouraged by the increasing flow of water.

We hoped with all our might the rain would quit. It kept on coming down. Now at least what fell on the meadow had somewhere to go, though there were parts of the hay land so boggy that we could never cut them that year. Would we ever now have sufficient hay to feed our cattle in the coming winter? It was impossible to be hopeful.

Then the weather showed signs of change. Even before the rain actually stopped, the Old Man took action. "Bill," he instructed, "you put on a pair of chaps to keep your legs dry and go out there to mow hay. You keep on mowing no matter what."

Mowing hay in the rain was contrary to everything I had learned about haying. Again I wondered if the Old Man wasn't suffering a mite too much under the strain. "Still rainin,' Dad," I said casually, to make him realize what he was doing without letting him know I suspected the worst.

"I know it's raining, you silly ass! But if I cut the hay now, there'll be hay down to dry when the sun does come out. It won't come out for long, you can count on that, and we won't waste it mowing. We can rake as soon as we dare." He tamped his pipe thoughtfully with a calloused thumb, impervious to the burning of the tobacco he had already lit. "And," he added, "if it doesn't work, it won't make any difference. We won't get the hay up anyway."

The change held. Soon we were haying and none of us had ever known anything so good in our lives. We still had rainy days but little by little we made progress.

Other grief beset us. The stacking poles we used were several years old but, carefully laid up on blocks each winter, they gave every sign of soundness. Dry and light, they handled well and to cut new poles would have seemed most unwise.

We were halfway through the first stack and all pressing ourselves, knowing the urgency the weather had put upon our every move. I came in with a heavy load, some of it dangerously wet but not that much that the Old Man couldn't work it in by spreading it along the very edges of the stack. Hurriedly I set the blocks, unhooked from the sloop, picked up the derrick cable, and tightened the slings. I always looked back at this point for a signal from the Old Man, just to be sure he was ready.

He waved me on. "Git!" I urged the team and quickly the load lifted from the sloop, rising fast up the front of the stack. On it went, higher, over the lip, now a foot of clearance, now two, now five, and that's good enough.

"Whoa! Whoa, you horses."

In a clean, unbroken movement the load came to the end of the rise and swung in over the stack. The fore line tightened, grabbing the poles, arresting the swing. The load went on and I wondered if the Old Man would trip it now or catch it on the first swing back. He'd had trouble grasping the trip rope as it went by and he might not judge his moment to pull. I readied myself to unhook the second the slings would burst, spilling the hay.

My stomach wrenched into a knot as I saw the load go on, the left pole splinter apart halfway from the stack top to the peak of the derrick, the crash of shattering wood hard on the sight of the right pole swinging crazily, then plunging down, driving the broken end like a skewer into the hay.

The Old Man had thrown himself into the stack, head down, crouching for what protection it might give him. I'd seen him go from sight and the broken pole end follow him into the hay but whether hurt or not I couldn't know from where I was.

I backed the team to slack the derrick cable. Somehow in spite of the trembling that seized me I got the cable ring off the doubletree hook. I dropped the lines and turned to run for the back of the stack where the Old Man had a ladder when, brushing hay from the back of his neck, he rose slowly up from the stack to survey the damage.

"You all right?" I shouted.

"Oh hell, I'm all right." Then thoughtfully: "We ruined us a pole, didn't we?"

I gulped. "We sure did. I guess I made my load too heavy."

"Oh, no. In a summer like this all the loads are too heavy. I just misjudged the poles, that's all."

We untangled the mess then and shut down to fetch new poles, losing precious hours of stacking weather, followed by the inevitable shower just when the new poles were ready to go.

As if bad luck haying wasn't enough, we had to have it other ways. Bill and the collie had become inseparable companions. Wherever he worked she followed. If he was out with the mower, she'd make the first round or two with him, then find a sheltered place in a nearby bush to lie where she could see him, to join him again when it came time to return to camp.

We were cocking hay one afternoon when a threatening shower had stopped us stacking and compelled us to top up the remaining bunches. Bill worked from bunch to bunch near one of the islands of timber in the middle of the meadow. The old collie left him briefly to explore the bush along the edge and suddenly came running back to him, crying in an agony of pain.

Bill knelt with her, talking to her, trying to quiet her whimpers, at a loss to know what afflicted her. Her pain increased, she went into convulsions and in moments, her head resting in his hands, she died.

Then we knew. She had picked up a strychnine pill set out for wolves which, despite the Old Man's scrupulous efforts to recover all the poison he'd set out, had lain there since last winter.

Bill picked the old girl up in his arms and walked away across the meadow to the timber to find a place to put her away, hobbling along pitifully on his bad feet. The first spattering drops coming as he started, it was raining so hard when he reached the trees you could barely make him out.

We all put our forks at the stackyard to trod wearily back to camp. That night Bill didn't come for supper.

Occasionally we saw something of Gussy. He'd ride over once in a while to see the Old Man, or perhaps one or two of us would visit the Blaze to pass the time in the eternal wet. He was making no more progress than we were. He had also a share of bad breaks. One night a porcupine chewed the front guy line while the poles rested on the back line. When the first load went over, the front line tightened and snapped, the poles crashing to the ground behind the stack, shattering themselves and the stackyard fence at the same time.

Haying done that fall, we were terribly short of winter feed. So was every other cowman in the country and therefore there was none to buy, supposing there had been any money to buy it with after paying the costs of the haying. All we needed was a long tough winter and it would he a hard row to hoe indeed.

The Old Man knew he would have to ship every animal that could sell to advantage, maybe some that couldn't. The season dealt him one backhanded stroke of luck, if you could call it that: the bears had killed so many calves on the summer range that he had nearly a carload of dry cows and heifers in butcher-fat condition. They brought a better price, with more poundage, than they would have had their calves been with them.

Roger and I, of course, had to leave the camp before the end of haying to return to school. In the last few days I was almost sure I looked forward to it. I had grown sick of hay and sick of fighting it in bad weather. Our every hour revolved around it. We fed it to our horses, we pitched it on our stoops, we cocked it up in the face of oncoming rain, we even slept on it.

The Old Man drove us out of camp to our mother's house in Williams Lake in the first week of September and for the first time in many weeks we slept in a proper bed. No sooner there and surrounded by comforts, I fell in an agony to be back on the ranch. I would have traded the soft mattress of my mother's house for the jack pine poles and swamp grass of camp on the instant, were it my choice to do so. Unhappily it wasn't, though wisely so, no doubt.

WE WERE BROTHERS

A new story by Eldon Lee

Eldon Lee, born in California in 1923, was raised on an isolated ranch in the rugged Central Cariboo from age five. He was home-schooled with only his younger brother, Todd, for companionship. At 19, Lee enlisted in the Royal Canadian Air Force and became a bomber pilot. He returned to ranch with Todd for several years, then went on to become a doctor, practising medicine both in his beloved Cariboo and in other remote areas of British Columbia. He is the author of numerous books about the Cariboo, some co-written with Todd, who became a minister. Lee now resides in Prince George and was presented with the Jeanne Clarke Memorial Local History Award in 1998. In Eldon Lee's brand new story, told with humour and love, he pays tribute to the closeness of brothers growing up together in the Cariboo's natural playground.

Todd and Eldon Lee developed deep bonds of brotherhood and affection growing up on a Soda Creek ranch.

"We were brothers and we were that close." The old man put his forefinger and thumb together. "I was there when he arrived a new baby, and I was there when he gasped his last breath."

But wait, whoa! I *am* the old man, Eldon Lee; and my brother, Todd Lee. And our entire lives were entwined with a love and devotion that started when we were children.

I was the older brother and I assumed responsibility for my younger brother. Todd was the more daring, but the more fragile, and it was I who got up from bed with him at night when he became croupy. It was I who saved him from drowning in a deep hole in Knife Creek. And it was I who dragged him from a runaway horse. He was the one who steadied me when, spurred on by the eccentricities that plague the near-genius, I went too far in correcting others. He was the one who dared more when dangers presented themselves.

We studied together, rode horses together, and slept in the same four-poster bed with our collie Duke between us. We wore each other's clothes and shared money or valuables equally. Our ranch was the centre of our world, and our world ended a half-day's journey by horseback. School was our home; our desk, the oval oak living-room table. Our only lights in darkness were gas lamps with glowing mantles. We had our own language, about 1,500 words, complete with grammar—and we conversed quite freely in it. For example, *wey mula eos saknet* meant, "we should go now."

In winter we fed the cows and horses, and in spring we rode horses over the range as we watched the cattle. In summer we helped put up hay for winter's food. All year long we milked our cows 7 days a week, at 7 a.m. and again at 7 p.m. It was a rare day that found either of us missing from that ritual. We sat on a stool, head resting on the cow's warm flank, and made milk fly into a three-gallon bucket.

During the spring and summer, we put gallons of milk through the hand-operated milk separator. Night and morning its high-pitched whine broke the pastoral stillness. From one spigot came a large stream of skim milk, and from the other trickled thick, yellow cream. The milk went for cottage cheese and a soft, white homemade cheese; some went to the pigs and chickens. The cream went to a gallon-sized butter churn, and to almost every dish served at the ranch dining table.

Milking cows was only one of the many events that deepened the bond between two brothers. One experience, oddly enough, involved us boys and a lunatic old racehorse called Babs. The psychologist would call it *folie à trois*, a delusion shared by three. At any rate, this adventure shaped our future.

It all began on a warm summer's morning when my brother and I collected our blueberry pails and made our way to the horse barn. There we found Grandad holding the halter of an old, brown nag already saddled and bridled.

"Whatever you do, don't let this horse get to running," said Grandad, as he handed us the reins. "He's an old racehorse and if he gets to running, you can't stop him."

Grumbling to ourselves, we mounted the horse, took the reins, and seized our chance for berry-picking. Old Babs' shambling gait took us away to the blueberry patch about a mile from the ranch barn. Two types of blueberries grew there—a high-bush, which was more productive, and a low-bush, which had tastier berries. The low-bush berries were dark blue and somewhat tart. They added flavor to the blander high-bush berries.

As we busily picked, old Babs stood, a disgraceful picture of a ranch horse. His back was bowed, his long tail was tangled, and he had spavins on his legs. His lean hips stood out like fence posts and his belly sagged. His neck drooped, with the ears falling to the outside. Most horses would nibble at the grass or make a threatening motion toward the flies buzzing around them, but Babs simply stood in the sunshine without moving a muscle.

After an hour our cans were filled and we mounted the horse again—this time with myself in the saddle and Todd behind me. We made our way to the road that led to the barn. Babs rambled along and Todd, in exasperation, gave him a kick in the sides and said: "Come on, you old plug. We'll never get home this way."

I shouted a warning: "Don't get Babs running! If he runs, we can't stop him."

"This old plug can hardly walk, let alone run," said Todd scornfully, and he gave the horse another urging whack on the flanks.

Babs hadn't felt this sort of activity for many years. He roused himself up and began a slow and jolting trot. We were pleased, but a little taken aback as the trot was quite jarring, and made us bounce up and down. The trot became stronger, and we became a bit alarmed when the blueberries started to fly out of the pail and turn to thick jam on the saddle leather beneath our denims.

"We'd better stop him," said Todd. "I'm having trouble holding on to my berries."

"He won't stop," I said. The old racehorse quickened his pace to a faster trot, and then to a gallop.

"Stop him!" said Todd.

"I can't! I think he's going to run away!"

It was then that Babs seemed to hear the roar of the thousands gathered around the racetrack, the thunder of hooves, the urging of jockeys. His back straightened, his head came up, his sagging belly became taut, his spavins ceased to hurt and his tail flew in the air as he pounded down the wagon road with a dust cloud behind him.

"Hang on to the berries!" I shouted, but my shouts were as a sparrow's cry for all the effect they had. I heard Todd's berry pail go clattering on the road, and my own flew in the air to land heaven knows where.

"Stop him, stop him!" cried Todd. "I'm going to fall off!"

"I can't stop him! He's got the bit in his teeth!" And indeed, I could not stop him unless I pulled out his teeth. "Hang on," I told Todd. "He's running away!"

Babs continued his wild gallop down the wagon road, dust flying. His neck was horizontal now, his nose pointed toward a distant goal. I was sliding around in the saddle and hanging on desperately. Todd dashed from side to side, and forward and back, with a layer of blue-berries making a slippery paste underneath his denim-clad bottom.

Babs could hear the crowd, the roars. Through his mind went the theme: *I can do it! I can do it! Even though my jockey hasn't much talent, a good steady horse can overcome. Legs, do your stuff. Heart, mind, lungs, wind ... I can do it! I can win the Kentucky Derby! I'm leading the pack! I'm out in front! All I need to do is maintain this speed ...*

The crowd's roar grew faint in his ears as he concentrated on the final quarter-mile.

"I can't hold on any longer," said Todd. "Stop him!"

"Hang on. It's not much further. I can't stop him, but hang on."

At this point I realized I was alone on the thundering horse. A wail arose from the road behind, attesting to contact between Todd and the solid ground.

"Stop, you old fool!" I screamed in frustration and desperation. I could see the barnyard gate barring the road ahead. But Babs never faltered. His eyes were on the race's end.

His breath came in gasps. Lather flew from his withers and his heart pounded. At full speed he crashed into the gate.

The laws of motion took over, and I flew over the blueberry-lubricated saddle, over Babs, over the gate, and into the soft barnyard soil 20 feet ahead. There I stopped, every muscle clamouring to have its message of pain and distress heard. I looked up the road to see Todd limping along, crying in great gusts of hurt and anguish and anger.

Babs stood in the wreckage of the gate, his sides heaving, lather dripping onto the ground. His chest pounded and his legs trembled. But his back was straight, his stomach was taut, and his head was up. He could see himself being led into the winner's circle and the wreath of flowers being draped around his neck. He could hear the crowd applauding his victory.

In our misery and our wrath, Todd and I gazed at this lunatic horse that had practically killed us. Our blueberries were scattered to the wind, the skin had peeled off Todd from buttocks to neck, and I was a mass of horse droppings and pain.

Then we too saw the glory: we saw Babs, the racehorse, no longer a shambling refugee from the glue factory, but standing straight and proud, nostrils distended, head up. And we heard the roar of the crowd, the praise, the adulation, the shouts of "well done!" And we realized then that we could do it too. We could achieve the impossible, for we had ridden the horse that just won the Kentucky Derby.

The portent of our experience with the crazy old racehorse was to be fulfilled in the future. In the meantime, our everyday life was filled with work on the ranch, home study, and what recreation there was available—mostly horseback riding, playing ball in the summer, and skiing in the winter. Our daily routine started when we were aroused from our four-poster bed by our grandfather, who would announce: "Six-thirty, boys ... time to get up."

After we were up and off to do our chores, Duke, our collie, would roll over on his back in the middle of the bed and catch a few more winks. At eight o'clock, after the horses were fed, the cows milked and the milk run through the separator, we gathered around the breakfast table. First giving thanks for the bounties provided, we tucked into porridge with real cream, eggs, homemade sausages, hot biscuits, fried potatoes, fruit and coffee—again, with thick, real cream. As growing, busy boys, we probably required 6,000 calories a day.

At nine o'clock brother Todd and I, under the stern eyes of our mother, started school work. Usually a whole day was spent on one subject: English literature on Monday, math on Tuesday, Latin on Wednesday, social studies on Thursday and science on Friday.

Lunchtime gave us an hour's remission from study. At this time we fled school, raced to our saddle horses, and were off grouse hunting, fishing, or simply riding the range for sheer enjoyment. Then it was back to the grind until 3:30 in the afternoon. In the winter, cross-country skiing on our five-foot-long wooden skies carried us for miles across field-and-forest trails. On weekend nights, if there was a moon, brother Todd and I donned our skis and flew down the 100-foot slope from the root-cellar roof to the frozen creekbed below.

In early summer the lure of a fishing expedition became totally irresistible on the Hills and Paul Ranch. During the lazy days of June, Todd and I saddled horses, tied lunches on behind and, with two large dogs following, galloped away to the fishing holes of Knife Creek as it coursed through Murphy's meadow two and a half miles away. Here the creek meandered in idle swings and turns. At each bend, deeper water was found, and it was in these that our six-foot-long willow poles, fishing lines, and worms were pressed into action. The trout could not resist, and by lunchtime each of us had 10 or 12 trout on a forked willow branch. Sometimes we would splay two trout and broil them over coals.

After lunch, our dogs swam to cool themselves while the horses fed on lush grasses and lazily swished their tails to ward off bothersome insects that buzzed about. Sometimes Todd and I would strip off our clothes and dive into the stream, which was usually not more that a metre deep. Once Todd, a poor swimmer, got caught in the current of a deep hole and went under the water. I remember that while he was under, he was still pluckily stroking to save himself. He might well of drowned had I not pushed him to shore, where we both choked and coughed and gasped for breath.

Sometimes, when riding the range looking for cattle, we came upon a likely looking trout stream where a half-dozen fat trout lay fanning themselves in the water of a shallow hole. We knew exactly how to relate to this. We cropped the longest strawberry runner available, bashed a luckless cricket, tied it to the end of the runner and, fixing the other end to a willow pole, let the cricket bait drift temptingly down in front of the trout. Reaction was explosive—the same as might be found at Mother's cry of "dinner is on the table" heard by two hungry ranch boys. The fish seized the bait. A whip of the pole and the half-swallowed lure came flying out of the water. With any luck, a plump trout was attached to it.

One adventure that stands out in my mind came on a cool day in early May. Our school lessons well in hand, we'd asked our mother for permission, and received it, to take a long-planned trip to the 108 Mile Road, 12 miles to the east. This road had a romantic past, beginning in 1862 when it served as a shortcut from the Cariboo Wagon Road to Horsefly, Quesnel Forks and, ultimately, Barkerville and the goldfields at Williams Creek. At the midpoint was a stopping place called, fittingly enough, the Halfway House. Our ride was calculated to strike the 108 Mile Road between this early settlement and Lac la Hache (lake of the hatchet). Brother Todd and I mounted our saddle horses, Dickie and Tony, and set out.

A mile into our journey we came to Knife Creek, which was in spring flood. "Feet out of the stirrups," I shouted at Todd, bringing my own feet up on Tony's shoulders.

Horses are fairly good swimmers, but have been known to roll over in fast water. It's better not to have a foot caught up in a stirrup if this happens. Todd already had his feet on Dickie's shoulders, and the horses plunged in short lunges across the seven-metre-wide crest and clambered out the far side, dripping water from their bellies and tails.

We turned to keep the sun directly in our faces, and in this way we knew that we were travelling in an easterly direction; we didn't need a compass. Our horses always had an unerring instinct about directions, and in a blinding snowstorm or utter darkness would turn and head for home. Their direction finders seemed to steer them around difficult, forested areas, swamps, and ravines, but eventually, even under the most adverse circumstances, they would arrive at the barnyard gate.

The timber was now of scattered aspen and pines rooted on rising terrain, with the occasional small pothole surrounded by thick willows. "Look there," said Todd. Not 20 metres from us stood a great, old cow moose in the brush. She was grey and thin from scant winter rations and motherhood, for beside her was a new calf, light brown in color and standing steadily on long, thin legs. It could not have been more than three weeks of age. The cow turned and trotted into deeper cover while the calf took a final look and galloped after the mother. To our surprise, it gave little bleats of *maa, maaaa*, probably saying: *Wait up for me, Mom. Not so fast. Is it time for lunch yet?*

A moment later a squirrel took up a furious chatter a hundred metres to the side, sounding an alert to his family and brother squirrels: *Move! Run for your lives! Moose are coming! Moose!* Our horses took no notice of this disturbance and we proceeded eastward. The countryside grew wilder with fallen trees, ravines, and in one place, a canyon. Thick patches of alder, spruce and willow covered the canyon's slopes and depths. Fortunately, the canyon and wild forest soon turned away all in a northerly direction, leaving our way clear.

At noon our horses snorted and sneezed to let us know that "time" had been called. Time for lunch, time for rest, time for a nap. We loosened saddle cinches, took bridles from horses' mouths, and then looked to our own comforts. We placed dry pine grass against the base of a pitch stump, added a few twigs and branches, and soon we had a fire with flames and sparks shooting upwards. We heated ham sandwiches on the sharpened ends of alder sticks, and ate apples and cake for dessert. Hot tea from a thermos finished off our lunch.

There was a rattle to one side, and we turned to see a grumpy porcupine sitting at the base of an immature pine tree. The white, debarked areas further up the tree gave evidence of our friend's eating habits. "I bet I can catch him," said Todd.

The porcupine started to climb and Todd raced over, seized the quill-laden tail in his gloved hand, and slid the other hand under the porcupine. He grasped the opposite foreleg, then *voila*! He lifted the porcupine in his arms, taking care to keep a respectable distance between his chest and the thousands of quills on the porcupine's back. Our little rodent was not frightened, but he was twice as grumpy and, when released, he made his way to a nearby pine tree, where he climbed to a low branch and complained mightily at the manners of some people found even in a forest solitude.

Finally, there it was: a straight, gravelled wagon road running north and south. One moment we were lost in a forest, and in the next, we had found civilization. There was even a fingerboard sign giving directions and distances to spots like Spout Lake, Murphy Lake, and Lac la Hache. Our spirits rose. Even our horses brightened up as they broke into a trot, then a gallop. We raced down the road towards the few scattered log buildings of the Halfway House, where we turned west. Two hours later, just as the sun dipped below the shadow of the hills, we pulled up before the barn gate of the Hills and Paul Ranch.

Now, years later, I remember with satisfaction this ordinary day's journey of two teenagers and their reluctant horses. Forgotten are details of exotic places, rich food, fine hotels and deep sleeps in soft beds. Our day's journey through the forest, our lunch by the flaming campfire, then dinner and sound sleep in our ranch home holds more appeal than all of these. Time has its habit of winnowing out the tiny kernels of true worth from a mountain of chaff, and the remarkable from the merely humdrum. This was a remarkable journey; one to be remembered for years, and the cost—not one cent!

Life passed tranquilly. Summer saw us harvesting the hay; fall, rounding up the cattle; and winter, feeding hay to the cows and horses. All year round, we read books and listened to music—both modern and classical—from hundreds of wax records played on the spring-powered phonograph. Of girls, we could only dream about wondrous curves and soft voices. There was one girl, only five miles away, who was tall, 18 years old, with the requisite number of curves, but she was mainly interested in older men and not two bashful, awkward youths. Our dogs made frantic trips back and forth whenever her female dog went into heat, but for us there was no encouragement.

When I reached 18, I wrote my final government exams and graduated from high school. There was no grad party or grad exercises, but I had my family's appreciation for a job well done. That fall, when the hay had been stacked, I went off to my first job as a labourer for McGregor Light and Power. This was by grace of Hirohito, since the Japanese were threatening our west coast and had even shelled a lighthouse. It was felt that western Canada and Alaska would be safer if a telephone line was built farther inland.

Brother Todd put aside his studies and came with me. We were not politically correct for the times: we asked the supervisor, whose name was Strachan, if that might be a German name. He informed us curtly that Strachan was Scottish, and that we'd better mind our tongues if we wanted to stay on his crew.

We boarded at the 70 Mile House and worked 10 hours a day for 65 cents an hour. The 70 Mile House was managed by Mrs. Porter and her husband Matt, whom she always called "Porter." Matt was the postmaster and a boozer, and Ma Porter would periodically, within our hearing, berate him for his faults. Sometimes this occurred at two o'clock in the morning. Ma, bless her heart, took Todd and me to her commodious bosom and fed us the most fabulous meals imaginable. She scrounged far and wide for fresh eggs, butter, sugar and beef—all in short supply due to wartime rationing.

We paid 50 cents for each meal, and a dollar each for beds in a large room that served as sleeping quarters for the 15-man crew. At night my faith was tested, for it took a lot of courage to bring out my New Testament and read a chapter in the midst of this homespun and rough-mannered work crew. I also had to hand the book to Todd and make sure that he read as he had promised to, and after that, make sure that he joined me in evening prayers. Todd, in his shyness, would have easily backslid had I not been firm.

I found out something about the average working man. These rough-hewn men had a true sense of appreciation for others who were sincere in their beliefs and held to their values. Not one word of rebuke or scorn was ever said, and, at our vespers time, coarse language and talk either subsided or stopped. The foreman, a 50-year-old family man, sensing that we were callow youths with no worldly experience, gave a serious homily on "women of easy entrance," and the importance of avoiding the bottle, gambling and bad company. Such a talk from a respected older person can be very effective in influencing young men, and has helped many to make sound choices when faced with temptations.

At the end of November, Todd returned to the ranch and grade 12, and a month later I left the crew. The outside temperature was 25 degrees below zero. There was two feet of snow, and I had a terrible bout of tonsillitis. Also, I had lost my enthusiasm for telephone lines. With increasing frequency my thoughts were on the war, and finally I came to a firm decision. I would join the Royal Canadian Air Force. The crew was still pushing northward and had erected telephone poles as far as 141 Mile House. They wished me well in my visit with Adolf.

On a clear February day at one o'clock in the afternoon, to tears from my mother and grandparents, brother Todd and I mounted our horses, Dickie and Tony, to meet the bus at the 141 Mile House, eight miles away. Halfway to the highway and chattering with the cold, we stopped and built a fire to warm ourselves. We didn't say much. We were so close that we didn't need to put our feelings into words. But we both knew that this could be the last time we would see each other, and we felt this parting deeply.

Todd said later that looking back to see the empty saddle on Tony and me walking away was the saddest moment in his life. For me, it was a time of sadness at parting, but also of excitement about a new venture. I was yet to realize that it would be a venture that would change my life; in two years I went from simple ranch lad to the role of bomber pilot in one of the greatest air forces of the world. I went away a boy and came back a man.

Two years later I alighted from the bus at 141 Mile House, where the venture had begun. The closeness between Todd and I was still there, but it had changed. Many of my war experiences could not be shared completely. Our old collie, Duke, who had occupied my position in the four-poster bed, was banished to the floor, where he complained mightily. We were now men on our own ranch, successful futures foreseen with old Babs so long ago looming before us. For four years we operated two ranches, then it was Todd's turn to leave—for university. A year later, I sold the ranches and cattle, and followed him. Our mother was proud: as a result of her teaching on the ranch, we were both "A" students at university.

Todd took advanced degrees at UBC in social work and the Christian ministry. I spent 13 years in study and finished as a medical specialist with numerous degrees.

We were boys together, young men, responsible citizens, family men; then we aged. I remember that spring long ago when the river was in flood and I hesitated to try and run it in the canoe. Todd, who loved to challenge his brother, stepped into the craft and emerged downstream, eyes flashing and a smile on his lips. Silently, I exulted.

So it was at the end. He went first, just as he had always dared to in our lifetime. I stood, unable to save him. And at the end, the nurse beside his bed said, "Has he gone?" and handed me a stethoscope. I listened. There was no breath, no heartbeat. And then came a lone beat—a strong, final beat—and in my sadness, I rejoiced. He had arrived at the calm waters ahead. It was I who was left to follow later.

Brotherly hijinks land Eldon and Todd Lee
in front of a cow-town judge.

High Noon in a Cow-town Court

from *Stories from the Cariboo: He Saw With Other Eyes* by Todd Lee

More brotherly escapades are confessed in this amusing reminiscence taken from Stories from the Cariboo, *this time by the other brother, Todd Lee. Recalling the days of his first appointment as a United Church minister in the 1950s, Todd writes that Williams Lake, home of the world-renowned Williams Lake Stampede, was "a dusty cow town … poised somewhere between a railroad whistle stop and a town with a possible future." It was then the largest cattle-shipping point in the province and was undergoing a boom of expansion and road building. In this story, Todd's memory carries him back to the Williams Lake of the previous decade, when he and Eldon, a couple of ranch teens hankering for excitement, took a ride that landed them in a clash between old modes of transportation and new on the streets of the "big city." Todd Lee died in 1995.*

It was one of those occasions when many of the folk of Williams Lake get together around groaning richly laden tables in the Elk's Hall. As the newest minister in town, I was to pronounce a blessing over the culinary delights and the women whose hands had prepared them. I was seated at the head table, near the front of the packed room. I turned to introduce myself to the gentleman on my left and then the lady on my right. When she told me her name, something rang a bell in the recesses of my memory.

"Haven't we met before?" she asked pleasantly.

"I'm not sure ..." I replied. "You *do* look familiar. It might have been before I left for university." Then it came back to me. We *had* met before, years before ... only that time she was riding a horse. My mind faded back over the years ...

There comes a time when feeding cows on a wild hay meadow ranch loses much of its thrill. Such a time came to my brother and me in March of 1947. Three feet of snow lay deep and crisp and even on the meadows of Lazy Lee Ranch, which was named more for alliterative effect than for our style of labour. Winter *was* receding, albeit too slow for our and the cows' liking. Cabin fever was advancing faster than the snow receded.

The cows, disenchanted with the quality of hay we served up on the feed-lot, had taken pre-emptive action and had preceded us to the stack-yard. When we arrived, we found the fence down and the haystack spread over a half acre with three hundred cows methodically stamping it into the snow. It was the last straw.

Surveying the damage done by these rebellious animals, Eldon blurted out with "Hey, let's take the day off and go to town. These ungrateful hay-burners can pull their lunch out of that mess themselves!"

"Yeah—I'll vote for that." It had been four months since we'd seen the bright lights. "Bright lights" meant Williams Lake, population six hundred, boasting of street lights up and down Oliver Street and

Railway Avenue. There was even a neon sign over Tyson's Drug Store. But it was a lot more exciting than March in a backwoods pasture.

I contemplated the excitement of playing a game of pool at Mac's Billiards, listening to the juke box at the Maple Leaf Hotel Coffee Shop, and eating a restaurant-cooked meal at the Famous Cafe. We might even catch a glimpse of one of those fair creatures rarely seen around a Cariboo swamp ranch—a girl!

However alluring the bright lights were, getting to the bright lights was another matter. The previous November we had blown all of our available assets on a 1932 Chevrolet roadster, whose main attractions were wire-spoke wheels set in the front, a rumble seat in the back, and a convertible top, which had a disconcerting habit of converting spontaneously while we were driving down the road. In addition, Andy Westwick, the previous owner, had attached a triple-throated, old-style Greyhound Bus horn under the hood.

The Department of Highways did not consider our nine-mile section of road worthy of being plowed in the winter, so "Betsy" had to be parked at the 150 Mile Garage, under the kindly eye of Jack McPhail, who saw the car's ancient workings as a source of constant revenue.

With light hearts we saddled our horses and rode down the mountain, the monotony of the trip being broke at the end when a browsing moose spooked at our approach and trotted through the yard of the 150 Mile Elementary School just as the children were out for recess. The chorus of shrill screams emanating from the playground brought delighted grins to our faces.

As one might expect, Betsy, ignored for nearly four months, was not inclined to be communicative; she wouldn't start. The battery was dead and even the crank which Eldon spun vigorously failed to elicit the slightest response.

"We have ways to make you talk!" Eldon warned the reluctant roadster. Removing the spark plugs, he put a generous squirt of raw gasoline into each cylinder. The flash of a lighter held to the open head brought a satisfying "whoosh." When this was repeated twice, we screwed back the plugs, opened choke and throttle and spun the crank. Betsy came to life with a roar, announcing to all within a quarter mile that its exhaust pipe and muffler had parted company.

We tied our horses to a tree across the road from the 150 Mile Hotel, to wait our return with as much equanimity as possible. Off we went for the "metropolis," dodging pot holes and gunning the motor to race through deep, muddy ruts before we got bogged down. Finally the town of Williams Lake in all its glory came into sight.

Our first stop was the court house. We were aware that our licence plate had expired, along with both our driver's licences. That would be our first item of business, but to our surprise, the court house door was locked and a sign told us why: CLOSED.

"Hey, how come? It's only 3:00 p.m.!" Eldon protested. "Hmmm ... it says, 'Open Monday to Friday.' What day is it anyhow?"

"Oh gosh—it's Saturday!" Since we worked seven days a week feeding those hungry cattle, one day was no different than another. We had forgotten that civil servants worked only five days a week.

"Oh well," Eldon shrugged, "We'll take care of all this the next time we come to town." We trooped back to our car.

"Hey! The Lees! When did you dig out of the snow?"

The cheery hail came from our friend Gordie Hyde, a "town" friend who later became a United Church minister, posted—as I was—to the Cariboo.

"Hi Gordie—good to see you. How do you like our chariot?"

"Super." Gordie crossed the street. "Say, can I take it for a spin, I've got a drivers licence."

"Sure ... but mind the brake. You have to shove it to the left or it catches the gas pedal on the way down."

Gordie slid behind the wheel; Eldon chose the middle, and I was left to twist the crank. Moments later we were off with a throaty roar and a shower of gravel, as Gordie let out the mustang clutch.

We turned off Oliver onto Third, dodging the quagmire in front of St. Peter's Anglican Church. Then it happened—a lady on a big bay saddle horse appeared in the centre of the street.

"Better stop—that horse looks skittish!" Eldon warned.

Gordie hit the brake; the brake hit the gas pedal. Betsy let out a terrible roar and shuddered so hard the roof converted on the spot. Confused, Gordie somehow hit the horn button, adding a triple-throated trumpet blast to the din. Then the motor died.

In horrified silence we watched the big bay rear up on his hind legs, whinny with fear, and pirouette in one flowing motion before bolting down the nearest alley.

"Hey—good rider!" I exclaimed.

"Yeah—I'd be lying in the mud if it had been me!" Gordie gasped. "Here, Eldon, you'd better take over."

We made our way to the Maple Leaf Cafe and caught up on all the gossip that had happened since our last trip to town while the latest hits played on Benny Abbott's juke box in the background. Our coffee cups were refilled by a provocatively cute waitress. The time passed quickly.

"Wow, look at that clock!" Gordie exclaimed finally. "I'm late for a meeting. See you guys. Thanks for the car ride."

"Anytime!" I called after him, then, "Say, Eldon, we've got time for a game of pool before supper. Let's go."

We headed for Mac's Billiards, which took us past where we had parked Betsy down the block.

"Oh, oh!" Eldon came to a stop. "We've got trouble!"

Indeed we had. Two uniformed constables were showing a marked interest in our little roadster. Even as we watched, one leaned over and rubbed mud off the licence plate.

"Maybe they'll go away," I suggested hopefully.

"Are you kidding?" Eldon led the way to the offending car.

"Ah ... good evening, officers. Nice spring weather, isn't it?"

They looked at us without enthusiasm. "This your car?"

"Yep. Doesn't look like much, but it gets us there," Eldon replied, patting Betsy's rumble seat.

"Are you aware that your licence plate expired last month?"

"Well yes. But I can explain. You see it's been laid up all winter. We drove in today to get the licence renewed."

"On Saturday?"

"Well ... um ... we didn't realize the Motor Vehicle Branch was closed on Saturday."

The constable looked pityingly at us and moved within sniffing distance. "Let's see your driver's licence."

Eldon produced his from his wallet and handed it over. I could see we were digging ourselves into a legal black hole.

"This licence expired last month, too." the constable said with grim satisfaction.

"We ... I was going to get that renewed today as well ... uh ... We don't come to town very often."

The constable had his book out and was writing busily. Finally he handed us three tickets.

"Uh ... what's the third one for?" I asked, reading them over Eldon's shoulder.

"Just what it says—driving in a manner dangerous to the public."

"Huh? What's that supposed to mean?"

"We had a citizen complain. She said you were dead drunk and driving like fiends. Scared her half to death!"

A light went on—the rider whose horse had bolted! She must have galloped straight to the police station.

"You'll note you're required to be in Magistrate's Court on Friday the 17th of March at 11:00 a.m." The other constable spoke for the first time. "Oh, by the way, we'll have to impound your car."

"Impound ... ? Hey, you can't do that!"

"Sec. 23 (1) of the Motor Vehicle Act. 'Unlicensed vehicles are subject to impoundment by the Crown.'"

"But ... but we've got to get home! Our horses are tied to a tree ten miles out!"

The constables exchanged glances. One shrugged. "All right, we'll stretch the law a bit. But get that car out of town right now and don't bring it back until it's licensed."

We drove out of town, our spirits matching the gloom of the dusk of early evening. I was thinking of the meal we'd missed and the dubious one of cold potatoes and warmed over moose parts that waited us at the ranch house.

"What a bummer!" I groaned.

"Darn it all! We didn't even get our game of pool!" Eldon complained.

"Say ... that constable said not to bring the car back into town ... he didn't say anything about us."

"You're right." Eldon's face lit up. "There's a road leading up into the trees ... we could park there ... walk back to town ... "

We'd just placed our order in the Famous Cafe when in walked the two constables and sat down across from us. We looked at them; they looked at us. One half rose from his seat, but the other held up his hand and grinned. Nothing happened, but somehow the joy had gone out of our meal.

We played a desultory game of pool, then walked out of town, fired up Betsy and plowed our muddy way back to the 150 Mile House and our horses.

We were up early on the 17th, not at all in the light-hearted spirit of St. Patrick despite some Irish blood on grandmother's side. Luck was with us, though. We were able to hitch a ride into town and arrived only a half hour late.

In spite of the fact that court was to start at 11:00, we counted on "Cariboo time" and thought it prudent to first visit the Motor Vehicle Branch. Minutes later we headed for the court, safely in possession of renewed driver's licences and a new licence plate. Our greatest concern was that we now had $23.50 between us and Magistrate Hart was known to be fond of the sentence of "thirty dollars or thirty days." We appeared to be the sole offenders that day, as the only occupants of the court room were the two constables and the Magistrate.

"This Magistrate's Court is now open. God save the King!" intoned one constable.

Magistrate Hart adjusted his glasses and read the first charge: Driving a 1932 Ford without a valid licence plate. "Guilty or not guilty?"

We exchanged glances. "Not guilty, your worship," Eldon replied. "We don't own a 1932 Ford ... never have."

Magistrate Hart looked over his glasses, "Can you prove that, son?"

Eldon fished in his pocket and came up with the vehicle registration, handed it across the Bench.

"Hmmm ... 1932 Chevrolet ... Constable?"

"Sorry, sir ... it was so muddy ..."

"Hurrumph! I'd have thought, Constable, that you could tell a Chevrolet from a Ford. Even I can. I'll have to throw out this charge." He picked up the second ticket.

"It says here, young man, that at the time of the complaint you were driving without a valid driver's licence. How do you answer that?"

"Not guilty, sir. I wasn't driving," Eldon answered.

"I wasn't driving, either," I added quickly.

Magistrate Hart again looked at the constables. "Your complainant made an identification, of course?" he enquired.

"Well, now that you mention it, she just said there were three wild drunks roaring around town ..."

"And the three were drunk when you questioned them?"

"Well, no, they didn't appear to have been drinking ... not these two, anyway.

"And the third?"

"Oh ... we saw only two."

Magistrate Hart turned to us. "You boys have drivers' licences now?"

"Yes sir!" We both held them out. "Case dismissed! Now, what about this dangerous driving charge?"

"I think I can explain that," Eldon said, "We turned the corner and there was this rider coming down the street ... we didn't mean to scare her. I told Gordie to stop."

"Did you come to a full stop?" the magistrate asked.

"Yes sir, the driver came to a full stop."

"Well, that's all the Act requires. Case dismissed. Constable, I believe that's all for today, is it not?"

"Yes, your worship. This court is closed. God save the King!"

Magistrate Hart gathered up his papers and left. The constables grinned and shook hands with us. "Okay, you kids, cool it, huh? Next time we just might be more accurate."

We left the court just as the noon whistle sounded, hardly daring to believe that justice had been so kind. It was time for celebration. Throwing caution to the wind, we opted for class and lunched in the luxurious Lakeview Hotel Dining Room.

How the years have rolled by. My brother and I attended universities in far cities and travelled the world, but as fate would have it, both of us ended up living in the North, I as a minister and Eldon as a medical specialist. Neither of us forgot, however, the day when the lady's horse was spooked, our apprehension of impending prosecution, and the euphoria of acquittal at High Noon in a Cow-town Court.

THE MECHANICS

from *The Road Runs West: A Century Along the
Bella Coola/Chilcotin Road*
by Diana French

*Road improvements in the mid-to-late 1900s solved many
transportation problems in the Cariboo–Chilcotin region, but
increased vehicle traffic required support systems to maintain
those vehicles. Enter the mechanic, a kind of magician who
had the power to make problems disappear and who exercised
a subtle tyranny over those who depended on his powers. One
such monkeywrencher, eccentric as only the truly gifted can be,
was Harold Stuart. His work got done, and done well, but on
Chilcotin time and no other. Diana French introduces Harold
and captures the unique pace of a typical business day at his
Redstone shop in this excerpt from* The Road Runs West.
*French left her home on Quadra Island in 1951 to teach in a
one-room school in Chezacut, a community of three ranches.
She later settled in Williams Lake and worked as a reporter,
then editor, of the* Tribune. *She is currently on the board of the
Open Learning Agency and is curator of the Museum of the
Cariboo–Chilcotin.*

For over seventy years Redstone was the mailing address for the Bayliffs, Blisses, everyone else within twenty miles, but as far as the dot on the map was concerned, Redstone was Stuart's. That's what it should have been called anyway, since the outcropping of red rock it is named for is twelve miles up the road. Except for some years going to school in Vancouver, Andy and Hettie Stuart's son Harold, born in 1921, and daughter Christina, two years younger, spent their lives at Redstone.

Harold was born to the Drummer's beat. He operated his garage for over forty years and he was outstanding on two counts. First, he had few peers as a mechanic. He could fix anything. If he didn't have the right tool, or the right part, he'd make it. He was expert at "mickey-mousing"—making emergency repairs to get the motorist home. His emergency repairs often outlasted the vehicle. Second, Harold was stubborn. In a country of pig-headed people he had no peers. He would do anything to help a neighbour, but he couldn't be rushed, pushed or coaxed to do anything he didn't want to do, and everything was done his way, in his own sweet time. If customers didn't like it they could stuff it, and he let them know where.

Andy bought his first truck in 1923, and he had two when Harold quit school in 1939. Harold began driving one of them and found it was easier than anything else he could do to earn a living. He liked monkey wrenching so he started doing his own repairs. Harold operated on Chilcotin time. "If something buggers, it only takes time to fix it. Nothing is lost if you can't fix it, only time. If you can fix it, you've saved money," he figured. Word got around that he was handy and he began fixing things for neighbours and for people whose vehicles broke down on the road.

After Harold started mechanicking, traffic had to elbow its way through the Stuart establishment, dodging bits and pieces of equipment and vehicles of various vintages crowding the right-of-way on both sides of the road. For over forty years assorted government officials tried to get Harold to clear the roadway but he never did; it just kept getting narrower. Eventually they moved the road.

Harold didn't have a proper garage building, just a little log cabin crammed with tools. His parts department was outside and he had an eclectic collection of artifacts piled all over the place.

It looked like a junkyard run amok, but he had everything he needed in that pile and he could find it if he searched long enough. He had a gasoline pump too, though he rarely sold gas. There was a sign on the pump saying "Honk for Service" but if anyone honked it made him mad and he wouldn't serve them.

Harold was self-taught and thought of himself as a diagnostician. "I can always find out what's wrong with something but don't hurry me, I have to play around with it until I find out how it works," he explained. He said there were two or three things he knew he couldn't do. No one ever found out what they were. He delighted in being rude to people he didn't like, and he didn't like big shots. "They want things done on Sunday when they know they can't get it done anywhere else. Americans are bad, sometimes if they're really in trouble I help them, but I give them hell. The worst are the snots who don't know me on the street in town, they walk right by without saying boo, then come crawling when they're stuck. They can stay stuck."

Harold did the big work outside. Even the most macho old-timers marvelled at his ability to do what was often delicate work in sub-zero weather, bare-handed, lying or kneeling in the snow for hours on end. He was a night person to boot, and working until the wee hours in the morning when it was coldest. Rain and mud didn't faze him either. He bought a big steel building from the Puntzi air base when it closed, and he took it apart and got it home, but he never got around to putting it up.

Harold's idea of money was elastic. He charged what he felt like, and rates varied from friend to foe. Sometimes he would do an incredible amount of work for little money, sometimes he would charge an incredible amount of money for little work. He didn't charge his Tsilhqot'in customers at all if they were broke but if he caught them faking, he charged them double. He soaked big shots. Once an

American tourist wanted a certain bolt. Harold rooted around in the parts pile and found one. He charged 25 cents for the bolt and $5 for hunting for it. In later years the store was broken into so often Harold put heavy wire on the windows, but few thieves had enough courage to tamper with the parts pile.

Harold's sister Christina was a fair mechanic too, and when it came to independence, they were a matched pair. After Harold married, he and his wife Marcella and their eight children lived down the road from the business. Christina lived in the big house across the road from the store.

One hot August day, Ed Wallace, the Anglican minister, was returning to Williams Lake after a week visiting his west Chilcotin parishioners. He left Tatla Lake at 10:00 a.m. in plenty of time to get home for supper. It was a sunshiny day. A few cauliflower clouds watched his dusty progress and all was well until a tire went flat about ten miles short of Redstone. His spare was a sorry thing, unlikely to get him home, so he stopped at Stuart's to get the flat fixed.

There was no sign of life at Redstone. A vagrant wind was sending dust devils down the road and making strange frying noises as it rose and fell in the cottonwoods by the river. Wallace walked across the road to the store. Inside it was as cluttered as Harold's shop, and it was dark after the bright sunlight. Wallace heard thumping noises, and found Christina sorting mail in the post office cubbyhole at the back of the store.

"He's at the shop," she said without looking up.

Wallace tiptoed out, blinking in the bright sunlight, and went back across the road.

"Hallo there," he ventured.

"Hallo there," replied a muffled voice. Harold emerged from under a derelict truck.

"It's a beautiful day," the minister said. He knew better than to jump right into business.

Harold agreed. Conversation came to a halt while he fished a battered package of cigarettes out of his shirt pocket, shook one out, put it in his mouth, and exchanged the package for a long wooden match which he lit with his thumbnail.

He was a gnome of a man, husky, dark-haired, unkempt. In later years he grew a big, bushy, slightly evil-looking beard. This day his blue jeans were black and shiny and grey woollen underwear peered over the collar of his shirt. (There were two kinds of Chilcotin men, those who wore long johns, and those who did not. Those who did rarely shed them on the theory that what keeps heat in keeps heat out. Harold was of this persuasion.)

With his smoke lit, he was ready to chat. Wallace told him all the upcountry news he could think of, then edged over to his car and opened the trunk.

"Troubles?" Harold asked.

Wallace showed him the tire. Harold inspected it, agreed it was "bad sick" and took it over to the shop. He was just starting to work on it when a dusty pickup truck rolled in, so he stopped to visit with the newcomer. As the cigarette ritual was repeated, Christina strolled across from the store and plumped herself into the conversation. She, too, lit up a smoke. They discussed the weather (great for the haymakers), foreign cars (we won the war but the Volkswagen is Germany's revenge), and the state of the road (the grader is at Chezacut). The latter topic gave the newcomer a chance to state his problem.

"Those damn rocks on Ross's Hill got my oil pan," he said.

When his smoke was done, Harold scrunched himself under the pickup to inspect the damage. Then he went into the shop, poked around, found what he wanted, crawled back under the truck, and began pounding at the oil pan. Christina toed her cigarette into the dust, went over to the shop, and began patching Wallace's tire. Work was proceeding nicely on all fronts when a blue delivery sedan screeched in and a young woman leaped out.

"I didn't think I'd make it here," she yelled.

Harold popped out from under the pickup and Christina dropped the tire. As the dust settled it was obvious the car's engine was steaming.

There was more conversation; more cigarettes were smoked. When the car cooled down, Harold lifted the hood. Muttering about "a sick hose" he headed for the parts pile. Christina finished her smoke and crawled under the pickup. She was dark and chunky like her brother and often as untidy. This day she was wearing a dark green sweater and a brown skirt that might once have been pleated. Her dusty bare legs stuck out from under the pickup as she banged on the oil pan. Harold's mining expedition was successful. He returned with a piece of hose and went to work on the car.

Time was sliding by and Wallace still had a three-hour drive ahead of him. At 2:00 p.m. he decided to patch his tire himself. The woman was conversing with Christina's legs but the pickup driver hovered over Wallace offering advice and encouragement. By the time the tire was repaired and remounted, Christina and Harold had traded jobs. She was bum-up under the car hood and he was toes-up under the pickup.

"What do I owe you?" Wallace asked Harold's toes. "Nothing," they replied.

As the minister left, a truck full of people pulled up to the store. Christina abandoned the car to tend to them and the two garage customers followed her, their feet making little puffs of dust as they crossed the road.

Looking Back with Irene

from *Looking Back at the Cariboo–Chilcotin*
by Irene Stangoe

One B.C. books website says Irene Stangoe has an "easy reading style that [speaks] from the heart. Irene has earned her place among the most popular of central B.C. writers." Stangoe entered the world in 1918, and 32 years later helped her husband Clive become the youngest publisher in the history of the province when they bought the Williams Lake Tribune *in 1950. They spent their first six years living in a tiny apartment above the print shop, frosty in winter and dusty in summer, raising two children to the "steady thump, thump, thump of an old Country Brower press downstairs." The Stangoes sold the newspaper in 1973 and moved to Chimney Lake, but Irene continued to write for the paper for more than 44 years, launching her "Looking Back" column in 1975 to spotlight the fading history of the Cariboo–Chilcotin. Many of her articles were published in a series of books, including* Looking Back at the Cariboo–Chilcotin. *In the following excerpt from that book, Irene gives us, with true regional flavour, a humourous, self-deprecating look back at the pitfalls of running a small-town newspaper. Irene currently resides again in Williams Lake. She received a national award for best historical story in a community newspaper from the Canadian Newspaper Association in 2000. Clive died in Williams Lake at the close of 2005.*

Irene Stangoe helped husband Clive, youngest publisher in the history of B.C., run the *Williams Lake Tribune* from 1950 to 1973.

"Renovate? RENOVATE?? You're out of your mind, woman," bellowed local historian Alf Bayne, who was also Williams Lake's only dentist.

We stood facing one another belligerently in the tiny *Tribune* office. The year was 1950.

"American tourists would drive hundreds of miles to see something like this," the angry dentist continued. I stared with disbelief at the old splintery wood floor, the flyspecked brown walls and the rusty wood heater that Clive and I had acquired along with the newspaper, the *Williams Lake Tribune*, earlier that year.

"But, Alf," I spluttered defensively, "I have to WORK in this."

Sadly he left our historic office, mumbling, "No one has a sense of history any more. Women!"

It was the coldest winter on record when I travelled up to the Cariboo via the Pacific Great Eastern Railway to join my editor husband in February. I remember looking out at the awesome Fraser Canyon bathed in frigid moonlight as I cuddled down in my berth, thankful for the potbellied stove that warmed the wooden coach, and the dim light from the swaying old-fashioned lamps.

I didn't know then that the "Please Go Easy" had a reputation for occasionally losing a train here and there, and I slept blissfully unaware that slides had blocked the rails several times during the night. It took thirty hours to get from Squamish to Williams Lake, and it was 45 below when I arrived, having warmed up from a shuddering 54 below. (Would you believe it was 72 below at Exeter Station near 100 Mile House?)

There was ice on the windowsills *inside* our tiny apartment over the newspaper plant, and frost formed on the walls as we struggled to heat the uninsulated rooms with a sawdust burner stove and one small oil heater, and stuffed toilet paper around the single-paned windows to try and stop the icy air from creeping in.

We lived there six years, freezing in winters, roasting in summer. We patched up the holes in the masonite walls, tried to squeeze our worldly goods into two small cupboards, tried to ignore the inch-thick dust that sifted in from the unpaved streets in summer, and tried to remember not to flush the toilet too often (it overflowed the septic tank in the backyard and triggered a frightful outcry from our back shop staff of 2½ people).

Somehow we even found room for the two children who came along. "That's the way to bring them up," boomed Lillooet publisher and good friend Margaret "Ma" Murray one night as Ward and Elaine slept peacefully through the din of a cattle sale party.

Why not? They had been brought up on the steady thump, thump, thump of the old Country Brower press downstairs as it pounded hour after hour, grinding out the weekly *Tribune* two pages at a time. "How do you stand the noise?" visitors often asked. And I truthfully answered, "What noise?"

Up until 1950, a newspaper was something I read in the evening and used to wrap the garbage the next morning. But then it became something I laughed and cried over and worked impossible hours to create. Faced with deadlines I learned to do impossible things, and had some of the most fascinating and most shattering experiences imaginable.

One of the first incidents occurred on a day early in 1950 when I was alone in the *Tribune* office. The door burst open and a local businessman stood in front of me trembling with the violence of his emotions, his face white with anger.

"I'm going to sue." He spit out the words one by one. It was over an innocuous reference to his store in an anonymous letter to the editor, if I remember correctly, but I was scared silly. I was new to the game and apprehensive over every misplaced comma, so I had visions of Clive's dream, a newspaper of his own, vanishing with the printing of those few short words. Luckily it didn't happen.

For two years running we goofed on Daylight Saving Time and told our readers to put their clocks back when it should have been ahead, and the following year were a whole day out! We hunkered in our apartment the following Sunday, wondering how many people would be late? early? for church, and died a thousand deaths.

It was on a day in 1950 that Maple Leaf Hotel owner Benny Abbott sang the whole chorus of "Good-night Irene" to me as we stood before the teller's window at the Bank of Montreal, and the red of my face matched our bank statement. It could only happen in the Cariboo.

The year 1950 was also the only time we missed a deadline. Jim Stitt, our back-shop foreman, went on holiday and Clive was left to struggle with our temperamental, antiquated linotype, which I swear was held together with baling wire and chewing gum.

Thursday's deadline came and went, then Friday's. Subscribers phoned, came to the office, and stopped us as we slunk down the street. By Saturday the editor had bags under his eyes from the sleepless nights, but still struggled valiantly on. At one o'clock in the morning even I got into the battle and discovered what Jim did when he stood on the little platform at the back of the linotype, and fed little squares of metal called "matrices" into the &!*$t# machine.

Sunday was definitely not a day of rest, and Clive laboured on in the dingy cobwebbed back shop, attempting to find out even more about the innards of a linotype. When Jim came back to work Monday morning and asked brightly, "How did the paper go?" we had to admit sadly that we didn't know. It still wasn't out.

Those were the days when we had to "stuff" the newspaper by hand; that is, insert the pages into one another. It was a backbreaking, time-consuming job that had to be slogged through until the mountainous stacks of pages were reduced to neat piles of completed newspapers. John Gibbon, our halftime student worker, was a whiz at it. He could put those pages together faster than anyone in the shop and although I tried and tried, I could never beat him.

I never dreamed during those hectic first years that this was a historic time in the newspaper game and that the pounding press, the linotype, and the hand-set type would soon be things of the past. Who could imagine the *Tribune* would one day be produced on a massive offset press capable of printing and folding thousands of copies an hour; that the back shop would be a bright room full of computerized equipment operated by a couple of petite gals in jeans or miniskirts; or that reporters would sit glued to computers in the quiet newsroom tapping out copy to be transferred by electronic wizardry into printed stories ready for "paste up." Although technology has changed and despite the marvellous things that can be accomplished with computers, the newspaper business will never be able to completely eliminate the goofs that appear in the written word.

I had written nothing more exciting than a high school essay before, but in 1950 I became the *Tribune*'s social editor (among other things) and for years suffered through an incredible number of horrible "typos" that somehow seemed to creep into my wedding write-ups.

I became quite philosophical about minor mistakes such as the bride carrying *moses* instead of roses, and *bowels* of carnations decorating the bridal table, and these would produce only low moaning sounds of anguish. But when I became hysterical, the editor knew that something tragic had happened. Like the time the wedding couple in question exchanged *cows* at the altar; yes, COWS, not vows.

Someone sent that charming little "bon mot" to Will Bennett at the Vancouver *Province* and he commented in his "Good Morning" column that "I know Williams Lake is the biggest cattle-shipping point in the province, but even I was surprised to find they were exchanging cows at weddings."

Clive's classic typo story revolves around a special event in the Roman Catholic church in which we reported—on the front page yet—that "Holy Mess" was celebrated. We only twigged to the mistake when a subscriber came in to gleefully scoop up twenty copies. He wasn't an RC but his wife was.

But despite the dust and deadlines, they were happy years in a small friendly town where everybody knew everybody else and we never locked our doors; when keeping cows off the main street was one of the village commission's most pressing problems, and raising the price of haircuts from 75 to 85 cents was front page news.

Wonderful, marvellous memories to look back on some forty years later, to remember the people I met and interviewed, particularly the pioneers who helped shape this country, and to be able to pass along some of their history.

PIONEER DOCTOR

from *Don't Shoot From the Saddle:*
Chronicles of a Frontier Surgeon
by D.A. Holley

A doctor is intimately acquainted with his community.
Who better than Dr. Al Holley, a surgeon in the Cariboo
from the 1930s to the 1960s, to shed light on the true spirit of
the Cariboo–Chilcotin people? His autobiographical Don't
Shoot From the Saddle *reveals the self-reliance, ingenuity and*
humorous bent of the colourful characters who were his patients
and his friends. With his own fondness for a joke and his unique
problem-solving abilities, the Doc fit right in. Committed to
improved medical care in the Cariboo–Chilcotin, he established
an intensive care unit in Quesnel—the first in the province.
Holley was also a horse rancher, cowboy, dog musher, Justice
of the Peace, and even an actor who played a stagecoach driver
and doctor in restored Barkerville, now a living museum of the
Cariboo gold rush. Holley died in 2000. The following samples
from his book conjure not only the people, but also the country
they travelled and the history they made. One reluctant patient,
Paul Krestenuk, happens to be the very man Rich Hobson and
Pan Phillips were told of in "Unexplored Territory" (p.120) by
their guide, Andy.

Doc Holley practised from a tent, bringing medical treatment to remote
villages.

In early days in Quesnel we had a radio station, but the station was not too flush and on occasion it sold radio time to citizens who provided their own program.

One of these home-grown productions was funded by Owens Department Store and featured the two young Chinese Owens boys singing cowboy songs, accompanied by themselves on guitar. Sometimes their old man joined in on a three-stringed Chinese violin. It was bloody awful.

We had some respite, though, when one of the boys broke his wrist. Doug Lahay gave him a shot of anaesthetic while I manipulated the fracture. I put on a cast from his armpit to his fingertips. Doug remarked that it was a pretty long cast for a small fracture.

I told him, "Shut up and look after your anaesthetic. We are going to have some peace and quiet on Sunday mornings for awhile around here."

One night we were finished a case in the operating room about midnight when Doug was on call. About that time a call came for him from a woman who thought she had pneumonia and wanted Doug to go see her at Brotherston's Cabins in West Quesnel. Doug changed into his street clothes and made the call.

The next day he told me that when he got there the door was locked, but there was a light on in a back window. He went around, looked in the window, and saw a man in bed with the woman. He yelled, "Open the goddamned door." They all went back to the bedroom, where he listened to her chest with his stethoscope, then turned her over his knee, pulled up her nightgown, and gave her a good shot of penicillin while her paramour looked on. Doug told me, "Damnit, if I go out in the middle of the night to see somebody with pneumonia, somebody is going to get a shot of penicillin in the ass."

The late Dwayne Witte was in for a check-up when I told him that I was a medical consultant, not a preacher, but that I would seriously recommend that he stop smoking and drinking if he wanted to live very long. Halfway measures would not do. He wondered if he could wait until after the Big Creek Stampede, which was coming up shortly and which we both attended. A few weeks later I had to phone Marion Vine about something and I asked how Dwayne was. He was in the other room and I heard her yell at him, "Hey, Dwayne, Doc wants to know how you are doing." In a minute she passed on the reply, "Tell him I quit smoking and drinking—but I still lie a lot." Dwayne was a great guy and a generous friend, with his old black hat and a pair of leather riding cuffs that he seldom took off. He made his decision about how he wanted to live and for how long; I didn't argue with him and he didn't last long.

The Emergency Room was always good for a little humour, mixed in with the various disasters and tragedies.

One morning the ER nurse asked me if I would mind seeing a young kid who had got run over by a car. This ten-year-old boy looked a little scuffed up, but not seriously hurt. His mother, however, was carrying on something awful. She was weeping and wailing and saying, "That Leon! He tells me, 'Why don't you learn to drive?' But he never teach me. Now look what happens."

I said to the kid, "Where were you when you got run over?"

"Up on the back doorstep," he replied. The nurse and I both retreated around separate corners, where we stayed until we could contain ourselves.

One dark night two highway workers came in. One had a fractured tibia. They were grumbling and cussing away. They said that they were in a turnaround, not even on the highway, and were out of their vehicle, standing beside it, when this old truck left the highway and came right for them. One of them jumped straight up, out of the way, but the other one did not jump high enough and the old pickup's bumper got him on the legs.

After I finished looking after them, ordering X-rays of the tibia, etc., I went into the next cubicle to check this old couple that had got shook up in a car accident. The lady hastened to tell me that they were driving down the road, John was driving real careful like he always does, when all of a sudden a Highways truck came right across the road after them. I checked them both over and refrained from comment. A few minutes later when their daughter came in, her first words were, "I do wish Dad would stop driving."

On another case I tried to be a good guy and it almost backfired. This 75-year-old farmer, who lived with his bachelor brother just across the Quesnel River, was in for his driver's medical exam. When I did his exam I found that his eyesight was really not too good, but I thought, "Oh, hell, Carl only drives a mile or two in and out of town once a week, in second gear, to get groceries and farm supplies." I guessed I could slip him through.

I was driving downtown two days later and was starting through an intersection when I saw this old GM pickup bearing down on me. I floorboarded her and just made it across with about a foot to spare or he would have nailed me. That taught me not to be so damned benevolent with some of these old-timers. The joke sure would have been on me.

Some of those old-timers were tough. Paul Krestenuk was an interesting example. He had come over from Russia during the Bolshevik Revolution, making his way across Siberia and then getting on a boat to cross the Bering Strait to Alaska. He worked his way inland, I don't know by what route, but he ended up in Cariboo country.

Paul started a trading post at the Carrier village of Nazko, 60 miles west of Quesnel. He traded with the Carrier for furs and built a store in which he sold groceries and dry goods. He ran a bunch of cows, using Native cowboys to help him. He cut hay on several wild meadows that he pre-empted. Paul also built a wagon road and winter sleigh road through the wild country to start another trading post at Kluskus Village, six days travel by team and sleigh from Nazko, with a crossing of the Blackwater River en route.

Paul pushed still farther: past Pan Phillips' Home Ranch, recrossing the Blackwater, past Eliguk Lake, to Ulkatcho Village to trade with the Ulkatcho, who ranged between there and Anahim. Not to be stopped, Paul even ran routes through Squinas Meadows, crossing the upper

Dean River and going almost to the Rainbow Mountains in what is now Tweedsmuir Park. He traded all along the way. Having ridden and taken pack horses through that whole country from the Nazko Valley to Bella Coola, I can tell you that there is some rough country to travel through. Paul did a lot of the maintenance work on the old government road from Nazko to Quesnel in the early days.

One winter Paul had a very bad belly ache and was in the Quesnel hospital. Dr. Baker wanted to take his appendix out. After supper Paul saw a nurse go by with a big tray of instruments. He asked her, "What for those things?"

"That is for your operation," the nurse said.

"Get me my clothes."

"I can't do that."

"You show me where they are and I get them myself," Paul said.

He left the hospital, went down to Fraser's Freight Barn where his horses and sleigh were, harnessed and hitched up his four-horse team, and left town for his place at Nazko.

When Paul told me this story he asked me, "You know how I cur'em up those appendix? Olive oil and turpentine—I drink olive oil and I rub that sore belly with turpentine."

I haven't seen that method described in the *New England Journal of Medicine* or the *Proceedings of the Mayo Clinic*, but Paul's cure could well be found under alternative medicine because it sure was a different approach.

Paul was never enthusiastic about surgery, I discovered. Sergeant John Stinson and his RCMP boys brought Paul to the hospital in poor shape and severe pain, and we admitted him to Emergency with a big incarcerated hernia. In no way could I reduce the hernia. It was solidly stuck. We put him to bed, elevated his pelvis, applied an ice bag, and gave him 100 mg of Demerol to relax him. I told him we would leave it for a couple of hours and if it would not go back in we would have to operate, otherwise he would develop gangrene of the bowel and we would really be in trouble. He was pretty worried. I went back about an hour later, prepared to call the OR nurses.

When I went into his room, I smelled the distinct aroma of Scotch whisky; Paul wore a smile you could see a mile, and he asked for his clothes. A half bottle of White Horse Scotch stood on his bedside table. Harvey Denamy had been up to see him and left him a bottle of his favourite Scotch. I checked for his hernia and it was completely gone, and the whisky smell was coming from his belly most noticeably in the area of his hernia.

Instead of drinking the Scotch, Paul used it to massage his hernia back in. He showed me how he had just massaged it over and over, pouring on more Scotch until it popped in. His pain was gone, he had a nice rest, and now he wanted to go home. I knew that big bulge was bothering him a lot before he came, and I would have liked to repair it while he was in. I could tell by the look on his face, however, that he meant it when he said he wanted out. The only way we could have kept him in would have been to forcibly restrain him, and I had no intention of doing that.

Stinson and his boys used to check on him whenever they were patrolling that way. About a year later he came to Emergency looking very ill and coughing. The duty doctor admitted him and he was eventually diagnosed with advanced tuberculosis. He died not long after. He made his living from the Native peoples and he died of their disease.

There were some other colourful Russians around Quesnel: Alex Loloff, Alex Bassoff, and Harry Gassoff. Loloff lived close to town, but I never knew much about him.

Alex Bassoff was one of the shiftiest looking old desperadoes you would see in a long time. He was a lean old cowboy, usually rode a good horse, and he slumped down in the saddle with his big black hat pulled down low so that his beady black eyes just peered out under the hat brim. He had a big, lean, slinky brown dog that followed along behind him.

Alex lived on Major Gook's farm at Dragon Lake for awhile, and we talked to him quite often. He had a habit when he was telling you something interesting of prefacing it with, "Honest-to-God, I tell you ..." He had a homestead away out near the foot of Dragon Mountain and used to ride back and forth between there and Gook's farm. Richard Gook told me of the time he chanced to be in at Bassoff's place and recognized two of his family's axes in the woodshed. He accosted Alex about the axes and said he expected to get them back. Alex told him a long story about needing an axe to cut out a bunch of trees across the trail. Richard reminded him that there were two axes. Alex gave his usual spit on the ground and said, "Honest-to-God, I tell you, it happened twice."

GANG RANCH COWBOY

from *Unfriendly Neighbours*
by Chilco Choate

*"So-called civilization and Choate never mix without dire
consequences. He remains in self-imposed exile to this day,
much to the relief of everyone that knows him."*
                    —*John Taylor of Telefilm Canada*

*An independent thinker and defender of the land he loves,
Ted "Chilco" Choate was born at White Rock, B.C., in 1935
and found his true home in the Chilcotin backcountry 16 years
later. For a time he worked as a ranch hand, and in 1955 got
his first wide-eyed look at the Gang Ranch. By 1956, he was a
cowboy on that ranch, and his sight was already jaded by his
keen observations. After his ranch experiences, Choate became
a big-game hunter and outfitter, wilderness guide and outspoken
conservationist and critic of B.C. land-use policy. He lives alone
by remote Gaspard Lake in the Chilcotin and communicates
with the world by solar fax machine. In this excerpt from*
Unfriendly Neighbours, *he shares with forthright wit and
wisdom some opinions on ranch practices, his early trials as
a junior cowboy and one thrilling ride of a lifetime.*

As a young man, Chilco Choate was a cowboy for the Gang Ranch, and he later became an outspoken protector of the vanishing Chilcotin wilderness.

So I had finally arrived at the Gang Ranch, the place from where at least half the B.C. cowboy stories seemed to originate. As we walked up through the yard that day, it was very noticeable that this was an old outfit—many of the buildings were beginning to sag and lean with the slope of the ground. The only new building I could see was a huge red barn, which resembled the barns that I had grown up with in the lower part of the province. There were all those red buildings spread across about sixty acres of land and close to 1,000 acres of hay fields within view. To this twenty-year old kid whose entire worldly possessions amounted to one saddle, a bedroll, and several guns, this place looked so impressive that it took my breath away.

We walked over to a large frame building, which turned out to be the office, store and post office. When we went through the door, we stepped right into the last century. The front part of the building served as the store and had one of those old-fashioned, horseshoe-shaped counters that kept all the merchandise smaller then a saddle out of reach of the customer. The counter was very wide so there was not going to be any problem of shop-lifting in this store. All of the merchandise that I could see was pure frontier ranch and cowboy gear.

The only person in the store was a medium-sized man who looked to have been in his mid to late 60s and when Shorty began talking to him, I noticed that he addressed him as Mac. A few moments later I was introduced to him and it was then confirmed that this was MacIntyre, or just plain Mac, the manager of the Gang Ranch. I had been hearing stories about Mac ever since I had arrived in the Chilcotin three years earlier. He came to the Gang Ranch as a young immigrant from Scotland and went to work as a ranch hand. From there he graduated to cowboy, then cowboss, and finally all the way up to become manager of the entire outfit. By then, Mac had been on the Gang Ranch for over 40 years, so he had seen and done many interesting things.

Mac was very quiet-spoken and after a few noticeably short and cool words with Shorty, he turned to me and started quizzing me about my background: where I had come from, what I had done, and who I knew. After telling him about my stay with Old Jack, Mac informed me that he remembered him very well from the days of the cattle drives that used to pass through the Gang Ranch country. As the cattle drives did not come this way any more, Mac had lost contact with many people from the Alexis Creek area and he seemed pleased that I was able to tell him some of the news from over in that area. I remember being extremely flattered by being able to relate so many mutual things to somebody of Mac's stature but at the same time I also noticed that he had cut Shorty completely out of the conversation, which seemed odd.

After we had been talking for a few minutes, the door literally burst open and a big, heavy-set man stepped just inside and hollered at us, "Who in hell put that bunch of crow bait horses into our corral?" As he walked further into the store he noticed Shorty and I standing there and he walked over and said, "By God, is it you again, Watson? I thought they had run you back out of the country." Although we all laughed at these remarks, I noticed that Shorty was beginning to get a hard look in his eye. Shorty then introduced me to this new fellow who turned out to be Jim Bishop, boss of all the cowboys on the Gang Ranch. His actual title was cowboss.

After he and Shorty traded a few more sarcastic remarks, Mac interrupted and said to Bishop in a quiet voice, "This young fellow here has just spent the past three years working for Jack Maindley, up near Alexis Creek," and he then just turned and walked into the back room where we never saw him again.

Bishop also cut Shorty out of the conversation but he and I had a good visit, as it turned out that he too knew Old Jack and several other people that I knew quite well. The tension in the store was getting so obvious that it became embarrassing and I was relieved when Shorty finally said it was time for me to mount up again as we still had twenty-eight uphill miles to go. As Showy led the way out the door, Bishop called after him and asked, "Hey Watson, are you sure you can find your way back up there?" At this remark, Bishop and I both had a short laugh, but I noticed that Shorty didn't even chuckle. As we were walking down the porch, I turned to nod and wave goodbye to Bishop when he gave me the whoa signal and then walked up to me and said in a voice that I suspected was calculated to accidentally reach Shorty's ears, "Ted, when you get tired of playing around up there, get in touch with me and I'll give you a real job in the cow camp."

When I caught up to Shorty at the corral his face was grey and there were tears in his eyes as he turned to me and said, "Someday I'll make that fat bastard swallow his snuff can."

Shorty got into the truck and instructed me to haze the horses after him. He wanted us to travel up to the timber-line (and thus off the Gang Ranch property) before we would eat our lunch. It appeared that we were not going to be challenged about access after all and that did come as a bit of a relief.

It was six steep miles up to where we were going to have lunch. As I rode up those hills that day I can still remember thinking that I had just walked into a very strange situation. No doubt my twenty-year old head was swollen beyond normal, because how many near-greenhorn kids had ever been offered the chance to ride and work with people like Mac and Bishop. It was common knowledge that every beginner was expected to work their way through the ranch hand stage before ever being even considered for the cow camp. A long time ago, even MacIntyre had been made to go through that initiation.

So this was my introduction to the Gang Ranch as it was then. Strange and interesting.

When I became a Gang Ranch cowboy, the first job Bishop assigned to me was to help three other riders with the spring horse roundup. In those days, nobody knew for certain how many horses there really were on the Gang. They had a herd of the best draft and saddle horses in this part of B.C., so our job was to locate and bring in as many as we could before horse thieves beat us to the slick colts. The area where we were horse hunting was an unfenced range covering about ten by twenty miles in size. It was two-thirds timbered, the rest being open benchland or natural meadows. The horse herd was spread throughout the entire area and we were quite sure that some bands had strayed or had been driven further afield by horse thieves than the range we were ordered to search for them in. For several days we hazed all the horses we found into what was once the "official" horse pasture about eight miles from the ranch. This had become a typical Gang Ranch pasture, as there were holes in the fences almost every mile, which explained why the horses were now ranging as far as they wanted to go. It did not take us long to realize that for every ten horses we put back into the pasture, we lost at least three of them before the next day.

As the junior cowboy in the bunch, I was soon taught that on the Gang Ranch it was considered to be below a cowboy's dignity to get off of his horse to fix a fence. That job was left for fence builders like Jim Russell and if there was no one assigned to that area, then to hell with it. I'm not sure what the score is on this subject today, but there was a time that if the boss told a cowboy to fix a fence, it meant that he was fired. Thus fences on the Gang Ranch seldom got fixed.

We worked on that "ten horses in, three horses out" project for about ten days. By that time we had so many horses in the holding pasture that we became worried that they might hit us with a mass escape, which would mean we would have to start all over again. When horses that have been used to being loose on the open range are corralled, it takes them a while to settle down to confinement again and, if they do get away within the first few days, they have a habit of running for many miles before stopping. I had some sympathy for them because it sort of reminded me of my school days.

Early one morning, just before we were to mount up to go out on the daily search again, one of the older cowboys rode in from the holding pasture and told us he could sense that our captives were getting restless. He suggested that perhaps we should run these ones down to the ranch right now while we still had them. We all agreed because we knew if we lost them, it would be somewhat embarrassing to have to explain to Jim Bishop how we had squandered ten days of hard work.

We quickly rolled up our gear and tied it to a pack horse. Our strawboss assigned an old Indian to lead the pack horse down to the ranch for us, which would mean that he would miss out on the wild run that everybody seemed to be so enthused about. On several occasions, the rest of the crew had told me that I was damn lucky to have been chosen to come out on the annual horse roundup on my first year here, because this was considered to be about the highest honour and achievement that a Gang Ranch cowboy could ever hope for. Every time somebody told me that, my head swelled up a little bit more. The old Indian was a bit grieved about being chosen to be the tail-end Charlie because he felt the job should have gone to me, since I was the youngest in the crew. Even though the old man did not have many more horse roundups left in him, I still did not volunteer to take his job.

One of the boys opened the gate and we were off. Most of the old brood mares had been through this before, so they knew exactly where we were headed. All we really had to do was haze the herd from behind to make sure none of the smarter ones tried doubling back and out onto the timbered range behind us. I had never been on such a ride in my life! It was eight miles downhill at a wide open run. We tore through those gullies, rock piles, and out across the open benches and my heart was in my throat all the way. Most of the time I just let my horse have his head and prayed that he wanted to live as much as I did. At times like that, religion can come back to a person real easy. If anyone had been watching from one of the hill tops, they would have witnessed a piece of cowboy heaven because it would have been the most wonderful sight to behold: 300 blooded horses streaming down out of the hills, with every mane and tail flying straight out and then three riders laying flat against their horse's necks, with never a stumble or a tumble. When daydreaming of rides like that, it's easy to imagine that at some distant time, God may have been a cowboy too, to let us get away with such a reckless run.

When we pulled up at the ranch corral, I almost fell off my horse because my knees were so sore. When I dropped my pants to find out why, I discovered that there were sores on the inside of my knees the size of dollar bills. I can still remember making a half-hearted vow to myself that the next time I was lucky enough to go on the horse roundup, I'd let the old Indian earn himself another feather. Maybe.

After the horse roundup was over, we joined Bishop and some other cowboys and began the summer cowcamp in earnest. Our first job was to round up the cattle on the spring range and brand the calves before herding them into the mountains. It took us about three weeks to locate 1,200 brood cows and brand their calves. This was not all the cows on the ranch that summer, but it was most of them. The rest would stay behind and get brought into the ranch on the last roundup, late in the fall. Bishop figured we were leaving behind as many as 300 head, but considering the size of the range they were hiding in, it might take us another two weeks to locate even half of them and we just did not have the time. There was enough grass left there that feed would be no problem for them.

A little incident at one of the branding corrals really raised my curiosity. On this lower spring range, the Gang Ranch had to share the area with small ranches from the Big Creek area. We were operating short-handed, so many times when we located a herd of cows, they would be intermixed with cattle bearing several different brands. As there were not enough riders to hold and separate the brands out on the open range, we would begin driving the small herds toward the corral. As we drove them along, the idea was we would drop the strays from the herd, one by one, before we arrived at the corral.

Well, several times we were not able to get the strays weeded out in time, so they got corralled right along with the Gang Ranch cattle. Every time that happened, I noticed that we branded every calf in the corral. I knew that this was not quite right. But I was told that we simply gave the rancher one of our unbranded slicks later.

This answer made sense, so I didn't give it any more thought until many years later when I was talking to one of the Big Creek ranchers whose calves I knew we had branded. When I brought the subject up, he listened to me for a while and then just shook his head and said, "If the Gang Ranch has ever given somebody around here a slick calf, then I've yet to receive my first one."

When most of the calves had been branded, we gathered up the entire herd and started hazing them towards their summer and fall pastures in the mountains to the south and west, a distance of seventy miles. We would be taking the herd up there in stages, as newly branded calves can only be driven ten or twelve miles a day. Even at that, we tried not to move them more than two days in a row. When young calves get tired, they have a fatal habit of sneaking away from the herd and finding themselves a nice cosy place to lay down and sleep. When they awake, their mothers are several miles further up the trail and a calf will never search forward for its mother; instead it will go back down the only trail it knows. I estimate that about eighty percent of the lost calves are found by their mothers; the rest are discovered by coyotes or bears.

What saves this situation from worse losses is the mother up ahead. When she realizes that her calf is no longer trailing with the herd, she lets us know about it. A cowboy must learn to distinguish which of those cows has really lost her calf and then let her slip back down the trail to locate her wayward brat.

All of this meant that we had to keep doubling back on our tracks to bring the re-united families back up with the main herd. There were only seven men in our trail crew, so it meant that we had our work cut out for us. For the rest of the summer it was going to be ride, cowboy, ride.

In most ways it was a great life, but it also left us mighty weary by the end of a day, as the heat, dust and flies took their toll. While we had been working at the branding corrals, one of the Chilcotin Indian cowboys had his wife doing the cooking for the crew, but on the trail, Jim Bishop took over that job and he also drove the big iron-wheeled chuck-wagon that also carried all of our loose gear.

For the first forty miles of this cattle drive, we followed very rough wagon roads for which our chuck-wagon was well suited, but by that time there were also a few damn fools who were beginning to drive their trucks and four-wheeled drives over the roads too. But that summer we were lucky and never met up with any of them, so we had the hills pretty much to ourselves. Bishop was a good cook and the rest of us tried to keep him at it permanently, but every few days he would climb back onto a saddle horse and delegate the cooking and chuck-wagon job to somebody else, usually me. I often wondered how some of the other men had survived so long on their own cooking. Some of them did not even know how to put together a stew or make a pot of coffee without screwing it up somehow. I mean we were travelling with some of the world's worst cooks.

The long days in the saddle soon took the glamour out of our life. Bishop expected to have to replace at least half the crew, because he felt that some of us were not going to be able to cut the hard work and low wages. Most of the crew had been promised ninety dollars a month and grub, which, even in those days, was still on the lean side. Our work day began at daylight when the wrangler went out to chase in the horses that we would be using that day. As soon as they were corralled, the rest of us would saddle up before breakfast and go to the creek and wash up, which meant splashing water on our faces. As soon as breakfast was over, we stepped straight into the saddle and would be gone for the day.

A working day might be anywhere from six to twelve hours. We normally packed a lunch of some sort, usually a piece of cold meat and a can of juice or tomatoes. Often there was no bread so most of the time cold pancakes served in its place but they didn't carry all that well. After five or six hours bouncing behind a saddle, those pancakes were often reduced to something that even a dog would have to be coaxed to eat.

We were expected to work seven days a week, but once in a while, one of the crew would be so weary that he would just say to hell with everything and take a Sunday off, to lay around camp to rest up a bit. When one of us did this, Bishop would dig out his "time sheet" and put a mark beside that person's name, indicating that there would be three dollars deducted from his pay cheque (if and when he got one). I can't remember a time when the entire crew took the same day off, but whenever someone did, the rest of us would refer to him as the "three dollar cowboy." His usual retort to that remark would be, "What the hell. With this outfit, we probably won't get paid anyway."

The Gang Ranch Compulsory Banking System was a continual topic of conversation any time two or more riders came together. I heard stories about how some of the men on earlier crews had worked for months at a time only to have Studdert flatly refuse to pay them anything. Some of them became so frustrated that they finally just rode away with nothing for their labour except bad memories. Bishop did not like to hear his crew discussing this type of campfire story and he always tried to play down the possibility that it would ever happen again. As for myself, I felt pretty secure because Bill Studdert and I had become good tillicums.

This problem of ranchers refusing to pay their hands was not that uncommon; there used to be many other ranches besides the Gang that pulled the same trick. The problem was that there were no labour laws that covered farm or domestic help, so they could do with us pretty much as they pleased. The only legal recourse we had was to go to town and hire a lawyer to collect the wages due. Even that was no assurance of a fair settlement because some of the ranchers had acquired a profitable habit of lying about how long the hand had been working. I had never met any cowboy who had tried collecting his wages through a lawyer, as most cowboys have a rather contemptuous feeling for the rule of law. Usually they left quietly, licking their wounds.

There was another reason why a hired hand would not hire a lawyer. Anyone who tried the lawyer route would damn soon find himself blacklisted throughout the ranching industry. Ranching is not a large industry and that type of information would travel quickly.

Some of the men I worked with told me that when they had been cheated by ranchers, they had their own collection system but when I asked them what it was, my answer was always just a laugh and shake of the head.

Some of the larger ranches provided a company store for their crew which, if abused, could lead to further hard feelings between themselves and their employees. On the Gang, as on some of the others, most of the crew lived in a cashless society. The company store, however, provided every hand with an account book, so he could draw items from the store in lieu of money. Since most cowboys who work on these places only do so because they were flat-assed broke in the first place, they are at the total mercy of the ranch store keeper. Some of those account keepers were very handy at padding the books in order to keep the hired help perpetually broke. The unscrupulous employer not only made money off them, but he also knew that a man with no money finds the road beyond the ranch gates is a very hungry place.

The company store has worked fine for some ranches, but for others who probably overdid it, it created a great deal of hard feelings, which sometimes came home to roost on them.

The problem was that if you think you are being cheated but you can't read or write, no one can tell you otherwise. So some of the hands made up their own accounts by pilfering ranch equipment. The ranchers would have been far better off if they had paid us in cash, and then we would have had to lay it out on the counter.

A gifted musician, Roger Law could outpick any guitar player in the
Cariboo–Chilcotin by age 10.

Almost Made the Big Time

A new story by Hilary Place

In this never-before-published story by Hilary Place, the decade of peace and love, music and drugs hits ranch country. Place was well positioned to stay abreast of the music scene in the Cariboo–Chilcotin: he owned a music store in Williams Lake and had a band that travelled the region playing for dances. He was also well prepared for handling a gifted teenaged guitar player who wandered into the music store one day and seemed to need a home. It was a "no-brainer" for Place, whose own parents had taken young Davey Anderson under their roof and raised him like a son when that boy needed help. In the spirit of peace and love that had been fashionable in the Cariboo–Chilcotin well before the 1960s, Place took Roger Law into his home, into his family and into his heart.

H is birth certificate reads:

Date of Birth: January 8th, 1946
Sex: Male
Name: Roger Anthony Law
Father: Joseph James Law (Hank)
Mother: Retta Pauline Purjue

His birth certificate, a small carving of a chickadee, a few cassette tapes and hearts full of memories are all we have left of Roger Law. Most of the memories are happy ones and they started in the early '60s like this ...

We were operating a small music store in Williams Lake under the name Place Music Co. Ltd. It wasn't a big business by any stretch of the imagination, but we were surviving. We sold records and radios, and we had a repair shop with a first-class repairman, Paul Locke. We also sold the odd musical instrument—especially guitars. It seemed like every second customer was a guitar plunker who would come into the store and treat us to yet another hashed-up version of "Wildwood Flower."

This particular morning the plunker was a young boy, probably 14 or 15 years old. He came in and asked if he could play a guitar. I asked him which one he wanted to play, and he chose the best one in the store. I handed it to him, and instead of "Wildwood Flower," I got "Heartaches," Chet Atkins' version, note-perfect, thumb pounding out the bass line, all harmonies correct and the chord pattern intact.

He just sat there and played and played. At noon he left for an hour and at one o'clock he was back. He sat and played some more. All his pieces were without a fault, in time, in key, without hesitation, and with feeling. I was thoroughly enjoying the concert, for indeed that was what it was.

Curiosity was gnawing at me as to who this young fellow was. I guessed that it was the young man from the Chilcotin I'd heard about, and a brief conversation with him confirmed this. He went on playing almost without stopping until it was time to close the store.

I asked him where he was staying, and he didn't seem to know.

"Have you got any money?"

He didn't.

"Where are you going to have supper?"

Wasn't too sure.

"Well, you better come home with me and have supper and we'll figure out what to do after that."

The upshot was that he stayed with us for the next four years. Our agreement was that he would go to school and behave himself. He would play in our band, the Saddle-ites, and the money he made playing was his to spend. We treated him like we treated our sons, and we never had a speck of trouble with him. He always did what he was asked to do and pitched in with everything we did.

Roger and our son, Martin, soon became great friends. Martin was playing a little trumpet at the time, and he and Roger were always making noise down in the basement. Martin soon acquired a set of drums and was pounding away on them. There wasn't much quiet around the house, but we enjoyed it.

Roger would sit in the basement and learn new Chet Atkins guitar solos. His method was to play the record over and over until he knew it perfectly, and then duplicate the sounds on his electric guitar. He had started doing this a long time before when he lived out in the Chilcotin. There the guitar was rigged up to a transistor radio so that he could get that "electric" sound. The technique was complicated and, at that time, unique. The "electric" guitar was able to deliver the sustained note to a much greater degree than the acoustic. It was also more suited to small-orchestra work, because it could produce far more volume. The art of the "electric" guitar was not just the execution of the music line, but also the control of the amplifier. This is where Roger really shone. All his playing was musically mature and controlled. There was no doubt in my mind that he had a rare and magnificent talent.

The Chilcotin is not just a geographic designation: it's also a state of mind. It seems that it requires a certain type of person to feel at home and be suited to the Chilcotin. This doesn't mean that all the Chilcotin's residents are the same, by any means, but rather the opposite. They are strong-willed and have different outlooks than their neighbour, certainly, but should that neighbour need help, it is always forthcoming. The early years of the Chilcotin produced some of the most unique pioneers this country has ever seen. Roger's father was such a pioneer.

Hank Law was born in Windsor, England. He left as soon as he finished school, and he headed for Canada. I don't know all the twists and turns Hank took to get to the Chilcotin, but when he did arrive, he got addicted to the place. He married Retta Purjue and set to work creating a family. Earning a living was tough going, so he headed to Vancouver and worked there as a carpenter. But he longed for the Chilcotin and made his way back as soon as he could. Hank took a place at Pyper Lake, and he and Retta lived there while Hank worked at the Puntzi Mountain Air Force Station.

Roger spoke often of the life they had at Pyper Lake. He said they stayed in a tent one winter when the weather was bitter cold. He recalled running down to the creek to get water in the morning in bare feet when it was 20 degrees below zero. He said you had to keep your feet moving or they might get frozen to the ground. But his life at Pyper was happy and it gave Roger an appreciation of nature that he never lost. He knew the proper Latin names for all the animals, and we learned some of them from him. *Ursus horribilis*, and *Falco peregrinus* and such like. We had lots of laughs about them, but it also showed a side of Roger that few knew.

As a result of his keen observation of all the animals and birds around him, he could mimic their quirks. He would often pretend to be a chicken and walk along with his head snapping back and forth, then scratch the ground with one foot and search the ground with one eye, exactly like a chicken looking for a seed. It was one of his favourite acts. He was an excellent raconteur and his stories about birds and animals were a delight. He was a reasonably good scholar, but not all that enthusiastic about school.

The principal advised him to take up woodworking, probably because Roger's father was a carpenter. I didn't know about this until one day I got an emergency call from the school telling us that Roger had been hurt in the woodworking class. He'd managed to run his thumb through the jointer and plane off most of the flesh. I got into a slanging match with the principal about it.

"Surely you must realize that this boy is going to be a musician," I said. "And surely you must realize that in order to be a musician it's preferable to have *all* your fingers. And surely you must take these things into account when you're assigning classes!"

I made myself as hard to deal with as I could. The poor old principal tried to get a word in edgewise, but didn't have too much luck. Eventually the situation resolved itself when the thumb grew back into shape by itself and didn't impede Roger's playing.

When he was a kid, he had raised an owl. He said he cleaned out the mouse population getting feed for his owl, and the owl kept getting bigger and bigger. Finally one day the thing was big enough to fly. Roger took it out in the yard and threw it up in the air. The bird was so shocked at this treatment that it forgot to flap its wings and it came down with a thump at Roger's feet. Roger gave it a good bawling out and held it up again. The owl got the message this time and started to flap its wings before Roger let go of its feet. This wasn't the way it was supposed to take wing, but it got airborne anyway. It headed off across the backyard in the general direction of the barn, flapping as hard as it could. When it saw the clothesline directly ahead, it stuck out its feet and grabbed the line in a death grip. Clutching the line, it immediately flipped over and found itself hanging upside down. The chickens were cackling, the dog was barking, and the goose took cover under the barn. As Roger said, "The whole barnyard freaked out!" Roger said he never saw such a startled expression on anyone's face as there was on that owl's. It hung there upside down until Roger went over and rescued it.

Roger took part in all of our activities; one main activity was doing repairs on the houses that we owned. We had four at the time, so there was always something to do. The one we had on South Lakeside needed a general upgrade, so we decided to do a complete overhaul on it. It was heated with oil, so we decided to put in a propane furnace and a hot water tank. There was no basement in the place. I got a chainsaw and cut a section out of the living room floor, eight feet by eight feet. Roger and Martin set to work after school digging the basement.

They were at it a few days before they got down eight feet so that I would have room for the furnace, but they made it. I decided to put in a concrete floor and do the walls with concrete blocks. All was in readiness. I called the concrete company to get a delivery, and they said "no problem." They were doing a school job just past our house and would bring our cement late the next afternoon. We dug a hole so the cement truck could dump directly into the basement, and we were ready when it arrived. Roger and Martin were out alongside the big cement truck, and I was in the house in the basement.

"Okay, boys, let her come."

Come it did. I soon had enough, so I hollered, "Shut her off!"

The concrete was still coming fast.

"SHUT HER OFF!!"

Panic was setting in. The concrete truck was still roaring and pouring. Obviously they couldn't hear me.

I knew that the only way I could get it stopped was to run outside and holler at the driver. It seemed that he was one of the boys' high-school buddies, and they were deep in conference about whatever it is boys that age discuss.

By this time my knee-high gumboots were starting to fill with concrete and I had a hell of a time getting them off so I could climb out of the basement, run outside and get the cement flow shut off. I finally made it and got it stopped. Then I went back in the house to look at the situation. I had five feet of concrete in the basement. It was setting up fast, as it had probably been whirring around in the truck for hours.

There was nothing we could do about it but have a good laugh, and order up a side-by-side furnace that only needed three feet of space, and rearrange the bathroom to accommodate the hot-water tank. This debacle seemed to hit Roger in the funny bone, but we were not finished with the job yet.

To install the bathroom we had to put in a septic tank and a disposal field. I hired a guy to dig the ditch down 18 feet from the house to where the septic tank would be. Roger, Martin and I were reinstalling the living-room floor while the guy was digging away outside. A little later, Roger went out for something or other. When he came back in, he was laughing so hard I thought he would bust. It seems that the guy was digging straight down 18 feet, as he had been told, and was already well out of sight. It took a few minutes to get him going in the right direction.

We weren't through with the house yet. We decided that with all the concrete and all the modern fixtures, it needed a new roof. I went over to Mackenzie's, the building supplies store, and told my friend Doug Stevenson I was in need of some cheap roofing material. It seemed that he had some bundles of white shingles and some bundles of blue shingles that he wanted to get rid of, so he gave me a bargain price. I bought half of them white and half of them blue. My idea was to do one side of the roof white and the other side blue. Martin and Roger were to put on the shingles after school. I wasn't able to get down to the house to see what they were doing for a couple of days, and when I did, I found that they'd worked out some kind of blue-and-white pattern that clearly put the house in the "different" class, to say the least.

But it didn't leak!

Roger was an exceptional musician. His father Hank was quite a player himself, and he got Roger off to a good start with basic training in chord patterns and timing. Hank and Retta had a little country band and played at stampedes and get-togethers in the Chilcotin. They called the band "Hank and Retta," but the name deteriorated to "Rank and Hetta." Roger was soon playing with them. When he was about 10 years old, he was the best guitar player in the Chilcotin. This did not always sit well with other guitar plunkers who practised for months to learn some hot lick, only to have this snotty-nosed brat come along and cut it off just right with ease.

Roger was playing for a dance with his parents one time at Anahim Lake. There was a little stage at the end of a small community hall and as the crowd went dancing by, Roger pulled off one of his hot licks and winked at a young cowboy who had been trying to do that lick for months. Young Cowboy showed his displeasure by hollering, "Up your ass!"

Roger thought this was funny, so he had a good laugh. Young Cowboy saw Roger laughing, so he circled back, and this time he hollered, "Right up your ass!"

Needless to say, this became our catchphrase whenever Roger pulled off a fancy bit while playing in our band.

That year we got hired to play for the New Year's dance at Lillooet. We thought this was a good idea as we didn't have to drive; we went on the train. It would be a new experience for the boys. Bill, our sax and banjo player, was to get on the train at Enterprise station, about 30 miles down the road. We all nearly had heart failure because when we got there, there was no Bill. He was a big part of the band. Just after the train pulled out of Enterprise station, I looked across the valley and saw Bill's car speeding down the highway, obviously trying to catch the train. Just then the conductor came along, and I asked him if it would be possible to slow the train down so that we could pick up Bill.

"Oh sure," he said. "No problem."

The train slowed right down, and Bill was retrieved at the next stop. The boys thought that was pretty neat. When we got to Lillooet, the people who hired us met us at the station with two big, deluxe cars and a truck. They loaded the instruments in the truck and took them to the hall while we were taken to the hotel in the cars. Roger had never experienced anything like that in his life, and he thought he had hit the big time for sure. We got a front-page write-up in the local Ma Murray paper and, although she scrambled up the relationship of the band members, we appreciated the kind words.

With Roger's playing, we started to get into more sophisticated music. At about the same time, we picked up a fine steel-guitar player who fitted in great with the boys. His name was Don McDonald and it was a pleasure playing with both of them for the next two years.

We played every Saturday night and quite often on weekdays too. It wasn't big pay, but it was enough for the boys to have a little spending money, and they experienced some night life. It soon lost a lot of its appeal for them.

After Martin graduated from high school, he and Roger went down to Kelowna, where Martin was to study with an artist by the name of

Zeljko Kujundzic. Roger looked for a job playing music, and was soon playing in a small local band. They lived in a tent and had lots of laughs. After the summer, Martin came home to Williams Lake and we had a big discussion about where he was going. He undoubtedly had a great deal of talent as an artist, but this was not a very good foundation for life. I suggested to Martin that he go for a teaching certificate. He could teach art, get a paycheque, and still be in the art business. That was exactly what he did, and so the fall saw him leaving for Vancouver.

It was a big jump for Martin to go down to Vancouver and get himself into UBC. He found a basement suite on 6th Avenue and Dunbar, and a job pumping gas at a service station, and he went at it. Roger, meanwhile, was playing and staying with some young fellows on 4th Avenue. He was the toast of the town and was living it up as much as possible. Martin could have been in on the good times if he'd wanted, but he stuck with the education business.

Roger tried to get going in the music business and spent a year or two touring around B.C. and Alberta with little western groups that had a habit of going broke when farthest from home. He told of one time being stranded in some little town north of Edmonton in the dead of winter. He was sitting in the lobby of a little fleabag hotel, waiting to catch the bus back to Vancouver. A sour-looking young man was at the desk. Just then the door burst open, and in came a tough-looking guy with a girl on his arm. The guy at the desk said, "I'd like to know what the hell is going on."

"Me too," said the fellow with the girl. "I'd like to know what the hell is going on."

"I want to know what the hell is going on, too," said the girl.

Back to the desk clerk. "What the hell is going on, anyway?"

"That's what I would like to know. What the hell is going on?"

Just then the bus arrived and Roger got on board. He never did find out what the hell was going on. Such is the life of a country musician.

Roger was a part of the rock band called Mother Tucker's Yellow Duck. It was an avant-garde group and was headed for the big time. Roger was writing some great songs and maturing as an artist. To give you some idea of his talent, on one occasion the opening act for a show at the Queen Elizabeth theatre didn't show up. Roger was contacted and, without any rehearsal or any backup, shoved out on stage to fill in. He told the audience about his life in the Cariboo as a child. He did his imitation of a chicken pecking for wheat. He told them stories about his pet owl. He played some beautiful Chet Atkins-style guitar. He sang some Beatles' songs and a song his dad wrote about his pony, and he played the guitar with his feet. He filled an hour and got a standing ovation at the end.

He married and had a son, but his personal life was falling apart. He was starting to use drugs and it was catching up to him. One of the top groups from the United States, Crosby, Stills and Nash, tried him out for membership in their outfit, but he blew the audition by turning up stoned. It wasn't too long before he had some close calls from overdosing.

And then, disaster. One time after a session on drugs, the music was gone. He just never had the magic again. He struggled along for a few years, and then gave up and went back to the Cariboo. He rented a cabin on South Lakeside in Williams Lake and set to work carving animals and birds. He was just as talented at that as he was with his music, but it didn't have the same attraction for him.

One day he borrowed his mother's car to go shopping in town. He never came back. He hit a truck head-on a few miles past 150 Mile House. He was killed instantly.

He always said that he would be playing his guitar at his own funeral, and that was exactly what happened. The songs were tapes that he had made, and they were beautiful. Then he was gone.

He was like another son to us. I guess he knew we loved him.

Everything You Need to Make a Ranch

from *Tell me a good lie: Tales From the Chilcotin Country*
by Paul St. Pierre

*Award-winning comic writer Paul St. Pierre has published
numerous books about the Cariboo–Chilcotin which, as
Alan Twigg of* BC BookWorld *observes, "showcase the humour
and stubborn independence of hardy people who instinctually
resent government, reflecting their resilience and sophistication."
St. Pierre's best-known book,* Breaking Smith's Quarter Horse,
*hasn't been out of print since its publication in 1966. In the
1960s he wrote scripts for an award-winning CBC-TV series,*
Cariboo Country, *which launched the acting career of
Chief Dan George as Ol' Antoine. Born in Chicago in 1923,
Paul St. Pierre grew up in Nova Scotia. He was Liberal MP
for the Coast Chilcotin riding from 1968 to 1972, and a B.C.
police commissioner from 1979 to 1983. St. Pierre continues
to maintain a mobile home in the Chilcotin, along with other
homes in Fort Langley and Mexico. In the following tongue-in-
cheek tale from* Tell me a good lie, *there's an undercurrent of
regret in the bantering tone—ranching has changed since Harry
Marriott's day, but somewhere along the way, in the midst of
modern concerns, has it lost its vital centre?*

ALEXIS CREEK—

We were in a ranch-house kitchen the other night hunting for the bottom of a whisky bottle when the question came up of what you need to be a rancher today.

Health and brains we didn't count. It's never been proven the first is necessary and the second can actually be a handicap.

We threw out stamina, endurance, and ambition, too. Those are just brag subjects.

As for expanded knowledge of new ranching techniques, the hell with them. Most ranchers in Chilcotin aren't running their places as well as they already know how to.

Love of cows and horses didn't count. There wasn't a rancher present who would admit to anything more than a bare tolerance of either.

We decided it was time to be practical, to discuss the priorities, the way the prime minister advises us.

These emerged as the priorities for ranching today, listed in the order of their importance.

The first thing to get was a pickup truck. Fact is, it's getting hard to remember if there were ranchers before there were pickups.

The pickup should have power brakes and power steering, a deer-gun rack behind the seat, and Farm Vehicle written on the side. In the box there should be a broken jack, a bale of hay, and a dog. Almost any dog that barks will do.

The next important thing is an accountant, preferably a smart one.

This accountant's job is to understand most of the federal and provincial government regulations. He should be tested occasionally.

If the accountant interprets regulations correctly just 50 per cent of the time, he is only guessing and you could do as well yourself. Find one that can read the regulations right at least two times out of three.

You will need a good tax lawyer, too. He will explain why heavy losses are your only hope. That will fit right in with what you're doing. Give him a piece of the ranch from time to time.

You will need to know all you can about feed grain subsidies and the Crow's Nest Pass freight rates. Study them for a few years. If you get good at them, you can quit ranching and become chairman of the Canadian Transport Commission, which is indoor work with no heavy lifting.

A good banker is next.

Find one who doesn't understand anything about ranching. That won't be hard.

It would be best if you don't know anything about finance and cannot tell a demand note for 9 1/2 per cent from a Rinso soap coupon. That way you and your banker will start out even, which is only fair. You can grow up together.

You will need a wife.

Find an attractive, intelligent, well-educated girl who likes carrying water in a pail and is happy to get laundry soap for a birthday present.

Raise a lot of kids. You will need the baby bonus to fix the pickup when they are young and you will find work for them to do from about the age of eight.

You will find the boys will work all right, up to the time they are old enough to pull the pin and head for Vancouver.

To keep the daughters cheerful, however, you will have to buy them at least one horse apiece, which they will spoil with love and cube sugar.

While you're at it, pick up some horses for yourself. They're not as handy as a plane or a motorcycle, but they sort of dress up the place.

Knowing your own ranch isn't enough; don't let yourself get cut off from the doings of the outside world. Buy a subscription to *Western Horseman.*

You will also need:

eighty-dollar boots;

a nickel-plated belt buckle;

some rope;

a set of moose horns for the living room wall, and

a cheque book.

Once you have put this all together you might try getting a cow and a bull together and see if anything happens.

How Red Lost the Ranch

from *Tell me a good lie: Tales from the Chilcotin Country*
by Paul St. Pierre

*Whatever modern ranching may have lost in the way of spirit
since its heyday, the humble, heroic spirit of self-sacrifice is alive
and well in the hearts of Chilcotin ranchers like Red Allison in
this next story from Paul St. Pierre.*

BIG CREEK—

Last Saturday, Red Allison and other friends of the late Ronnie Tomlinson came up to Twilight Ranch and, in the grove of golden poplar where Ronnie's ashes are scattered, they erected a small plaque in his memory.

It's four years since the guy died, which proves that people up here still haven't got a very good handle on that thing called time, but the thought was good.

There are a lot of thoughts about Twilight Ranch, Ronnie Tomlinson, and Red Allison: thoughts of hope, of sadness, and, in the end, with Red, something a trifle noble shining through.

My first note on Red Allison relates to a Williams Lake stampede of about twenty years ago. Red was drunker than fourteen hundred dollars and so was his companion. Fancying they had some disagreement, Red took a roundhouse swing at the chin of his buddy, missed by about a foot and a half, lost his balance, and tried to save himself from falling by grabbing his opponent's belt. The other fellow lost his balance and they both fell into the dust.

Red turned his big, pink, boyish face to the other and snarled: "Why can't you SHTAND up and FIGHT like a MAN?" Clearly, Red was a man of some distinction, and so it proved.

Over the years he did many things, always well. For quite a few years he ran the general store at Riske Creek in Chilcotin. When the big OK Ranch on the other side of the Fraser River was in absentee ownership, Red was manager, again for many years.

He raised a family and a good reputation but made no great amount of money. He had a little piece of land here, another little piece there. He has a little piece in the Clinton area now.

Also, for a number of years, he was a silent partner in the Twilight Ranch here at Big Creek. Ronnie Tomlinson, a very quiet Englishman from Yorkshire, couldn't raise enough money for a down payment when the place came up for sale. Red came in on shares.

Ronnie proved to be an excellent rancher. The Twilight grew just a bit better, year by year. Fences were renewed. New grazing leases were acquired. Land was cleared. Always it was done a little bit at a time because that's how the money to do it came in, one dollar at a time.

At about the time the Twilight began to look like a model small ranch, Ronnie complained to his cowboy one morning that he felt funny, somehow, and was going to lie down. Twenty minutes later he was dead of a heart problem that he never knew he had.

Since he was a bachelor and clearly had had no thoughts about dying in middle age, people were not surprised when no will was found. So in the normal process of law, the Twilight was sold, Red was paid off for his share, and the balance, a sizable bite out of a million-dollar bill, went to Ronnie's old mother in England.

Red would have dearly loved to have taken over Twilight. It was a ranch just of a size and type for him and his family to run. But a couple of things had happened since he first became a silent partner. Ronnie had repaid Red a fair portion of what he contributed. More, Ronnie had so improved the place, and speculators had driven all ranch prices so high, that it was impossible for Red to raise enough cash to buy Ronnie's share of the place from the estate.

Last fall, three years after Ronnie's death, I ran into Red at a Williams Lake cattle auction where he was buying, selling, and just poking around. It was a shame, I said, that he did not become the owner of the Twilight place, there in the shallow valley of the Bambrick Creek with the green pine hills standing over the yellow grass meadows.

"Oh, then you don't know the rest of the story," he said. He giggled. He is a big man, over six feet, and mostly made of muscle, but he has always had a high-pitched girlish voice and a girlish giggle. He must have had a hard time with both during school days.

No, I knew no more to the story.

Well, Red said, not long ago he got a call from a Williams Lake lawyer. This lawyer had taken over the files of another Williams Lake lawyer who had died, or gone to Heaven, Hell, or the Supreme Court, wherever it is lawyers go when they quit working.

"He had only just got around to going through these cardboard boxes full of the other lawyer's files and what does he find but Ronnie Tomlinson's will. There it is, all signed, sealed, and proper, and it leaves the entire ranch to me."

"What are you going to do, Red?"

"Well, the lawyer said a will is a will and this is a real one. If I went to court, I could overturn everything that had happened and get the Twilight. But of course, I couldn't do that.

"Can you imagine me asking some judge to tell Ronnie's old mother in England that she has got to give all that money back to me? I couldn't possibly do a thing like that."

So he told the lawyer to forget the whole business and let the tail go with the hide. His last tie with Twilight was cut last Saturday when he put the plaque in the poplar grove so men would remember his partner.

WE NEVER GAVE IN

from *Nemiah: The Unconquered Country*
by Terry Glavin and the people of Nemiah Valley

*Beautiful and remote Nemiah Valley in the Chilcotin, home to
the Nemiah Valley Indian Band, part of the Tsilhqot'in First
Nation, is a plateau of rolling hills butting up against mountains.
There was no road access until 1973. Because of this isolation,
the Band's first spoken language is Tsilhqot'in, not English. They
value simplicity and old ways, the slow pace of their sustainable,
small-scale ranching lifestyle, and the natural environment, which
they are battling to protect from encroaching logging interests.*

*Terry Glavin, an award-winning journalist, is a passionate
advocate for environmental protection and First Nations issues.
In* Nemiah: The Unconquered Country, *Glavin is sensitive
to parallels between this battle and the Chilcotin War of 1864,
undertaken by the Nemiah Band's ancestors. "We are the only
First Nations in Canada that fought and went to war to protect
our land," says Chief Roger William. It began when a member
of a survey crew, part of a work team intending to build a road
through the Chilcotin from the coast, en route to Barkerville and
the Cariboo goldfields, accused several Tsilhqot'in of stealing
flour. To intimidate them, he threatened to bring smallpox to the
area. The Tsilhqot'in, still reeling from an outbreak of the disease
brought in unwittingly only two years previously, rose up and killed
19 people, mostly members of the work crew. Although several
warriors were tried and hanged, the Tsilhqot'in consider the war*

a success: the road project was abandoned and the Nemiah Valley remained undisturbed for more than a hundred years. Now the Valley's uncut pine is coveted by logging companies, and once again the Tsilhqot'in are protecting their traditional lands. At the time Glavin wrote his book, the Nemiah people were expressing concerns about logging incursions and hinting at resistance. In 2002, the Band took their logging battle to court.

This is the first time an Aboriginal people has tested the concept of Aboriginal title since the Supreme Court of Canada ruled in 1997 that Aboriginal title exists by law. The outcome is expected to set a critical precedent for Aboriginal land claims. Legally, the Tsilhqot'in have to prove the land is theirs. Victoria's Times Colonist reported: "There have been times when the court sat at night, because Tsilhqot'in custom demands some legends and stories not be spoken while the sun is up. The court listened as Tsilhqot'in witnesses provided older place names, mountain by mountain and river by river, for the names on the current map of the land they inhabit." As this book went to print, testimony was still being heard.

In the following excerpt from Nemiah, even a sympathetic listener like Glavin has trouble communicating with his Nemiah Valley friends. For one thing, there is the mystery about what really happened in the Chilcotin War; for another, there is the difficulty of translation. This excerpt ends on a note of uncertainty, suggesting that there is a point at which two cultures coming together do not connect. The discussion is left open-ended to imply that for an understanding to be reached, more needs to be said. The dialogue is far from over.

Eugene had killed a white-tailed deer with the .22 he keeps in brackets fashioned from upturned deer hooves among the kerosene lamps, cowboy hats, cups and saucers, coats and saws that hang from the walls of the tiny cabin where he lives with Mabel and little Benson and whoever else happens to be passing through. Another thing was that Eugene's dog, King, had a limp from getting his paw caught in something while he was chasing jackrabbits across the pasture, but it didn't seem to bother him much and he kept going after jackrabbits. And Adam and Blaine and Willard, nephews to Eugene in one way or another, had come up to help put the hay in, and so had Dave Dinwoodie, a Mexican-born, Alberta-raised Montana resident from the University of Chicago who had arrived in the Nemiah Valley a couple of weeks earlier with a vague plan of staying on for as long as it took to learn how to speak Chilcotin. So lots had been going on, and it seemed like the important thing at the moment was to sit for a while and drink ledi, as Chilcotins around here call tea, and talk about the affairs of the world. And about how long it would take to get the hay in and how many haystacks these meadows might make.

There's more than 200 acres of swamp hay here. Much of it is thick with tangled willows or poplar or aspen, despite the best efforts of the beavers, which have cut timber from the sidehills and dragged it to the creek. They've cleared broad trails through the bush and built their lodges at every bend and oxbow, and there's clearly more beaver here than there ever were people. And this was swamp hay, not that "tame hay" they make down around Stoney that you can cut three times in a good year, and so the discussion went until Eugene stood up and said, "Well, you going to help me with that deer?"

So we headed off into the bush behind the cabin, with little Benson scurrying along behind. We carried the deer back from the trees where Eugene had gutted it the night before after hauling it down from the hills. We carried it past the square pole-corral of an old fish-drying rack down to a grove of small pines in the afternoon sunlight. The wind was warm and blowing strong from the south, and clouds unravelled across the sky. Mabel gathered pine poles for the drying rack, and Eugene went off to cut some young birch for more poles. He came back with enough to lash together a tripod with crosspoles balanced from it to the limbs of a small pine tree on the other end, and Mabel went to work on the deer. Benson did his best to help.

Mabel knelt and went to work on the hind legs, slowly and carefully cutting the hide away from the flesh, working her way up to the belly and along the sides. She lay the deer on its back and deftly skinned another hind leg, pulling the hide from the fat and the meat, like pulling sleeves from a child's arm. In her red kerchief, blue cardigan and tartan dress, Mabel hurried without effort. While her quick fingers worked their way along the belly she talked gently to Benson in Chilcotin, telling him how to hold the animal for her in the way that would make her work go easy. Eugene knelt beside her and cut sections of meat from the animal, passing each to me and pointing to the pole on the drying rack it should hang from. Willard and Blaine gathered firewood and built a slow blaze beneath the rack to keep the flies away.

Within an hour, Eugene was sharpening a stake at both ends to roast the animal's ribs over the fire, and we all sat around in the afternoon sun and the sweet smell of poplar smoke and venison. The ribs roasted in the flames and the smoke drifted across the meadows.

Mabel and Eugene sat together and talked and laughed quietly, the two of them being married now more than 50 years. They married in Redstone, her village, during priest time, one of the two or three times a year one of the Oblates from Saint Joseph's Mission made the week-long trek out to the far Chilcotin. It was the same day Pilip Pateece married a girl from Anaham and his old friend Ubill married Oolia Charlieboy, but they're all dead now and only Eugene and Mabel are left.

They have a dozen children of their own, enough grandchildren that they've just about lost count, and they live the old way with about 40 head of cattle, here or in the far meadow about seven miles further in, and down in Nemiah where they winter. Since they're getting on in years, their sons, maybe Benny or Boysie, bring them fish, and so does

Benson's dad, Edmund Lulua, who's sometimes called "Edmund Two" because there are two Edmund Luluas in the Nemiah. Sometimes he's just called Eetman after the fashion of Chilcotinizing outside names.

Eugene was born up the Taseko River, on the trapline, in a tent in the dead of winter. He and Mabel raised their own family out towards Tatlayoko in the northwest corner of the territory, where Carrier Lumber was hoping to start clearcutting pretty soon, but over the years he's spent more time down towards Xeni Lake where the swamp hay is richer and there's more of it. He's run his cattle here at Captain George Town and the Nemiah Valley for a dozen years or so, and before that it was in the Eagle Lake country for about fifteen years after moving south from the Tatlayoko.

Eugene sat quietly, whittling on a stick, fidgeting a little in his old workboots. He brushed his hands on his jeans and pulled his baseball cap low over his eyes in the piercing afternoon sun.

"Well, we say we don't want them to get all the logs," he said about the logging companies' plans. "Sometimes, we need it sometime. All of this would be open, no tree pretty soon. Game, he won't stay in the open like that, you know? Just like killing all the game. That's what we say.

"Game, I guess he got to have some timber, to lay down under the tree when the snow comes, rain. The log company, he cut all the tree, all the way."

He looks worried when he talks about it.

"I don't know what we would do with no timber. There'd be no more game, too. I don't know what we're going to eat."

So what do you do?

"Try to stop them. I don't know. We'll think of something, I guess," he says. And then something about it makes him laugh.

"I guess government, they don't want to stop it, but we'll just try, anyway," he said, and he smiled that broad smile of his, and his thoughts took him elsewhere.

"We got lots of time, eh? That's the reason, out here, living out here like this, it's kind of quiet. Now we go to town, and we want to come back in, eh?"

Eugene's been as far as Vancouver four times in his life, and it's about as far and as often as he cares to go. He says he doesn't like it there because there are too many people, too many buildings. The last time he was there was the time 30 Xeni gwet'in headed out in two vans and five pickup trucks on the thirteen-hour trip to Vancouver to formally submit their court case against the logging companies. That was December 14, 1989, and there were even more buildings then than the time he went before.

Like Eugene says, it's kind of quiet out here. The years carry in to one another with the seasons. People move with their animals from one meadow to the next, sell some calves and sometimes an older one to bring in some money, decide which heifers to keep and which of the fatter cows to hold back for milk in the springtime, and life moves slowly. With the dying day there wasn't much point in getting much work in, so back in the cabin after a meal of venison and rice and carrots and potatoes, Mabel and Eugene chatted away, with Mabel looking out through the cabin window as the last light of day fell over the fields.

Adam was asking when Captain George, son of the second Nemiah chief known to the outside world, was here last.

"It's over forty years, anyway," Eugene said, in English. "He's buried at Nemiah."

Eugene and Adam talked a bit in Chilcotin, and laughed. People seem to end up laughing whenever Captain George's name comes up.

This was his place at one time, and the cabin was here before Benny was born, Eugene said. That was more than forty years ago now, so there's no telling when it was built, but the story is that Captain George himself built it.

The sun went down over the mountainside and the horses grazed down by the shallows. Little Benson was looking at the pictures of Mabel's three-year-old copy of *Crochet World* magazine in one hand and a half-eaten deer rib in the other. He was the first to fall asleep.

The coyotes were the last.

They kept each other awake half the night howling to each other from the pine forests on one side of the meadows to the hills across the valley, and the owls took up their work in the frosty air before daybreak. By morning, southbound flocks of Canada geese were adding their voices high above Captain George Town, and we sat down to a breakfast of Mabel's deer steak and eggs and coffee.

The first job of the day was to harness the two workhorses to the rough-hewn haysled Eugene had cut from the pines and lead them across the deep creek with the haysled in tow. Eugene and Willard hitched the sled to the horses, pulled them around and headed them towards the creek to cross them at the shallows, with King following along.

"Did you see that dog running through the field?" Willard asked on his way across with Eugene. "Jumps right up in the air, like that," he said, throwing his hand above his head in sharp strokes, "just like a deer. Chasing something." The limp wasn't bothering him anymore, and the dog disappeared through the willows down to the south. In the distance, Tŝ'il?os rose in the morning mist with what we were certain was a fresh fall of snow on his peak.

With an uproar of hooves, the haysled splashed into the creek with Eugene at the reins. The pine pole uprights shuddered and heaved with the force of the tow, straining the baling wire Eugene had used to lash the whole thing together. King appeared out of nowhere and swam along behind, and the whole works floated downstream intact behind the snorting workhorses until Eugene guided them back up the bank and through the willows. He brought them to a dead stop and stood there proud and smiling, reins in hand. He caught his breath and said, "Sometimes I use a wagon, but with a wagon you got to take everything off before you stack."

Which is why he prefers the ?esdluŝ, which is the Chilcotin word for haysled.

"Sled's better than wagon," Blaine explained. "Wagon gets stuck, and it's too bumpy."

The haysled is only slightly less elaborate than Eugene's Frost and Wood horse-drawn haymower, and only slightly more sophisticated than his horse-drawn hayrake—24 half-circle rake teeth hung from an adjustable bar beneath a cast-iron seat, the whole business suspended between two iron wagon wheels and pulled by two pine poles harnessed to two workhorses. That's the extent of Eugene's heavy machinery, and he's proud of his machines, but later on, as he laboured with the haysled chains, his breathing was heavy.

"Just doesn't want to quit," Adam said. "He's a workingman. He just can't sit around."

Mabel walked out to the hill behind the cabin to cut some more deer meat from the drying rack, and the rest of us headed out for the day's pitchfork work on the meadow. Adam's GMC Sierra pickup was put into service to haul the sled, and that allowed Eugene to take it slow for awhile. We worked through the morning and the sun burned away the frost, and with only a few traces of cloud in the sky it's hot again soon enough and the grasshoppers are back. We managed about a dozen haystacks in each sledload, hauling the load back to the crib, where a 60-foot-high tripod rig lifts cables from underneath the haysled load in a kind of sling that pops up with a hard tug from the bumper of Adam's pickup. With each load pulled up and over into the crib, Benson jumped and tumbled around and tried to pretend, at least, that he was serious about keeping out of everybody's way.

After a lunch of deer stew, potatoes, carrots, rice, bannock, jam, cookies and coffee, we were back at it, and by late afternoon Benson was no longer alone in the growing haystack in Eugene's corral-sized crib. A convoy of pickups carrying Nemiah families from down the valley came to visit with Eugene to see how he was getting along, and Benson's leaps into the hay were followed by the somersaults of Erikk Lulua, Brenda Lulua, Celia Setah, Joline Marie William, Charlene William, Yolanda William, Geraldine William, Wesley William, Lois William and Linda Setah. Eugene sat at the end of the day whittling wood shavings in front of an open fire outside his cabin. Mabel was cooking deer stew in a big pot, trying her best to keep us all fed.

Eugene was rested and happy. He was getting his hay in and he had visits from his relations in the bargain, and he liked to hear them speaking Chilcotin still, even if some of them did have a hard time of it since they spent so much time speaking English. Little Benson was that way. He was four years old, but he could understand Chilcotin, even if he couldn't speak it all too well.

"I know a little bit about Chinook," Eugene said, in the slow and deliberate way he speaks. Chinook was the trading jargon used to speak to outsiders before the people learned English.

"My dad, he told me a little bit. I had a little book. Chinook words, with English. I lost it, though."

He looked across the field at the gang of Nemiah kids jumping from his haycrib fence into the haystack.

"Kids play with it. All wore out," he said, thinking again about that book.

He smiled and went on that it would be nice if he still had the book around to show people, at least.

"Anyway, I'm 73. Going to be 74 in November. I should be in good shape right now, but I got a sickness, you know. Diabetes. High blood pressure."

That was what the doctor had told him the day Walter took him into Williams Lake. The doctor told him about how those things can wear on a man's heart, and that's why he wanted to see Eugene again.

"Last time, doctor give me a pill. Say I pretty near had a heart attack. Doctor tell me, no work. Take it easy. Take it easy for five, six weeks. That was about five weeks ago now. But I can't just do that. I gotta work."

He smiled again.

"But I take my time," he said.

One of those broad smiles came over Eugene's face again, and he laughed. He sat forward on the woodblock in front of the fire and looked out across the fields, deep into the trees on the far side of the winding creek where Walter and I used his grasshoppers to catch trout a few days earlier.

Eugene talked about what had brought him to these hills apart from the hay for his cattle. "Moose, deer, coyote, fox, lynx, marten ... no. No marten. Mink. Some mink down here. Weasel. Wolverine ... not many wolverine. Sometimes you see them, eh?"

I asked him about the logging companies again, and what people were going to do. These very hills showed up on government forest service maps in Alexis Creek as timber available for P & T Mills. The government said it was all theirs as soon as they decided the best way to get across the Taseko River.

And then Eugene said, simply, "Samandlin."

This would be the Chilcotin War story Walter told me Eugene had. "Old people have story about that one," Eugene said. "Samandlin, he come up, I guess, Eagle Lake. He went all down that way east, I guess."

He sat comfortably on his woodblock and whittled away with his old hunting knife.

"They say, them old days, 'If he win at Eagle Lake, he win everything,' eh? He's going to get it all. Everything, I guess.

"But he lost. He gets killed."

Samandlin is the name that Chilcotin people, for their own reasons, have given to Donald McLean, a retired Hudson's Bay Company trader who was hired by colonial authorities to help command a group of white volunteers in an expeditionary force against the Chilcotin warriors of 1864. It may be that the name Samandlin evolved from a Chilcotin pronunciation of the French *monsieur*—some Chilcotins developed a familiarity with French from the days of the fur trade— coupled with an abbreviated pronunciation of McLean. Whatever the case, his killing was a crucial event in the incidents of 1864, and from the Xeni gwet'in point of view, Samandlin's death was the decisive encounter in the struggle for the defence of their homelands.

The Chilcotin War, as it's come to be known, was the only instance of significant military resistance to colonial authority waged by Aboriginal people west of the Rocky Mountains.

Apart from Metis resistance at the Red River, the Northwest Rebellion of 1885 and occasional skirmishing across the Canadian west, British and Canadian sovereignty was asserted west of the Great Lakes without much sustained bloodshed. But in the Chilcotin country, by the end of 1864, nineteen white men and four Indians were dead, and six more Chilcotin were to die on the gallows.

Most British Columbians are unlikely to have even heard of the Chilcotin War. And the popular accounts of it, such as they are, tend to present a story about a gang of bloodthirsty if tragic Indian characters engaged in a losing battle against the unstoppable march of civilization. But when all the 19th-century folktales are put aside, what clearly emerges is that the Chilcotins involved in the resistance clearly meant to wage war against hostile and unwanted intrusions from outside, and they more or less won, or at least fought the thing to a draw.

It was the construction of a wagon road from the coast that provoked the initial and most bloody encounter in the war. The road was a grand scheme hatched by a big-business speculator named Alfred Waddington. He proposed to move miners from the coast to the Cariboo goldfields in a relatively quick and inexpensive fashion, sort of a Coquihalla Highway of its day. In the Office of Lands and Works in the 1860s, no more regard was given to Aboriginal title than in the Ministry of Forests in the 1980s. The attack on the road crew in the Homathko Canyon went unquestionably in favour of the Chilcotins: fourteen roadbuilders killed; no Indian casualties. The ensuing encounters also went generally in favour of the Indians, and the road, which Waddington planned to put straight through the heart of the Xeni gwet'in territories, never did get built. And no road had made its way through the Xeni gwet'in country until the Canadian military engineers pushed their road through unmolested in 1973.

The war "ended," by most accounts, after five warriors turned themselves in and were hanged at Quesnellemouth, with the sixth dying at the end of a rope behind the old New Westminster jailhouse.

The official version of the story never held much water. Even a substantial body of white opinion at the time saw the hangings as a cowardly and deceitful response to peace talks the warriors appear to have proposed prior to their capture. To this day the Chilcotins are inclined to say they won, if the war really ended at all, and questions remain about who died on the gallows. After the main fighting was over most of the warriors fled into the mountains with their families, anyway, and they were never captured.

What is clear is that the heroic figure that shows up in popular accounts as Donald McLean had it coming to him when a bullet ended his life on a hill a few miles from Captain George Town, in the bush up by Eagle Lake. Eugene whittled some more, smiled, and began his story.

"One of the Chilcotin, I guess, they went up around Eagle Lake, around there. Nemiah. Kind of a dokdox, like, you know, his own way. A dokdox."

"Samandlin?" I asked. "A dokdox?"

"No," Eugene answered. "Chilcotin himself. A dokdox."

"So what's a dokdox, in midugh?" I asked, midugh being the word for white man, or the word for the white man's language.

"Just something ... like, you know what they call it. You know when somebody's coming. You find out right away, even you don't see him."

"Oh," I said, thinking this should have been clear to me a little quicker. "Indian doctor" is to Chilcotin what "witch doctor" might be to a Catholic priest. Chilcotin sometimes take an English word with a roughly equivalent meaning to a word of their own, put a Chilcotin spin on it and hand it back again.

"You mean, like a doctor."

Eugene "Yeah. Like a dokdox ..."

"Like an Indian doctor."

Eugene: "Like what we call Indian dokdox."

"So. A dokdox."

Eugene: "Yeah."

At that point I remember thinking that by now, Eugene must be reckoning that I'm a little slow. But he was kind enough to be patient and he continued on.

"So, Samandlin, he come over there, Eagle Lake. He went out on a trail. That's an Indian trail, huh? Indian had no horses, just walking, up in that mountain. He dig the wild potato up there, I guess.

"So they went down to check the trail, eh? Two guys went down there, to check everything. Then pretty soon, Samandlin. He's coming up that trail. He don't know that trail, but he's coming up that trail."

The brief encounter McLean was about to have with the Chilcotin people on that trail near Eagle Lake was not his first.

His relations with them went back twenty years, to the time he spent as a trader at Fort Chilcotin, a Hudson's Bay Company outpost on the Chilcotin River that operated intermittently between 1829 and 1844.

Most of their neighbours embraced the Hudson's Bay trade but the Chilcotins displayed little interest in selling furs to the HBC, and company officials were often vexed by what they described as the "audacity," "insolence" and "menaces" of the Chilcotins, who also show up in HBC records as "troublesome and disorderly." McLean didn't exactly contribute to improved relations, and it was under his tenure at Fort Chilcotin that the outpost was shut down and removed to Kluskus, in Carrier country.

McLean shows up as a "devoted family man" with a "reputation for fairness" in a popular account of the events of 1864, aptly titled *The Chilcotin War*, written by Kamloops journalist Mel Rothenburger, himself a descendant of McLean. McLean also shows up in a book of reminiscences written by the Protestant missionary R.C. Lundin Brown, entitled *Klatsassan*, after the reputed leader of the Chilcotin warriors. Brown describes McLean as a man who was "immensely popular for his kindliness, his unwearying energy, and the good will with which he undertook any work that wanted doing." This is the same man to which even the Reverend Brown attributes the deaths of as many as nineteen Indians prior to the outbreak of hostilities in the Chilcotin country, the same man who distinguished himself in the winter of 1849 by murdering an unarmed elderly Indian in a Carrier village near Quesnel because the old man didn't know where a murder suspect was hiding. During the course of that same "investigation," McLean's party shot and killed another unarmed man, fired a musket point-blank into the head of an infant, and shot the dead child's mother in the shoulder.

McLean was cleared by HBC officials as having behaved with "entire satisfaction" in the Quesnel murders, just as he has been rehabilitated by popular white history and the official story of the Chilcotin War.

It certainly wasn't McLean's kindliness that prompted colonial governor Frederick Seymour to hire him out of retirement at his ranch down at Hat Creek for the mercenary work that needed doing in Chilcotin country. And McLean was anxious to get on with his work. He put on his trademark bullet-proof metal vest, quickly raised two dozen of his own volunteers to head off into the Chilcotin, and was out scouting for the enemy on his own the day he died, defying explicit orders from expedition leader and colonial commissioner William Cox to stay back in camp with the others.

"He find the trail all right, that Samandlin," says Eugene.

"Then somebody, he take his knife out of its sheath, and cut from kind of a tree, right down on the trail. Leave 'em on a trail."

That was the trap.

At this point, Eugene takes a firm hold of his knife, holds his thumb against the dull edge of the blade to steady his hand, and cuts a thin slice from the stick he's whittling. He takes the strip he's cut and puts it on the ground in front of him.

"He put it on the trail," he says, pointing with his knife to the strip of wood on the ground between his feet.

"He leave it on the trail. That one, like this," he says.

Again, Eugene takes a firm grip of the short pole in his left hand, and pulls the blade of his hunting knife towards him with his right hand, peeling off a strip of wood and dropping it to the ground. He looks at the two shavings between his boots, then looks up, and starts whittling some more.

"So Samandlin come there, and he's a long time on the trail, I guess."

Eugene sits upright on his woodblock and looks down on the ground in front of him.

"He wanted to find out how long ago that one there. So he put it in his mouth."

Eugene picks up the shaving and puts it in his mouth.

"I guess, green tree, I guess. He want to find out. Maybe it's dry, maybe it's wet yet."

Samandlin takes the bait. A Chilcotin marksman takes aim.

Eugene's quiet for a moment.

"Pretty soon, somebody ... bang. Over there."

Eugene points towards the trees out behind the cabin.

"Well, that first one, I guess he miss. Two guys. So the second one, he shot him, Samandlin."

"Two guys," I repeated. "Second one shot him."

"Yeah," Eugene said.

"I guess he's going up a hill, eh? Kind of warm, eh? Kind of hot. So he took off his shirt, like that. Somebody heard they got steel shirts. I don't know what kind of shirt that is."

"I heard about that," I said. "I heard about it."

"So that time, he's not wearing his shirt, I guess. Bullet, he can't go in that shirt. It just fall down, I guess. But it was opened up. Right here."

Eugene points to his chest.

"Right here. That's where the Indian hit him, with a bullet. That's why he killed him."

Eugene slowly whittles a few more shavings from the sharpening end of the stick in his left hand.

"Who killed him?" I asked.

"Sachayel."

Mabel was standing by the fire. Eugene asked her the same question, in Chilcotin. She had been listening a while, turning some bannock on the iron griddle.

They talked back and forth in Chilcotin, then Eugene said, again, Sachayel."

He thought for a moment, and then he said: "Two guys, I know. I don't know which one."

Rothenburger names the marksman as somebody named Anukatlk, a scout that joined the warriors late in the war. The Reverend Brown says it was someone named Shililika.

Mabel was standing quietly at the iron griddle over the open fire. She glanced over and said to Eugene, "Hatish."

"Hatish?" asked Eugene.

"Hatish," Mabel answered.

"Hatish. Yeah," Eugene said. He nodded in agreement, but he looked uncertain.

"He was the other guy?" I asked.

"Yeah."

"Sachayel," I said, "but maybe Sachayel, maybe."

"Yeah," Eugene said. "Maybe that one. I don't know. Don't know for sure."

So maybe Sachayel, maybe Hatish, and then there are the names Anukatlk and Shililika, and I'm reminded about the clouded identity of the very leader of the Chilcotins who was hanged at Quesnel with the others. In the official court records he's identified as Klatsassin, sometimes known as Klatsassan, sometimes Klatsassine, and sometimes Klatassin. In Chilcotin, it's Lhasas?in, and Adam William explained to me one day that translated into the English it means "We don't know who it is."

It's not clear who might legitimately claim credit for shooting Samandlin but like Eugene said, the idea was that if he won at Eagle Lake, he'd win everything, that he'd get it all. But he lost. He got killed.

And Commissioner William Cox's expeditionary force of 50 men turned around and headed back on a quick march to Puntzi Lake, leaving Samandlin's body buried somewhere in the bush.

"Who was the dokdox? What was his name?"

"Oh, some kind of a dokdox. You know, just a dokdox."

"But we don't know his name?"

"No."

"But the people here knew he was coming, because the dokdox told them?"

"Yeah. Pretty near all of them were like that, I guess. Somebody coming they find out. Maybe he feel them, I guess. That's the way with dokdox. If somebody's coming, they feel kind of funny, I guess. That's how they know somebody's coming."

There's not too many people around that are like that anymore, he said.

"Them old people, though, that's what I mean. Indian dokdox. You know, when you get sick, he'll fix you up. That's why they call them dokdox.

"Same kind they got in Williams Lake," he said, like the doctor he was supposed to see that day he didn't show when Walter was waiting for him at the band office down in Nemiah Valley.

"Only different way."

Photo Credits

Front and back cover image by Chris Harris

Robert Keziere, p. 14; illustrations by Gwen Lewis, from *The Cariboo Story* by F.W. Lindsay, pp. 20, 23; engraved plates from *The North-West Passage by Land*, p. 26 top and bottom; Irene Stangoe, p. 40; Veera Bonner, pp. 44, 52; cover image from *Tenderfoot Trail* used by permission of Sono Nis, p. 80; Veasy Collier, p. 100 top and bottom; the Place family, p .128; Alan Fry, p. 138; Eldon Lee, p. 152; illustration by Gaye Hammond used by permission of Howard White, administrator for Caitlin Press, p. 164; Irene Stangoe, p. 180 top left, top right, and bottom; D.A. Holley, p. 186; Chilco Choate, p. 194; Martin Place, p. 204.

Acknowledgements

We gratefully acknowledge the following for permission to reprint previously published material. Every attempt has been made to acquire permission to reprint the stories appearing herein. We would be grateful for information that would allow us to correct any errors or omissions in a subsequent reprinting of the book.

Sage Birchwater, extracts from "The Country Was Still Raw," "Loozap," "To Have a Witchdoctor Sing With Granny," "I Take Him From Coyote," "Fire on Top of the Ice," and "Stone Rancherie" in *Chiwid*, published by New Star Books Ltd., Vancouver, BC, 1995. Copyright © 1995 by Sage Birchwater. Reprinted by permission of New Star Books.

Veera Bonner, excerpt from "Hanceville" in *Chilcotin: Preserving Pioneer Memories*, published by Heritage House Publishing Company Ltd., Surrey, BC, 1995, reprinted 2005. Copyright © 1995, 2005 by Veera Bonner, Irene E. Bliss, Hazel H. Litterick.

W.B. Cheadle and Viscount Milton, excerpts from "Chapter XVIII" and "Chapter XIX" in *The North-West Passage by Land*, sixth ed., published by Cassell, Petter, and Galpin, London, UK, 1865. Public domain.

Chilco Choate, excerpts from "Chapter 2" and "Chapter 10" in *Unfriendly Neighbours*, published by The Caitlin Press, Prince George, BC, 1993. Copyright © 1993 by Chilco Choate. Reprinted by permission of the author.

Eric Collier, "Chapter Six" in *Three Against the Wilderness*, published by Irwin Publishing, London, UK, 1959. Reprinted by permission of the Collier estate.

Diana French, excerpt from "The Mechanics" in *The Road Runs West: A Century Along the Bella Coola/Chilcotin Road*, published by Harbour Publishing, Madeira Park, BC, 1994. Copyright © 1994 by Diana French. Reprinted by permission of Harbour Publishing.

Alan Fry, "Wet Summer" from *The Ranch on the Cariboo*, first published by Doubleday, New York, 1962, reprinted by TouchWood Editions Ltd., Victoria, BC, 2002. Copyright © 2002 by Alan Fry. Reprinted by permission of TouchWood Editions Ltd.

Terry Glavin and the people of Nemiah Valley, excerpt from "Captain George Town" in *Nemiah: The Unconquered Country*, published by New Star Books, Vancouver, BC, 1992. Text copyright © 1992 by the Nemiah Valley Indian Band. Reprinted by permission of New Star Books.

Richmond P. Hobson, "Unexplored Territory" in *Grass Beyond the Mountains*, published by McClelland & Stewart Inc., Toronto, ON, 1951, reprinted 1998. Copyright © 1951 by Richmond P. Hobson Jr. Reprinted by permission of McClelland & Stewart Inc.

D.A. Holley, excerpts from "Silencing the Cowboy Crooners," "Half-Way Measures Will Not Do," "Can't See Too Good," and "Cowboy Remedies" in *Don't Shoot From the Saddle: Chronicles of a Frontier Surgeon*, published by Heritage House Publishing Company Ltd., Surrey, BC, 2000. Copyright © 2000 by D.A. Holley.

Agnes C. Laut, excerpt from "The Cariboo Road" in *The Cariboo Trail: A Chronicle of the Gold-fields of British Columbia*, vol. 23, Chronicles of Canada, H.H. Langton and George M. Wrong, ed., published by University of Toronto Press, Toronto, ON, 1964. Public domain.

Todd Lee, "High Noon in a Cow-town Court" in *Stories from the Cariboo: He Saw With Other Eyes*, published by The Caitlin Press, Prince George, BC, 1992. Copyright © 1992 by Todd Lee. Reprinted by permission of the Lee estate.

F.W. Lindsay, "Dusty Nuggets from a Miner's Diary" and "Discovery of Williams Creek" in *The Cariboo Story*, published by author, Quesnel, BC, 1958. Copyright © 1958 by F.W. Lindsay.

Olive Spencer Loggins, excerpts from "Journey to the Cariboo" and "Danger Comes Calling" in *Tenderfoot Trail: Greenhorns in the Cariboo*, published by Sono Nis Press, Victoria, BC, 1983. Copyright © 1983 by Olive Spencer Loggins. Reprinted by permission of Sono Nis.

Harry Marriott, "Riding Up the Road" in *Cariboo Cowboy*, first Heritage edition published by Heritage House Publishing Company Ltd., Surrey, BC, 1994, reprinted 2001. Copyright © 1994 by Estate of Harry Marriott.

Hilary Place, "Davey Anderson" in *Dog Creek: A Place in the Cariboo*, published by Heritage House Publishing Company Ltd., Surrey, BC, 1999. Copyright © 1999 by Hilary Place.

Bill Riley and Laura Leake, excerpt from "On to Soda Creek" in *History and Events of the Early 1920s*, published by Vantage Press, New York, NY, 1980. Copyright © 1980 by William Riley.

Robin Skelton, excerpt from "Before the Gold Rush" in *They call it the Cariboo*, published by Sono Nis Press, Victoria, BC, 1980. Copyright © 1980 by Robin Skelton. Reprinted by permission of Alison and Brigid Skelton.

Jean E. Speare, ed., "The Captive Girl" in *The Days of Augusta*, first published by J. J. Douglas Ltd., Vancouver, BC, 1973, and reprinted by Douglas & McIntyre, Vancouver, BC, 1992. Copyright © 1973, 1992 by Augusta Evans and Jean E. Speare. Reprinted by permission of Douglas & McIntyre.

Paul St. Pierre, "Everything You Need to Make a Ranch" and "How Red Lost the Ranch" in *Tell me a good lie: Tales from the Chilcotin Country*, published by Douglas & McIntyre, Vancouver, BC, 2001. Copyright © 2001 by Paul St. Pierre. Reprinted by permission of Douglas & McIntyre.

Irene Stangoe, "Looking Back With Irene" in *Looking Back at the Cariboo–Chilcotin*, published by Heritage House Publishing Company Ltd., Surrey, BC, 1994. Copyright © 1997 by Irene Stangoe.